SOS For Teachers

STRATEGIES OF SELF-IMPROVEMENT
For Teachers

JAMES D. LONG
APPALACHIAN STATE UNIVERSITY

ROBERT L. WILLIAMS
UNIVERSITY OF TENNESSEE

PRINCETON BOOK COMPANY, PUBLISHERS
PRINCETON, NEW JERSEY

Illustration facing page 1, a *Charlotte Observer* Illustration by Chip Martin, South Mecklenburg High School, is reprinted by permission of the *Charlotte Observer,* Charlotte, North Carolina.

Illustration on back cover, by Henry Martin, is reprinted by permission of the Chicago Tribune-New York News Syndicate, Inc.

THE AUTHORS

JAMES D. LONG (Ed. D. in Educational Psychology and Guidance, University of Tennessee) has been on the Faculty of Psychology at Appalachian State University, Boone, North Carolina since 1972. He is the author of numerous articles on self-management, behavioral objectives, and classroom management, and the coauthor (with Virginia H. Frye) of *Making It Till Friday: A Guide to Successful Classroom Management* (Princeton Book Company, Publishers), now in its second edition. In addition to teaching and writing, he is active in conducting workshops on classroom management and self-management.

ROBERT L. WILLIAMS (Ph.D. in Educational Psychology, George Peabody College) has been Professor of Educational Psychology and Guidance at the University of Tennessee since 1967. He is the author of 50 journal articles and five books, also dealing with classroom management and self-management.

Long and Williams have collaborated on a number of articles and books, notably *Toward a Self-Managed Life Style* (Houghton-Mifflin). They are available to conduct in-the-field workshops and seminars. For information, write to Princeton Book Company, Publishers, P.O. Box 109, Princeton, NJ 08540.

Dedicated to Lib, Blakeley, Jackie, and Todd

PREFACE

TEACHERS are beset by as many challenges as any other professional group, and perhaps more. They must concern themselves with organizing academic programs, maintaining discipline, utilizing community resources, serving as a good example—to name a few. Teaching is far from easy, even under optimal circumstances. Many teachers become exhausted as they try desperately to meet the numerous demands of the job. In popular terminology, some burn out. Others who manage to remain in the teaching profession never realize their full potential. This observation is distressing because most who choose teaching want more than mere survival. Teachers tend to be idealistic individuals who genuinely want to contribute to a better society.

The major purpose of this book, therefore, is to demonstrate how educators (especially teachers) can use their own skills in getting the most out of their professional and personal lives. Although the book focuses on the professional needs and aspirations of the teacher, the theme is not a selfish one. We believe that if teachers are to be of maximum service to others, they must first recognize their own needs. Additionally, they must be at the forefront in improving their own behaviors and in working for situational changes that will benefit themselves and others.

In brief, the text emphasizes how teachers can use self-improvement strategies to alter conditions within their school and classroom. Specifically, such problems as planning for effective teaching, maintaining discipline, coping with stress, becoming more creative, resolving interpersonal conflicts, establishing a meaningful home life, and many more are dealt with in the text. Our belief is that the strategies presented in the book can assist each reader in achieving a fuller measure of satisfaction from a most noble profession. The reader will not find a strategy for every problem he or she might encounter in teaching. However, the general principles of self-improvement described herein can probably be adapted to those unusual problems that lie ahead.

Few efforts are achieved without the support of others. Such is certainly the case with the present undertaking. For their encouragement and assistance in refining the book, we thank Richard Levin, Lib Long, Phyllis O'Donnell, Mary Powell, Jackie Williams, and Fred Wilson. Special thanks go to Sandra Thomas, presently a doctoral student at the University of Tennessee. Ms. Thomas gave extensive assistance in collecting information for the book and in the editorial refinement of the initial manuscript. Our typists, Joyce Harris, Teresa Johnson, and Marge Summer, were extremely efficient and conscientious in typing the various drafts of the manuscript.

J.D.L.

R.L.W.

CONTENTS

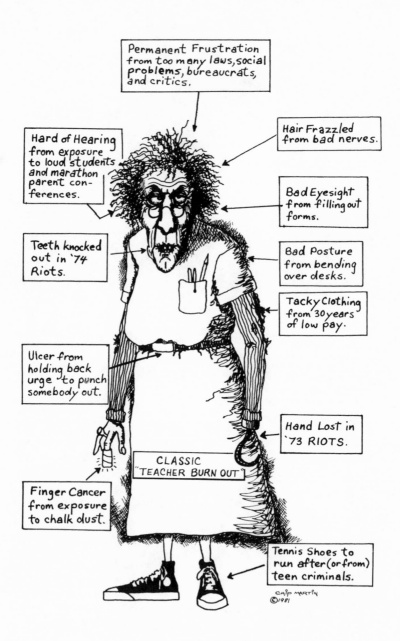

CHAPTER ONE

RAINY MONDAYS: AN INTRODUCTION TO SELF-IMPROVEMENT

IT WAS MONDAY morning, the beginning of a new workweek. As Bill sat sipping coffee at the kitchen table, he could hear the rain falling outside. "What a great day for sleeping," he thought to himself. "I'd like to crawl back into bed." Then, with a note of resignation in his voice, he sighed, "I guess I'd better get going. It's already 7:30."

Lately, Bill had been finding it more difficult to leave for work, especially on Mondays. The excitement and novelty he had felt last year as a first-year teacher were gone. Certain aspects of the job—such as teaching six fifty-minute classes a day, having a thirty-minute period for lunch, and a twenty-minute break in the morning and a ten-minute break in the afternoon—had become routine. He had experienced a few discipline problems with students recently, and that had been taking some of the luster off teaching. (If only the students could be more appreciative of his efforts.) He was also beginning to feel that he did not always have the support that he needed from the principal and from parents. In fact, Bill was beginning to sense that the cumulative impact of minor irritants was eroding his enthusiasm. Maybe, he thought, that was why he was hesitant about leaving for work. Perhaps it was not, though. It might just be the rain.

As Bill took a last sip of coffee, he pondered whether he might have changed more in the last year than he had realized. Maybe he was becoming one of those burned-out professionals everybody was talking about. Bill was determined not to let burnout happen to him. He glanced over at his wife. "Well! I'm not going to let the weather get me down," he said. Without another word he got up and quickly pushed his chair under the table.

Bill's wife knew him well enough to recognize that all was not well. "Let's talk tonight," she suggested.

"Fine, I've got some ideas about school I want to share with you. I'll see you around 4:30." Taking a deep breath, Bill walked toward the door.

SIMILARITIES AMONG TEACHERS

The situation described above may seem a bit melodramatic, but is it really atypical? If you look closely, you can identify a number of similarities between Bill and other teachers. Most teachers enter their first teaching assignments with considerable enthusiasm for testing innovative ideas and for working with students and associates. Typically, as the novelty of the new job wears off, the enthusiasm of the teacher also begins to wane. Also, as teachers begin to tackle problems that they never knew existed while in college, they lose some of their energy. Unfortunately, the decline in enthusiasm often occurs more quickly than it did even for Bill. A number of studies (e.g., Magoon and Davis, 1973; Mahan and Lacefield, 1976; Yee, 1969) suggest that shifts in attitudes begin even during student teaching. Magoon and Davis's research, for example, showed that individuals who had completed student teaching were much less positive toward education, students, parents, and colleagues than were those who had just begun their teacher-preparation programs. Among those who have been on the job for a few years, one-third strongly regret their decision to enter teaching and would choose another profession if they could start college anew (McGuire, 1979).

Although Bill had not yet encountered any major problems with others, he was conscious of the potentially additive effect of minor problems. His experience with minor daily problems is probably more characteristic of teaching than is exposure to singular, traumatic events. Nonetheless, some teachers do have to contend with physical threats from students—genuinely traumatic events. One survey (McGuire, 1979) revealed that one out of twenty teachers was physically attacked by students on school property during the 1978–79 school year. The rate is much higher in many inner-city areas. Twenty-five percent of teachers reported that they had personal property stolen at school and another twenty-five percent that they had personal property damaged at school during the 1978–79 school year. The threat of physical harm and loss of personal property is unlikely to add to the joy of one's teaching day.

● Slip Sliding Away

Have you ever made the comment, "That just burns me up?" Although that statement alone doesn't mean that one is suffering from burnout, it could be indicative of the need to take a closer look at yourself, your situation, or both. Most professionals agree that burnout progresses in stages. The early signs may be so innocuous as to go unnoticed. Phillips and Marriott (1980), for example, say that the beginning signs of burnout may be such simple occurrences as impatience or distractibility. Headaches, colds, and other minor maladies may be early physical signs that one is tiring of one's work. If these early signs go unnoticed, more serious problems may occur. According to Phillips and Marriott, the person may become more exhausted, experience a sense of being overwhelmed, and become more rigid in his or her thinking. Later signs include increased negativism toward home, work, and self. The end result is a depressed (burned out) professional who is no longer capable of doing the job or simply has lost all desire to do it.

Although many, if not all, teachers are exposed to circumstances that *could* result in burnout, most never reach a level of exhaustion that is irreversible. We believe that most teachers who lose the glow they had when they became teachers can regain it. ●

At this point you may be thinking, "Not all teachers lose their enthusiasm and develop negative attitudes toward teaching." This is true. Some teachers become even more positive and enthusiastic with time. They somehow manage to resolve the issues that were just beginning to concern Bill. However, even these special teachers have low points in their careers and from time to time they question their effectiveness. The critical issue in this text is not whether teachers occasionally get the blahs. All humans do. The critical issue is whether teachers can establish effective control over their lives and generally feel comfortable and enthusiastic about their work. Like Bill, most teachers would prefer to stay on top of their jobs: they want to grow personally and to feel that they are making a contribution to others. To date, too few teachers have been able to sustain their initial enthusiasm—let alone move to higher levels. Even those who appear to have gained control over their teaching often have done so at great personal expense. Need it be this way?

FINDING AN ANTIDOTE

In recent years a number of teachers have left the profession because of what is characterized as burnout. Possibly many more would have quit if the economic situation had not created such a tight job market. However, experts are now beginning to predict that the decrease in the number of people entering the teaching profession in combination with an upturn in the economy could actually lead to a teacher shortage in a few years (Lione, 1980). Well, one can dream!

With all the reports about the negative aspects of teaching, it is tempting to recommend that others not enter the field and that experienced teachers get out as quickly as possible and prepare themselves for more promising professions. If we were convinced that contemporary teaching was inherently a demoralizing profession, we would join the exodus. However, before we reach that point of resignation, we will consider some options that may still be available for salvaging your involvement in a noble profession.

Several options are available for combating the deterioration of teacher ideals and for fostering the continued development of desired teacher behaviors. First, teachers can work for changes in the educational system itself. A basic assumption in this approach is that teachers become products of the environment to which they are exposed. For example, a school system that solicits teacher ideas will cultivate the intellectual growth of its teachers. Conversely, a setting where teachers are told, "We don't do things that way around here," will stifle creativity. As one educator put it (Crockenberg, 1975, p. 189): ". . . the mindlessness, the intellectual docility, and subservience that have continued to characterize teachers are directly a function of the working conditions of teachers; more specifically, that teachers are denied the conditions necessary for the development of the mind because of the way in which schools are organized and controlled." The attempts of professional education associations, teachers' unions, PTAs, and community action groups to improve the working conditions of teachers and to give teachers more voice in school affairs are predicated on the belief that the teaching-learning process will improve once the conditions in the schools improve.

There is considerable merit in everyone working to create a more favorable school environment. Teachers should definitely be at the forefront of such activities. However, an approach that can serve as an alternative to, or be used in conjunction with, attempts to change the system is for teachers to work for self-changes. This is not to say that teachers should adjust themselves to unreasonable school environments. Rather, they should consider how their own behaviors influence the school environment. Teachers do not merely react to the environment and become good or bad teachers as a function of the environment. They also operate on the environment. Part of the way in which others respond to teachers is a result of how teachers behave. In other words, teachers bring something to the situation. Besides, self-control may be the most efficient way of producing environmental changes. If teachers can learn to resist the initial pressures to conform, for example, they may eventually produce changes in the environment.

● Turned On Again

Ann was in her fifth year of teaching. She was enjoying her job more than ever. She had become an ardent jogger, was active in her local teachers association, and was pursuing an advanced degree through night classes. Ann also looked forward to school, even when she was working out problems with students. Things had not always gone so well for her, however. There had been a time during the previous three years when her chief pleasure had been getting home in the afternoon so that she could have a glass of wine and start forgetting about school. Fortunately, at the beginning of the new school year Ann reappraised her life. She began looking for constructive activities to resolve her problems rather than trying to escape them. She also began to place fewer demands on herself. Previously, Ann had been so worried about being held accountable for the students' behaviors—in and out of school—that she had rendered herself unable to perform her job effectively. Her involvement with the teachers association helped her realize what a teacher can realistically expect to achieve with students. Her jogging helped her become more mentally and physically able to face problems as they arose. Finally, her efforts in pursuing a degree gave Ann a new enthusiasm about herself and about teaching. Ann knew that difficulties might lie ahead, but now she was on the offensive, determined to grow rather than merely survive and actively working toward goals. ●

The remaining chapters of this text emphasize how teachers can develop greater self-improvement skills and thus create the kinds of environments they desire. The self-improvement approach itself is not just a matter of exhorting yourself to "try harder," "be a better teacher," "get hold of yourself," or "don't lose your cool." Exhortation alone seldom produces lasting changes. Rather, self-improvement involves manipulating thoughts, behaviors, and environmental events to achieve outcomes related to effective teaching. The approach comes down to implementing specific techniques as opposed to mere exhortation.

PREREQUISITES TO SELF-IMPROVEMENT

Although the use of self-improvement approaches holds considerable promise, teachers vary drastically in their willingness to turn to self-improvement as a means of achieving desired goals. Their willingness (or unwillingness) to use self-improvement strategies is closely related to how they have come to think about themselves and their situation. For example, teachers who contend that they are not good at a particular activity are less likely to participate in the activity or, even if they do participate, are less likely to perform as well as they potentially could. Conversely, teachers who think positively about themselves are more likely to perform up to their potential and to receive positive reactions from others.

One of the foremost advocates of positive thinking in this century says (Peale, 1952, p. 11): "Any fact facing us, however difficult, even seemingly hopeless, is not so important as our attitude toward that fact. How you think about a fact may defeat you before you ever do anything about it. You may permit a fact to overwhelm you mentally before you start to deal with it actually. On the other hand, a confident and optimistic thought pattern can modify or overcome the fact altogether." What we are saying, in brief, is that what teachers believe will dictate whether they seek self-improvement as a means of achieving success. Therefore, before we examine the mechanics of self-improvement, we will look briefly at those beliefs which seem to promote the use of self-improvement strategies.

A BELIEF IN SELF-WORTH

The major portion of professional education courses is aimed at training teachers to help others. Examination of any number of educational psychology books, for instance, will reveal that students—not teachers—are the center of attention. Teachers are taught how to motivate students, how to instruct students, and how to evaluate student progress. They are continually reminded of the importance of the students' welfare. Obviously, understanding students is an essential aspect of becoming an effective teacher. Consequently, teachers seek educational experiences oriented toward understanding students. Courses in child and adolescent development are a part of most teacher-education programs. As a group, teachers probably have as much interest in helping others as any other group of professionals.

Overattention to students, however, can cause teachers to lose sight of themselves. Teachers need to understand themselves, how they are motivated, and how they can evaluate their own progress. Greater knowledge of students in no way guarantees that teachers can control themselves. Furthermore, teachers must begin to recognize their own importance. Their well-being should be a first consideration because of the influence teachers have on others. Jo Ann Norris, a North Carolina teacher-of-the-year, puts it this way: "Someone has said that the hope of the future lies in our children. I contend that the hope of the future lies in you and me, the TEACHERS of the children" (1980, p. 7). In her talks with teachers she has stressed the need for teachers to raise their self-image, recognizing their own value and the value of what they do. She contends that teacher performance is significantly associated with what teachers think of themselves. So do we.

• By Popular Demand

John was the principal of a new middle school that had been open for two years. The school had its share of problems ranging from truancy and vandalism to poor achievement. Yet, John liked to think of himself as being willing to help his teachers obtain the kind of training they needed to meet student needs. So, at the beginning of the second school year, John advised his teachers that he could arrange for a series of in-service courses that could be used for teacher-certification renewal and for graduate credits. John asked the teachers for their suggestions. Not surprisingly, the teachers asked for courses on adolescent psychology, behavior modification, individual instruction, and remedial reading. John's teachers wanted to know more about helping students. They made comments such as: "I need to be able to get inside the students' heads to know how they think." "Some of today's kids just don't seem to be motivated. We need courses on how to get these students interested in school." "We need class work on how to identify and help problem students."

Although John realized that teachers had needs of their own, no one mentioned a need for courses on stress reduction, self-analysis, assertiveness training, group dynamics, or anything generally related to self-enhancement. Several teachers mentioned the need for a course on games for students. No one requested recreational activities for teachers. John wondered why the teachers focused all their attention on helping students. Had the teachers been indoctrinated to think only of others? Were they afraid to admit personal problems? What is your assessment? ●

A Belief in the Potentiality of Self-Control

Many individuals feel that their problems are largely a function of the "system" and that the "system" is too big and impersonal for them to take on. These individuals possess what psychologists call perceived external locus of control. Teachers with this orientation are apt to contend that others choose their students, select their texts, determine their teaching assignments, and, in general, control their lives. They often see themselves as being small cogs in a vast bureaucratic machine. They feel helpless to do anything about their situation. More and more they yield to external forces.

Possibilities for self-improvement, of course, are minimal

so long as teachers feel that the major forces controlling their lives lie outside themselves. What teachers must do is to develop more of a perceived internal locus of control. In other words, they must start asking, "If I cannot transform the system, what modification is possible within my particular teaching situation at this point?" "What control can I exercise over my life?" Williams and Long (1979) suggest that a shift from external to internal locus of control evolves from successfully completing self-change activities. In brief, success seems to foster the belief that individuals can control themselves.

• There Is a Force

Hanna Levenson, a noted psychologist, has developed a Locus of Control Scale (1974) to assist individuals in determining how they perceive the controlling forces in their lives: are their destinies controlled by themselves, by powerful others, or by chance factors? On Levenson's scale the perception that an individual is in control of his or her own life is reflected by agreement with such statements as "When I make plans I am almost certain to make them work" and "I can pretty much determine what will happen in my life." The conception that others are in control is reflected by agreement with such statements as "People like [me] have little chance of protecting our personal interests when they conflict with those of strong pressure groups." Individuals who believe that their lives are controlled by chance are apt to agree with such ideas as "To a great extent my life is controlled by accidental happenings" and "I have often found that what is going to happen will happen."

An alternative to using Levenson's Locus of Control Scale would be to log the statements you make about critical events in your life. How often, for example, do you talk about luck determining your fate? Do you complain about the influence of powerful others on your life? Or do you consider most often how you can bring your own abilities to the resolution of problems? A personal assessment with these and similar questions should help you evaluate your own orientation to the controlling forces in your life. •

In suggesting that teachers can change certain factors of their professional lives, we do not want to give the impression that teachers should assume total responsibility for producing change in every aspect of school life. Teachers, obviously, are not responsible for all the ills of our educational system any more than they are responsible for all of its achievements. We know that you will agree, however, that teachers can take much credit for the advancement of education. You will undoubtedly also agree that teachers occasionally contribute to the problems. Unfortunately, teachers are as reluctant to accept blame as they are to take credit. In a recent survey (Long and Mamola, 1978) of 1,200 teachers, no teachers mentioned themselves when asked: "What are the sources of your major school problems?" The system, parents, principal, and students were identified as the sources of a variety of problems. Possibly the teachers' responses grew from a desire to help others. On the other hand, the teachers may have claimed to be problem-free because they feared how others would react if they accepted any blame. In either event the failure to assume at least some responsibility for their problems precluded any need for the teachers to change. We think, however, that when teachers can recognize their potential to exert control over their lives, they will also be able to define clearly where their own responsibilities to others begin and end.

A COMMITMENT TO MOTIVATION AND KNOWLEDGE

Many teachers have the idea that self-improvement is simply a matter of wanting to change. They tell themselves and their students: "You can do anything if you want to badly enough." This philosophy can create two problems. First, it inhibits searching for alternative ways of producing change. Who needs to look for alternatives if desire *alone* will suffice? Maybe this philosophy partially explains why one study (Blair, Jones, and Simpson, 1975) revealed that during a given month 40 percent of the 746 teachers and administrators questioned had not looked at a single professional book and 14 percent had read no professional magazine articles.

Second, the belief that motivation is sufficient for self-control can leave teachers immobilized when they fail to solve their problems. All teachers want to do a good job in teaching. Many give up entirely when their good intentions prove insufficient for the job. Teachers must have something going for themselves besides motivation. They must also know how to achieve their goals. Therefore, much of the rest of this book will be devoted to exploring strategies that can be used in achieving the goals teachers want for their lives. This combination of motivation and knowledge can lead to successful self-management. Either ingredient by itself will be inadequate.

● Who Needs It?

A barrier to applying self-improvement to teaching, one that we hope to remedy in this book, is simply not knowing where to begin and how to proceed. You may have already identified several facets of your teaching behavior that probably should be changed. Where do you start to change? How do you identify which changes would be fundamental to other changes? Even if you know what you want to change, how do you go about changing it? If you can answer these questions, you may not need our text. However, if you want to change, have accepted responsibility for change, but simply don't have a very clear idea of how to proceed with that quest, our text should help. ●

A COMMITMENT TO GROWTH

You may have gotten the idea that self-improvement strategies can eventually lead to perfection. In reality, perfection is an unattainable and often counterproductive pursuit. Many individuals enter the teaching profession with the idealistic aspiration of helping *all* students. They want to be liked by all students and to see all students make significant academic improvements. We have not found this to be the case under the most optimal of academic circumstances for even the most experienced teachers. You simply cannot be responsible for the child's total environment; people and circumstances both in and out of school can negate your noble intentions. However, because some individuals are unprepared for these failures, they lose heart about their teaching when such failures occur. The response is, "If I can't be a really top-notch teacher, why bother trying to improve my teaching skills?"

You will find a world of difference between those strategies which you can describe while in a teaching-training program and those strategies which you can implement when you are first thrust into an actual teaching situation. A tremendous amount of on-the-job learning must occur in every profession. You certainly will not begin your professional career as a perfect teacher, and, as a matter of fact, you will never achieve such perfection. The theme of our text is "growth," not "perfection." Growth is a realistic expectation for *any* teacher, whereas perfection is a realistic expectation for *no* teacher.

CONCLUDING COMMENTS

During the course of their professional training, prospective teachers get exposed to a variety of strategies directed at helping them work more effectively with students. Most future teachers are also introduced to the problems that exist in the schools and are given suggestions on how to confront those problems. Almost all begin their career with high expectations. Unfortunately, few teachers are taught how to maintain their enthusiasm when their initial efforts meet with resistance. Perhaps techniques learned in college are abandoned as unworkable because teachers have never learned how to analyze and control the factors that sustain behavior change. This inadequacy need not exist.

Self-improvement strategies are available for the myriad of personal and professional problems that lead teachers to burnout rather than growth. A recent review (Glasgow and Rosen, 1978) of self-help manuals, for example, uncovered more than seventy-five self-help books published in a five-year period. Numerous case studies and experiments were also conducted during that time. The topics ranged from increasing one's assertiveness and reducing anxieties to managing child behaviors and improving one's physique. Although many of these works are of dubious value, teachers have yet to tap the worthwhile resources that are available. Too few teachers have learned to ask, "How can I help myself?" Certainly, self-improvement is no panacea. Any approach has obstacles and pitfalls. Self-improvement does offer hope, however, and lasting changes begin with hope. In the chapters that lie ahead, the hope and potential of self-improvement will be examined in detail.

We will be talking about how to manage minor as well as serious discipline problems, stress, time demands, professional relationships, lesson planning, and a variety of other problems that beset teachers. We will also discuss ways in which teachers can use self-improvement techniques to develop hobbies and interests unrelated to work. We believe that the ways in which teachers are spending their non-teaching hours may be contributing significantly to the burnout phenomenon. Our hope is that the techniques described in the remaining chapters will aid teachers in maintaining or in rekindling the fires that led them to select teaching as a career.

REFERENCES

Blair, G. M., R. S. Jones, and R. H. Simpson. *Educational psychology,* 4th ed. New York: Macmillan Publishing Company, Inc., 1975.

Crockenberg, V. "Poor teachers are made not born." *Educational Forum 39* (1975): 189–198.

Glasgow, R. E. and G. M. Rosen. "Behavioral bibliotherapy: A review of self-help behavior therapy manuals." *Psychological Bulletin 85* (1978): 1–23.

Levenson, H. "Activism and powerful others: Distinctions with the concept of internal-external control. *Journal of Personality Assessment 38* (1974): 377–383.

Lione, L. H. "Teacher burnout: The next crisis in the classroom?" *Charlotte Observer,* October 12, 1980: 1B.

Long, J. D. and C. Mamola. "Perceived problems in teaching." Paper presented at the 2nd Annual Meeting of the Research and Development Association for Education, Alexandria, Va., November 1978.

Magoon, R. A. and T. B. Davis. "A developmental validative study of a semantic differential scale for studying attitudes and values." *Education and psychology: Past, present, and future.* Columbus, Ohio: Charles E. Merrill, 1973.

Mahan, J. M. and W. E. Lacefield. "Student teacher educational attitude changes in year-long placements examined from a cognitive dissonance framework." *Teacher Education Forum 4* (1976).

McGuire, W. H. "Teacher burnout." *Today's Education 68* (1979): 5.

Norris, J. A. "I'm the best teacher I know!" *N.C. Education 10* (7) (1980): 6–8.

Peale, N. V. *The power of positive thinking.* New York: Prentice-Hall, Inc., 1952.

Phillips, T. J. and K. A. Marriott. "Burnout." *Programming* (May 1980): 36–39.

Williams, R. L. and J. D. Long. *Toward a self-managed life style,* 2nd ed. Boston: Houghton-Mifflin Company, 1979.

Yee, A. H. "Do cooperating teachers influence the attitudes of student teachers?" *Journal of Educational Psychology 60* (1969): 327–332.

CHAPTER TWO

THE SECOND TIME AROUND: DEVELOPING AN APPROACH TO SELF-IMPROVEMENT

AS JOYCE was loudly admonishing two boys for horseplay in her classroom, the father of one of the boys entered the class to pick up his child early. Ted overslept and was fifteen minutes late getting to work, and as he rushed into the building he accidently collided with the principal. The one day that Liz was at a loss about what to do in language arts, the supervisor came for a surprise visit. You can conclude in each of these instances that:

A. It will never happen again,
B. The teachers should be happy they have it so good,
C. The teachers should start looking for other work,
D. Murphy's law (sometimes interpreted to mean that if things can go wrong they will) is in operation.

If you picked D, you *might* be correct. Murphy's law does sometimes seem ubiquitous. However, we really believe that "none of the above" (a choice you were not given) is correct.

Educators, including the student teacher who is spending her first day in the classroom as well as the forty-year veteran, will surely make mistakes. Seldom, however, is a mistake so great that it cannot be overcome. The misfortune is that some individuals let one mistake undermine a multitude of potential successes. They feel guilty and lament what went wrong when they could be concentrating on how to handle similar situations in the future.

What teachers obviously need is an approach that not only can help them reduce their mistakes but also can help them develop confidence about facing tomorrow. Possibly, the major reason why so many teachers "burn out" is that they have no systematic way of viewing themselves positively or of managing their difficulties. Even those who resolve a problem on the spot often do so without conscious awareness of their approach and may have difficulty with an identical problem in the future. This chapter, therefore, is designed to offer teachers a plan that is largely under their own control: one for developing their self-image as they go about managing the many problems that arise in teaching. The plan includes strategies for assessing personal strengths, setting goals, identifying what it takes to reach those goals, and measuring progress toward goals. Although the present chapter describes how the model can be used in getting a broad perspective on one's teaching, subsequent chapters demonstrate in detail how the model can be applied to specific problem areas in teaching.

ASSESSING YOUR STRENGTHS

One of the most perplexing issues in self-improvement is determining where to begin. You may feel that something needs to be done to improve your situation, but you may be so overwhelmed by day-to-day problems that you do not get around to deciding *what*. Or, even if you attempt to improve some aspects of your life, your efforts may be thwarted by doubts about the real importance of what you are trying to change. Individuals who have just been involved in controversy or who have just made an error in handling a problem are especially prone to question the usefulness of all their efforts. Teachers, for example, say that their self-concepts drop considerably when they question the meaning of teaching (Hendrickson, 1979). Individuals can let feelings of inadequacy become so extreme that they eventually *do* render themselves ineffective in working with others. Thus, we want to provide a framework to help you put your errors in perspective as well as to provide the morale needed to sustain your self-improvement activities.

We strongly believe that changes in one's life are best made from a base of strengths rather than from a catalog of deficiencies. Immediately focusing on what has gone wrong in your life may immobilize rather than motivate. You may decide that there is so much to be changed that the task is practically impossible or that there is so much wrong that your situation is hopeless. For the time being, we will forget about what might be wrong and focus on what is right. From that base we can work on adding skills to your repertoire.

● I'd Give a Thousand Dollars to . . .

Did you ever want to trade places with someone else? Most of us have. Yet, have you ever considered that someone else is probably wishing that he or she were in your shoes? The fact that you are about to obtain a degree in teaching (or already have) is something not achieved by a majority of the U.S. population. It represents a goal toward which families are willing to invest thousands of dollars. What you have already done by merely attending college is something generally valued in this society. The chances are also good that you have extensive training in a particular content area, such as art, music, physical education, mathematics, reading, or science. Many persons seeking information about your discipline would actually consider you an authority in that area. Also, if you have a teaching position, you are envied by many others. Not everyone who wants a job as a teacher gets one. So, before you bemoan your fate as a teacher or prospective teacher, why not take stock of what you have that others would like to have? ●

No matter how much difficulty you perceive yourself as experiencing, we would wager that you are doing more things right than wrong. We realize, however, that you could

easily lose sight of those "rights" in the midst of daily confrontations and disappointments. It is critical, therefore,
that you determine what is right with your situation (be it
that of a teacher in training or of one already in the field) so
that you can build on that base. Unfortunately, few persons
have been trained to recognize and use all the assets they
possess. The following pages describe a number of strategies
that should assist you in that quest.

TAKING INVENTORY

A logical starting point is to take an inventory of your
strengths. Your strengths could include abilities, skills, or
traits you deem helpful in realizing your full potential. Perhaps you have skill or aptitude in sports, music, art, speech,
mathematics, or equipment repair. Do not overlook any
area of your life as you inventory your strengths. If you experience difficulty thinking of yourself in positive terms
(most persons do), you can use a descriptive word list to get
you started. Table 2.1 contains descriptive words that may
be of value to you. To use the table, circle the adjectives (a
minimum of 10) that best describe you. You can also ask
friends to check the words they think best fit you.

If you prefer working with others in determining your
strengths, the Multiple Strength Perception Method (M.S.P.
Method) developed by Herbert Otto (1966) should be of
interest to you. In the M.S.P. Method a target person enu-
merates his or her strengths aloud before a group. The
group members are then asked to identify all additional
strengths they see in the individual. The group in effect
"bombards" the target individual with a list of his or her
strengths. At the request of the target person, the group members also identify what they believe is keeping the individual from reaching his or her full potential. The focus,
however, is on the use of strengths—not on obstacles per se.
The results of the strengths bombardment appear to be
1) increased awareness of one's strengths and 2) an enhanced
self-concept. Participants in Otto's M.S.P. Method also

TABLE 2.1

ADJECTIVE CHECKLIST OF POSITIVE CHARACTERISTICS THAT PERSONS OFTEN OVERLOOK ABOUT THEMSELVES

Accepting	Devoted	Judicious	Proficient
Accommodating	Direct	Just	Progressive
Active	Discreet		Punctual
Adventuresome	Distinctive	Keen	
Affable		Kind	Quick
Analytical	Efficient	Knowledgeable	
Appreciative	Effervescent		Realistic
Approachable	Empathic	Liberal	Reasonable
Artistic	Energetic	Likable	Receptive
Assertive	Enthusiastic	Lively	Refreshing
Astute	Expressive	Lucid	Reinforcing
Attractive			Reliable
	Fair	Mathematical	Responsible
Beautiful	Forgiving	Motivating	
Bold	Friendly	Musical	Sensible
Bright			Sensitive
Bustling	Gentle	Natural	Sharing
	Giving	Neat	Skillful
Calm	Glowing	Nice	Sociable
Capable	Gracious	Nimble	Spontaneous
Charitable	Graceful	Novel	Stable
Cheerful			Strong
Clear	Handsome	Objective	Succinct
Compassionate	Helpful	Open	Swift
Competent	Humane	Optimistic	
Concerned	Humorous	Organized	Tactful
Confident		Original	Talented
Congenial	Imaginative		Thoughtful
Conscientious	Independent	Patient	Trustworthy
Considerate	Inductive	Perceptive	Tenacious
Cool	Industrious	Persuasive	Theatrical
Cooperative	Innovative	Pleasant	
Creative	Inquisitive	Poetic	Understanding
	Insightful	Poised	
Deductive	Instructive	Positive	Vigilant
Democratic	Interested	Practical	
Dependable		Pretty	Warm
Determined	Jovial	Productive	Wholesome

report increases in work productivity. Increased confidence seems to lead people to undertake tasks they have previously put off trying.

A variation of the group use of strengths bombardment would be to use the method with a trusted colleague. You and your colleague could take turns at strengths bombardment. (It surely beats finding faults.) Start by enumerating your strengths and by having your partner add to the list. Then switch roles and help your partner assess his or her strengths. If you have reservations about this approach because it sounds like bragging, never mind. You are simply looking at your virtues. You can reduce feelings of bragging by avoiding comparative statements. Braggarts are prone to say, "I am the best at ———," as opposed to "I am good at ———" or "I'm improving at ———." The first statement antagonizes others and makes people hesitant to assess their strengths. The latter statements permit you to feel good about yourself without implicitly putting others down.

Another potential source of information about your strengths is your own students. Teachers often avoid seeking input from students for fear of being inundated with criticism. Because an avalanche of criticism is not tempting to any of us and is certainly not a good beginning point for self-improvement, why not initially solicit input from students regarding what you are doing that is helpful to them? You could preface your request by indicating that you want to do more of those things which help them learn and feel confident about themselves. Then, your question might be, "What am I doing that makes you feel good about yourself and helps you learn?" With this base of student support, you can later take on those areas in which you are not facilitating students' personal and academic growth.

• Ever Think of Keeping a Serendipity File?

Kay was depressed. Lately there seemed to be no end to her self-deprecating thoughts. She kept lamenting, "Why can't I do anything right?" "Why am I not good at anything?" All her assets—her earned degrees, her family, her good health, her attractive appearance—were overlooked. As Kay sat brooding over a lesson plan for the next day, a note fell from her text. It was a note from Billy with the message, "You're the nicest teacher in the world." Kay went to the closet and began sorting through papers from days past. She uncovered notes pointing to a number of personal strengths. Over the past five years Kay had received hundreds of short, laudatory notes from students. "How could I have forgotten these?" she thought. At that point Kay resolved to take stock of what others thought about her. She began to save all the nice messages passed on to her. She even began writing more notes to students. Later on, when Kay began feeling sorry for herself, she would look at the student messages. This approach helped. Billy's thoughtfulness gave Kay the impetus to take a new look at herself. ●

POSITIVE EXPERIENCES

Focusing on your positive experiences represents another strategy for gaining greater insight into your strengths. You might begin using this strategy by considering your most recent positive experiences. For example, what nice thing happened to you today? It would probably be easier to say what bad things happened. Individuals may have a number of positive experiences during a day with only a single negative occurence, but when asked "How was your day?" the response invariably is "Terrible." The positive events get taken for granted, while the negative ones receive disproportionate attention. Recollection of negative experiences places emphasis on one's weaknesses. To avoid this dilemma, try talking about all the nice things that happen to you. Emphasizing the good points of your day will cause others to enjoy being around you even more. You might even want to write down your positive experiences if this approach is more reinforcing to you. In either event focusing on your positive experiences will give you a good base on which to build your next day.

If you are unable to think of any recent positive experiences, do not despair. You can go farther back in time. Maslow's concept of peak experiences (1962), for example, represents one useful way of uncovering positive happenings from the past. Maslow's emphasis, however, is on the happiest or most ecstatic moments in your life. Yet, these moments can serve to highlight your most outstanding assets. Think back on your life. What especially pleasant events stand out? Were they related to outstanding achievements, approving comments from others, interpersonal interactions? Now consider why these moments occurred. Undoubtedly, your strengths were involved in producing these peak experiences.

Another form of positive experience from the past is known as the Minerva Experience. Otto (1966, 1968) describes these Minerva Experiences as highly formative events that contain positive emotional components. Unlike peak experiences, Minerva Experiences need not be your most blissful moments. Any happening about which you have felt positive could be classified as a Minerva Experience. One way to recall Minerva Experiences is to think of an age span—for example, ten to twelve—and try to recall the positive happenings during that span. Otto says that recall of one Minerva Experience will often trigger recall of others. Eventually, an entire network of experiences may unfold. What positive experiences can you recall from your childhood? Do you see how this recall process could influence your present development?

RELATING GOALS TO STRENGTHS

From this point on, the major focus of our model is extending your strengths. In this chapter we have considered strengths assessment from a broad perspective. However, when you identify a particular problem area in your teaching, you should designate strengths related to that specific area. For example, if you are having difficulty leading class discussions, you should first try to identify your discussion-related skills and then determine the logical step for extending those skills. You may feel that your class focuses on relevant issues, that you ask provocative questions concerning those issues, but that you are inclined to disagree with most student responses to your questions. Thus, your first goal in this area might be learning to respond more supportively to student comments. This goal would be a logical extension of the class-discussion skills you already have. We are obviously defining goals as desired extensions of your present skills. In fact, a goal may simply be the strengthening of a relatively weak skill or the application of a skill in the classroom that you already employ in other situations.

In this section we will suggest some ground rules for determining areas where goal formulation would be appropriate. We know that you want to be a successful teacher. This section should give you some assistance in determining what it will take beyond your present skills to actualize that aspiration.

ESTABLISH PRIORITIES

One of the first considerations in goal setting is to establish a priority for your goals. Not uncommonly, teachers become involved in a multiplicity of goal-related activities. They frequently find themselves moving busily from one activity to the next with little thought given to the importance of the activity. However, treading a wheel cannot be equated with productivity. A strategy that is better than to increase activity per se is to determine those goals which merit the expenditure of effort. In other words, you should identify those broad goals which are most important to you. You can begin by making a list of all the goals you would personally like to achieve. If you have doubts about the goals that are most important to you, a review of Table 2.2 should help. You can establish your priorities by ranking the goals in Table 2.2 from *most* to *least* important. Any other goals that you deem worthy of consideration can be added. Additional goals could include those set by others (e.g., administrators, parents, students) that you believe are essential to your success and happiness.

TABLE 2.2

BROAD PRIORITIES

Rank (High to Low)	Goal
_____	To manage my time and work schedule more effectively.
_____	To improve classroom discipline.
_____	To enhance my interpersonal interactions in the school.
_____	To become a more creative teacher.
_____	To control the way in which I react to problems (to reduce stress).
_____	To increase my personal interests/activities outside of school.
_____	To broaden my academic competencies.
_____	To improve the academic skills of my students.
_____	To contribute to the social development of my students.
_____	To become more self-confident/assertive.
_____	To do more long-term planning.
_____	To improve my professional contacts outside the classroom.
_____	Others

REFINE YOUR GOALS

Now that you have set priorities among your goals, a second step is to look for subordinate goals that comprise your broader goals. For example, subordinate goals for enhancing interpersonal relations might include identifying at least one positive quality in each of your students, offering more praise in class situations, participating with students in recreational activities, expressing appreciation to the principal when support is given to you, and developing a team approach with a colleague. Refining your goals will give you a high degree of goal clarity and should be more effective in helping you to alter your behavior. In fact, reviews covering years of goal-related research (Locke, 1975; Steers and Porter, 1974) have shown that greater goal specificity is consistently related to 1) improved performance and 2) higher job satisfaction. Researchers (e.g., Latham, Mitchell, and Dossett, 1978; Terborg, 1976) believe that specificity enables individuals to improve performance because specific goals suggest *specific* actions. For example, wanting to identify the positive qualities in your students immediately suggests having discussions with the students about their interests and abilities, reviewing the students' past accomplishments, and meeting with parents. These plans should eventually contribute to reaching the broader goal of improving interpersonal relationships. Reaching an important goal should contribute significantly to your job satisfaction and perhaps to your general happiness.

CHALLENGE YOURSELF

Another consideration in goal setting relates to the difficulty level of your goals. Should your initial goals be difficult or easy to attain? One researcher (Locke, 1968) has found a positive relationship between difficult goals and improved performance. He suggests that difficult goals increase the likelihood that one will work toward goal attainment. However, an extremely difficult goal might be so far beyond your present performance level that you would have minimal chances of attaining it. That would quickly undermine your self-management endeavors. A reasonable solution to this dilemma would be to select moderately difficult goals and raise your expectations as you experience success.

Not everyone is willing to take the risks inherent in

seeking challenging goals. A person's initial achievement motivation affects the difficulty level of the goals he or she selects (Alschuler, Tabor, and McIntyre, 1971; McClelland, 1965). Persons with high motivation to achieve generally set moderately difficult goals for themselves. Conversely, persons who fear failure may set extremely low or extremely high goals for themselves. Unfortunately, easy goals often do not produce behavior changes or improve performance. High goal setting would seem to involve great risks, but actually it reduces risks because no one expects people to reach impossibly high goals. The excessively high goal setter can say to himself or herself: "I failed, but so what? No one else could have done it."

If you believe that your own feelings about success and failure have inhibited you from setting appropriate goals, do not despair. Individuals can change their orientations toward higher achievement. Recognizing your fears about success and failure and establishing challenging, but not impossible, goals are requisites for productive change. Later in the chapter more will be said about techniques that can move you toward successful attainment of your goals.

● How Much Is Too Much?

Joan, a third-year teacher, recognized that in an effort to control her seventh-grade class she was becoming increasingly critical. An analysis of her verbal interactions with students showed that about 5 percent of her remarks (ten per day) could be categorized as approval, whereas 20 percent were negative. She wanted to reverse this relationship but had reservations about the impact on student behavior. She wondered if students who had been accustomed to punitive measures would view approval as a sign of weakness. She did not want students to take advantage of her. Joan also feared that too radical a change might be viewed with skepticism. She could just hear her students saying, "Oh, Ms. Wilson is just being nice to get more work from us." Yet, Joan was determined to become more positive. She decided to begin by doubling the number of positive comments she was making. Joan felt that an increase of one or two positive statements would give her little personal satisfaction and probably would have minimal impact on her students. On the other hand, she reasoned that ten additional positive comments would be rewarding to herself as well as to her students. She did not think that this shift in her verbal behavior was so great as to create any new problems with students. What do you believe happened? Did Joan set her initial goal too high or too low? ●

ACCENT THE POSITIVE

It is generally best to state your goals positively. The setting of positive goals is preferable because, typically, positive actions bring the greatest fulfillment to your life. Thinking in terms of what should *not* be gives an unpleasant aura to the entire concept of self-management. Teachers particularly have become disillusioned with admonitions for them to be content with living austere, sacrificial lives. An early Southern newspaper account describing the desired code of conduct for female teachers vividly reveals the unacceptability of the negative approach:

> . . . I promise to abstain from all dancing, immodest dressing, and any other conduct unbecoming a teacher and a lady. I promise not to go out with any young man except in so far as it may be necessary to stimulate Sunday-school work. I promise not to fall in love, to become engaged or secretly married. I promise to remain in the dormitory or on the school grounds when not actively engaged in school or church work elsewhere. I promise not to encourage or tolerate the least familiarity on the part of any of my boy pupils.

Even if there are some things you would like to refrain from doing, you can still work within a positive framework. Suppose, for example, that you want to reduce the number of critical remarks you make. You could set your goal to increase the number of positive statements to others. You cannot be critical and positive simultaneously. Similarly, if you want to be less aggressive, try setting a goal of becoming more assertive. Assertive behavior allows you to respond to frustrating situations without attacking others. It is much easier to take positive actions than always to restrain yourself. Most of us do not even like to think about our negative qualities—let alone focus goals around them. The idea is to establish goals you care about achieving and not merely to think about what you do not want to do.

MANAGING ENVIRONMENTAL EVENTS

By analyzing your strengths and setting goals for yourself, you can probably achieve many self-management gains. However, a third strategy—managing environmental events—can add immeasurably to the control you have over your life. Whereas the first two strategies focus mainly on the impact that feelings and aspirations can have on behavior, the third strategy focuses on the importance of factors external to the self. All human behavior is preceded and followed by environmental events. These antecedent and consequent events have a major impact on how people feel as well as how they behave. Obviously, then, consideration of how you can control environmental events should be an integral part of your self-management endeavors.

CONTROLLING ANTECEDENT EVENTS

The events that precede behavior, referred to as antecedent events, serve to set the occasion for different types of behaviors. For instance, the ringing of a doorbell sets the occasion for going to the door; a nod or smile sets the occasion for continuing a discussion; and a frown signals the presence of unwanted behavior and sets the occasion for other actions. Attempts to control antecedent events as a means of achieving self-control have been widespread. Israel Goldiamond (1965) was among the first researchers to demonstrate the usefulness of the strategy. Stimulus control is the name he gave to the approach. Goldiamond used the approach initially to show how a young man could control his own weight by limiting the number of places where he ate. By avoiding eating while watching television and while studying, the young man was able to reduce the control these stimuli had on eating; eventually, the antecedent stimuli of turning on the television or opening a book no longer set the occasion for eating. Other researchers have shown how stimulus control can increase study behavior (Beneke and Harris, 1972; Fox, 1962). Subjects associated certain locales exclusively with studying, so that studying, not other behaviors, was precipitated when the subjects entered those locales.

Teachers are well aware of how antecedent events influence student behaviors. Teachers, for example, know that seating certain students near each other can set the occasion for disruptive behavior. They also understand how changing instructional materials, altering the lighting, and improving the decor of their room can affect students. Yet, teachers are less familiar with ways in which antecedent events affect their own actions. Perhaps you have begun to think about how certain events shape your day. Maybe you have noticed how being prepared for the first five minutes of class sets the occasion for how you perform the remainder of the hour. Or you may have noticed how a complaining colleague can start you to complaining. These and numerous other antecedent events can enhance or destroy the joy in teaching.

Basically, antecedent events are controlled in two ways: 1) by providing stimuli that set the occasion for wanted behaviors, and 2) by limiting the stimuli that precipitate unwanted behavior. If you wanted to increase the likelihood of a given behavior, you would need to identify stimuli that trigger the behavior and ensure their presence whenever the behavior was desired. The antecedent stimuli would not "make" you behave as desired; they would merely improve your chances. Suppose that you wanted to increase your input at faculty meetings. You would need to identify those events which would facilitate your active involvement in the meetings. Studying the agenda prior to the meetings, sharing your ideas with a colleague before the meetings, and sitting by supportive persons could all be related to how actively you participate once the meetings are underway. Expecting to be loquacious without arranging events in advance could be disappointing.

If you wished to reduce a behavior, you would need to identify and limit the presence of stimuli that precipitate the unwanted response. Suppose that you tend to get angry when parents question the approach you have taken with their child. Such a reaction could be the result of when and where you meet with parents, the presence of other persons, or lack of advanced preparation. A different reaction might be forthcoming by changing the place of the meeting, being prepared to discuss successes as well as failures, rehearsing how you might respond to various questions, and identifying something good about the parents' questions. You will note that even when you have eliminated the stimuli that precipitate unwanted actions, it is still appropriate to provide stimuli that support alternative actions. In either event the purpose is always to control your own behavior.

● Alice in Wonderland?

Alice's biggest problem each day was getting to work early enough to get a few things done before the students arrived. It seemed that every day she rushed into her room around 8:15. Shortly thereafter, students would begin arriving. The students either had things to tell her or they needed help with a lesson. Alice found it impossible to attend to the early arrivers and get organized at the same time. While she would be searching for an attendance sheet or scoring a paper, students would be asking questions. Invariably, Alice would get angry and shout, "Please get in your seats! Please leave me alone for just a minute!" The anxiety generated before classes ever began seemed to carry over until midmorning. Alice had frequent morning headaches. She also knew that she was being unfair in not giving students some undivided attention.

Alice decided to deal with her problem by changing some antecedent events. She began by changing her routine prior to leaving school. Instead of leaving as soon as the school day ended, Alice stayed for an extra fifteen minutes. She arranged her desk, organized reports that had to be submitted the next morning, and laid out materials she would be using the next day. By doing these tasks in the afternoon when no students were around, Alice felt that she would be better prepared to handle unexpected events in the mornings. Alice also changed events at home. Prior to retiring each night, she selected the clothes she would wear the next day, prepared a midday snack, and organized her briefcase, instead of hurriedly doing these tasks in the morning.

Can you guess what happened? Headaches, fussing, and "rushing about" all began to diminish. In fact, Alice began arriving at school relaxed. She even had time for a cup of coffee and a chat with colleagues before meeting her students. ●

MANAGING CONSEQUENCES

Whereas setting the occasion for specified behaviors is important, what happens after behaviors are emitted (the consequences of behavior) is equally important. If a behavior gets no attention or is punished, it will probably not be continued. Only when behaviors are positively reinforced (rewarded) are they likely to continue. Perhaps the first order of business in arranging positive consequences for desired behavior is to determine exactly what you find reinforcing. Approval from others, knowledge of progress, activities (e.g., movies, sporting events), and tangibles (e.g., money) are among the consequences that many teachers find reinforcing. A perusal of Table 2.3 should help you identify some potential rewards that can be applied to your own behaviors. Any event, so long as it maintains or increases the frequency of the behavior that it follows, meets the definition of a positive reinforcer. If a colleague tells you, "I'm glad you brought up that point," and you raise similar points in the future, then the colleague's comment is a positive reinforcer. Of course, other consequences, such as administrative reactions to your comments, could be influencing your behavior as well. Where a number of consequences follow a behavior, you will need to note the consequences that seem to be exerting the most influence. You can try manipulating each consequence in the future to determine exactly what is controlling your behavior.

TABLE 2.3

SELF-REWARDS THAT CAN BE APPLIED FOR ENGAGING IN APPROPRIATE GOAL-RELATED BEHAVIORS

Telling yourself "I have done an especially good job on. . ."
Making a note of your achievements in a "Personal Achievement File"
Recording your progress on a wall chart
Sharing your achievement with a friend
Arranging for your spouse to praise you when you have exhibited a desired behavior
Submitting a progress report to your supervisor
Listening to music
Relaxing in an easy chair
Taking a nap
Watching television
Reading a book
Attending a movie
Taking a walk
Going for a ride
Having an ice cream cone
Buying an article of clothing
Awarding yourself a token (e.g., a point) that can be "cashed in" later on a desired reward

A second consideration regarding the control of consequences is the availability of given reinforcers. Unfortunately, many teachers depend almost exclusively on tentative, illusive consequences. In a survey involving 1,200 classroom teachers (Long and Mamola, 1978), 85 percent of the male teachers and 90 percent of the female teachers indicated that seeing student progress and receiving appreciation from students and parents were highly rewarding aspects of teaching. The same teachers, however, listed lack of student interest, low achievement, and lack of respect from students as major problems. The trouble with this situation was that the teachers were depending on others to deliver the desired consequences. Teachers must be ready to apply their own reinforcers when others are nonsupportive of their constructive behaviors. A less attractive, yet accessible, reward is better than permitting desired acts to go unnoticed. When a "Thank you" from a student is not forthcoming, you might try sharing your achievement with a colleague, making a note about progress with the student, or giving yourself a few minutes of pleasure reading.

Closely related to the preceding paragraph is the question of who should deliver reinforcement. You may be thinking that consequences are less reinforcing if you apply them. Contrary to popular belief, consequences need not be applied by others in order to be reinforcing. Bandura and his colleagues found that self-administered consequences can be as potent as externally administered consequences (Bandura and Perloff, 1967). In fact, Bandura has suggested that self-application of rewards may actually be superior to externally administered reinforcement. The critical factor is not who applies a consequence. The most critical factors are that reinforcers be applied consistently and as soon as possible following the behavior to be influenced.

MEASURING PROGRESS

No self-improvement design would be complete without establishing procedures for measuring progress toward your goals. Many teachers, however, overlook the need for objectively evaluating their own behaviors. They feel that they can subjectively estimate their own progress. Unfortunately, the multiplicity of ongoing events causes teachers to lose track of their behavior. One highly noticeable occurrence may lead a teacher to think, "I'm not making any progress" or "Everything went well today." At other times changes occur so gradually that teachers do not realize how differently they are behaving. Evaluation of progress, or lack of it, need not be based on a guess. Many refined strategies are available for making accurate assessments. Two of the strategies most applicable to teaching are discussed below.

SELF-MONITORING

Monitoring one's own behavior is highly consistent with the theme of self-improvement and is becoming an increasingly popular method of evaluation. A variety of devices are available to help teachers increase the accuracy of their self-monitoring. Perhaps the most sophisticated device is the videotape. A videotape of yourself demonstrating a laboratory procedure or conducting a discussion can help you see yourself as others see you. However, simply viewing yourself interacting with others could be meaningless unless you focus on specific behaviors. One means of focusing on specific behaviors is to code various behaviors and to concentrate on those when viewing the videotape. Thomas (1971) found, for example, that having teachers code their positive comments as either "specific praise," which included giving a reason for the praise (e.g., "Good job, you solved this one correctly"), or "other praise" enabled teachers to direct their attention to specific behaviors they wanted to change and subsequently to make marked changes in those behaviors. In an earlier study, Birch (1969) found that pre-service teachers who did not look for specific behaviors while viewing videotapes paid attention primarily to their appearance and to obvious mannerisms of speech and gestures. Good and Brophy (1977) have also suggested that positive self-change with videotapes is unlikely unless teachers focus on reaching specific goals.

● Health Majors Do It

R. K. Means (1977), a professor of health education at Auburn University, is a strong proponent of videotaping. Means reports that his university has been using videotaping for a number of years as a way of improving teaching. At his university health-education majors prepare lessons for videotaping as a part of their teacher training.

The lessons range in length from ten to thirty minutes. In advance of each presentation the presenter submits a description of his or her topic, the teaching technique to be used, and the intended grade level to be taught. The lesson is then videotaped as it is presented to a class of peers. Each member of the class gives the presenter a written evaluation of the lesson. The evaluations that focus on evidence of preparation for the lesson, relevance of the lesson to assignments, organization, discussion skills, and value to the intended group serve as a reference when the presenter reviews his or her tape at a later date. Means says that faculty and students endorse the videotaping technique as one of the best learning opportunities available. Have you had an opportunity to see yourself teach? ●

If the idea of videotaping sounds unappealing, you might experiment with audiotaping. Like the videotape, an audiotape permits the counting of specific verbal behaviors and the assessment of time spent in a given behavior. The audiotape has the advantage of less time required to set up. An audiotape recorder also is much less "imposing" in the class. It can prove useful in monitoring such behaviors as speech interruptions (disfluencies), intonation, and succinctness in making a point.

Should neither the videotape nor audiotape be practical for measuring progress toward your goal, a number of other devices are available. You could try recording behaviors on index cards, with a wrist counter (e.g., a golf-stroke counter), or with a pocket counter. These devices are appropriate for making frequency counts on various behaviors. Behaviors of short duration that have a discrete beginning and end can be assessed via a frequency count. Approval and disapproval, questions and answers, and smiles and frowns are examples of behaviors that readily lend themselves to frequency count. For behaviors of longer duration, a stopwatch can be an appropriate self-monitoring device. A stopwatch is useful for logging the time spent in working with students, the time taken in responding to a question, the time spent grading papers, and other kinds of continuing behavior. Regardless of the device, the purpose is always the same—to let you know where you have been, where you are now, and where you are headed.

In addition to monitoring your behavior via various self-managing devices, you will probably find it helpful to graph your behavior on a daily basis. You can construct graphs from the frequency counts of your behaviors or from your logs of time spent in given behaviors. Simply plot the days on the horizontal axis and the frequency or amount on the vertical axis. Such graphs will permit you to make a quick assessment of how you are progressing. Seeing behavior improvement on your graph should prove reinforcing. In fact, graphing will go a long way in sustaining your self-management efforts.

FEEDBACK FROM OTHERS

Self-improvement does not mean that you have to be totally self-sufficient in managing your own behavior. You can get help from others. Teachers are in a unique position to receive feedback from others. One readily available source is the students. Students can tell you if you are helpful when they ask questions, treat all students with respect, are impartial in assigning grades, tell them when they have done especially well, introduce interesting topics, use sufficient examples to illustrate material, and so on. As a matter of fact, students probably are in the best position to judge the quality of your work. Early studies (Gage, 1963; Tuckman and Oliver, 1968) reveal that teachers can make substantial improvements in teaching based on feedback from students.

Colleagues and supervisors are also important sources of feedback. Colleagues can be especially helpful in giving feedback regarding your behavior in meetings, your interpersonal skills, and your emotional control in and out of the classroom. Supervisors can provide information related to your use of creative ideas, your relationships with parents and administrators, and your contributions to the system. Do not overlook the opinions of supervisors and administrators because, like it or not, they can affect your career. It is easy to make false assumptions about their views. For example, a recent survey (Long, 1979) comparing teachers who were judged by their supervisors as being either successful or unsuccessful revealed no significant differences in the way they perceived their success. Although some teachers were in jeopardy of losing their jobs, they rated themselves as successful and indicated that others viewed them similarly. A number of those judged as successful also misjudged how others evaluated them. If teachers are ever to understand how others see them, they must establish a workable means of achieving feedback from others.

Feedback can be potentially useful regardless of its source. However, adherence to certain guidelines can increase your success in obtaining usable feedback. First, be specific with the requests you make. For example, it is much better to ask "Do you feel free in disagreeing with me about. . . ?" than to ask "Am I an open person?" Second, listen carefully when others talk. Quick disagreement with others will signal that you are not really interested in hearing what they have to say. You can ask for clarification, of course, by interjecting "You think" or "You are saying," but try withholding a negative reaction. Consideration of the feedback for a few days before making any reaction may help you to see the wisdom of what others have to say. Third, ask for information that is relevant and limited to your goals. You can overburden others with too many requests. You can also be overwhelmed by too much feedback, especially when it is negative. Finally, ask for plans of action. If the person giving the feedback feels that you are moving toward your goal, ask how he or she thinks you can continue making progress. If changes are needed in your behavior, ask for specific suggestions on how the needed changes might be achieved. Research strongly suggests that teachers will change their behaviors when they are given relevant suggestions. Brophy and Good (1974) contend that "most inappropriate teaching is due to a lack of awareness in the teacher rather than to any deliberate callousness or inability to change." Few things can lead to greater self-awareness than properly solicited feedback.

SUMMARY

This chapter has been devoted to the development of a model for self-management. Specifically, the chapter has described how the assessment and use of strengths, goal setting, environmental manipulation, and measurement of progress toward goals fit together into a meaningful approach for managing one's life. Table 2.4 provides a thumbnail sketch of ways in which each step of the model can be applied. Although the model will never free teachers of all difficulties, it should prove useful for managing most problems confronting teachers. The model, however, offers more than a means of resolving problems. It offers a means by which teachers can find greater fulfillment in their jobs and lives. No claims are made that the model or any variation of it is the only way of achieving self-improvement. One thing is certain, though: the route to professional success depends more on you and your own planning than anything else.

TABLE 2.4
A MODEL FOR SELF-IMPROVEMENT

(STEP 1) Assessing Your Strengths	(STEP 2) Relating Goals to Strengths	(STEP 3) Managing Environmental Events	(STEP 4) Measuring Progress
A. Take inventory of your strengths via: 1. Positive adjective checklist, 2. Multiple Strengths Perception Method, 3. Identification of positive past experiences (Peak Experiences, Minerva Experiences).	A. Establish broad priorities for your life. B. Develop specific goals from your broad priorities. C. Establish goals that offer a challenge (i.e., moderately difficult goals). D. State goals in terms of positive outcomes.	A. Control antecedent events by: 1. Providing stimuli that set the occasion for wanted behavior, 2. Limiting stimuli that set the occasion for unwanted behavior. B. Manage consequences by: 1. Determining what is positively reinforcing, 2. Applying positive reinforcers to goal-related behaviors.	A. Monitor own behavior via: 1. Videotape, 2. Audiotape, 3. Mechanical counters (e.g., golf), 4. Paper and pencil techniques. B. Obtain feedback by: 1. Making specific requests, 2. Listening attentively without negative reactions, 3. Seeking limited amounts of information, 4. Asking for suggestions on ways to continue making progress.

REFERENCES

Alschuler, A. S., D. Tabor, and J. McIntyre. *Teaching achievement motivation*. Middletown, Conn.: Education Ventures, Inc., 1971.

Bandura, A. and B. Perloff. "Relative efficacy of self-monitored and externally imposed reinforcement systems." *Journal of Personality and Social Psychology* 7(1967): 111–116.

Beneke, W. M. and M. B. Harris. "Teaching self-control of study behavior." *Behavior Research and Therapy 10* (1972): 35–41.

Birch, D. R. "Guided self-analysis and teacher education." Unpublished doctoral dissertation, University of California at Berkeley, 1969.

Brophy, J. E. and T. L. Good. *Teacher-student relationships: Causes and consequences.* New York: Holt, Rinehart, and Winston, 1974.

Fox, L. "Effecting the use of efficient study habits." *Journal of Mathetics 1* (1) (1962): 75–86.

Gage, N. L. "A method for improving teacher behavior." *Journal of Teacher Education 14* (1963): 261–266.

Goldiamond, I. "Self-control procedures in personal behavior problems." *Psychological Report 17* (1965): 861–868.

Good, T. L. and J. E. Brophy. *Educational psychology: A realistic approach.* New York: Holt, Rinehart, and Winston, 1977.

Hendrickson, B. "Teacher burnout: How to recognize it, what to do about it." *Learning 7* (5) (1979): 37–39.

Latham, G. P., T. R. Mitchell, and D. L. Dossett. "Importance of participative goal setting and anticipated rewards on goal difficulty and job performance." *Journal of Applied Psychology 63* (1978): 163–171.

Locke, E. A. "Personal attitudes and motivation." *In* M. R. Rosenzweig and L. W. Porter (eds.), *Annual review of psychology.* Palo Alto, Calif: Annual Reviews Inc., 1975.

————."Toward a theory of task motivation and incentives." *Organizational Behavior and Human Performance 3* (1968): 157–189.

Long, J.D. "Sources of reinforcement in teaching." Unpublished manuscript. Appalachian State University, 1979.

———— and C. Mamola. "Perceived problems in teaching." Paper presented at the 2nd Annual Meeting of the Research and Development Association for Education, Alexandria, Va., November 1978.

Lovitt, T. C. and K. Curtiss. "Academic response rate as a function of teacher- and self-imposed contingencies." *Journal of Applied Behavior Analysis 2* (1969): 49–53.

Maslow, A. *Toward a psychology of being.* Princeton, N. J.: Van Nostrand Reinhold, 1962.

McClelland, D. C. "Toward a theory of motive acquisition." *American Psychologist 20* (1965): 321–333.

Means, R. K. "Instrument for accountability: The videotape." *Health Education 8* (2) (1977): 7.

Otto, H. A. *Explorations in human potentialities.* Springfield, Ill.: Charles C. Thomas, 1966.

———. *Human potentialities: The challenge and the promise.* St. Louis, Mo.: Warren H. Green, Inc., 1968.

Steers, R. M. and L. W. Porter. "The role of task-goal attributes in employee performance." *Psychological Bulletin 81* (1974): 434–452.

Terborg, J. R. "The motivational components of goal setting." *Journal of Applied Psychology 61* (1976): 613–621.

Thomas, D. R. "Preliminary findings on self-monitoring for modifying teaching behaviors." *In* E. A. Ramp and B. L. Hopkins (eds.), *A new direction for education: Behavior analysis 1971.* Lawrence, Kans.: University of Kansas, 1971.

Tuckman, B. W. and W. F. Oliver. "Effectiveness of feedback to teacher as a function of source." *Journal of Educational Psychology 59* (1968): 297–301.

CHAPTER THREE

A BIRD IN THE HAND: PLANNING FOR A YEAR AND A DAY

MS. GIVENS was recognized as one of the brightest teachers on the Hillcrest School staff. She was known for her provocative ideas and vivacious personality. Both students and faculty generally enjoyed her presence. Her classes were often characterized by stimulating discussion and unusual happenings. Almost everyone felt that Ms. Givens had much to contribute to students' academic and personal growth.

Despite the significant pulses in Ms. Givens's intellectual endowment and teaching style, she often seemed to get bogged down in day-to-day teaching responsibilities. Her desk area was inundated with stacks of papers; she frequently had to stay up late at night to grade student papers or make out student tests; typically, she was late in returning students' work to them; she was often seen working at the duplicating equipment just before materials were to be distributed in her class; and students often did not know what to expect in her classes from one day to the next.

Ms. Givens's general problem seems to be one that characterizes many teachers—inadequate planning. We have seen numerous teachers become physically and emotionally drained, not because teaching is inherently overwhelming but because their planning strategies were not commensurate with the complexities of the role. A new teacher (perhaps even an experienced teacher) has some very important questions to answer as he or she approaches the school year with its daily pressures and opportunities. How should the physical space in the classroom be organized? How does one determine what to teach from day to day? How are instructional activities selected? How does one handle the grading of student papers? Should tests primarily be used for instructional or evaluational purposes? How should routine activities—such as money collection, intercom announcements, restroom excursions, pencil sharpening, and paper distribution—be managed to minimize their disruptive impact? How can materials and supplies best be stored? How does one ever find time to answer these questions? Do not despair! We're going to provide some assistance right now in your quest for answers.

GENERAL GUIDELINES

THINK SMALL

Teachers who aspire to do everything will probably accomplish little. They will constantly be overwhelmed by the complexity of their plans and will usually fall short of their goals. Each morning's optimism will quickly fade into cynicism as their daily goals fail to be met. It is easy to be victimized by their own ambitions as they formulate long- and short-term plans. For example, teachers aspire to have an academic program that is individualized, in terms of both student interest and skill level. That is a very noble goal, but one that will have to be approached gradually if you are starting from scratch in the classroom.

If you identify modest goals for your class, you are likely to approach the school year and each school day with a much greater sense of confidence. Teaching each child to throw a ball might be a very appropriate goal for a physical education teacher, but attempting to teach children to scale Pike's Peak or swim the English Channel is likely to produce a sense of uneasiness about what the day will bring. This apprehension makes it even less likely that one will be able to attain one's daily goals. We are quite confident that modest goals contribute to psychological comfort and that psychological comfort contributes to success.

Obviously, there are some very big tasks to be faced in teaching. However, even in approaching gigantic tasks, the principle of "thinking small" still applies. One of the first things to be done is to divide the large task into a series of small tasks. Then arrange those tasks in order of priority. Then deal only with the first small task—not with the entire major task.

The "thinking small" concept can be illustrated in the establishment of learning centers. Many teachers employ learning centers in which students operate independently of direct teacher supervision. If you are using learning centers for the first time, start with only one. Develop that center thoroughly before attempting to launch others. Students should know specifically where the center is located in the classroom, when to go to it, what to do after they get there, and what to do when they finish. Because center work is largely independent activity, be sure that students have the requisite skills to carry out the center tasks independently. After one center is operating smoothly enough to require little of your time, add another. However, attempting to launch several centers simultaneously increases the likelihood of a logistical breakdown—which could undermine the credibility of your center system.

• Building a Learning Center

A learning center provides a collection of visual, auditory, tactile, and manipulative materials designed to teach, reinforce, or extend a single concept, or a group of related concepts. A center is designed to operate with minimal teacher supervision, allowing a child to learn individually and at his or her own pace. It sounds wonderful, but how does one put together such an auspicious arrangement?

First, think in terms of the skill area that will have top

priority in your classroom. Although your students will have a multiplicity of needs that might be addressed in school, do not attempt to make all those needs top-priority items. For example, your mathematics students may have serious reading deficiencies, but is your primary aim to teach reading or math skills? Assuming that math is considered primary and reading secondary, you should develop your first center around a math-related theme.

Another fundamental issue is whether the center will basically be used to teach new skills or to strengthen skills initially taught through other modes. If the center is to be used for teaching new skills, you will need to provide programmed and self-instructional kits. If the center is to be used to strengthen formative skills, you will need to provide activities that allow students to apply the skills in different ways. Simply asking children to work umpteen identical problems does little to promote maintenance and generalizability of the skills. It would be especially appropriate to provide tangible items, such as rulers, play money, math games, and math puzzles, for children to use in applying skills initially learned from the textbook and/or class instruction.

Having selected the concept focus and instructional materials for your center, you are now ready to consider a good location. A basic consideration is how to minimize disruptions between the center and the remainder of the room. We suggest that you begin with an area on the periphery of the room and use chalkboards, bookcases, and dividers to separate the center visually from the rest of the classroom.

For a center to be most successful it should also be an inviting area for students. Rugs, pillows, record players, filmstrips, projectors, paintings, and an array of colorful, understandable instructional materials contribute to student enjoyment. The activities at a center should involve something other than conventional seat work. Manipulative activities are quite interesting to young children, and activities involving group research and discussion are especially reinforcing to older students. Centers should provide a great deal of immediate feedback (checklists, answer codes, self-correcting puzzles) in order to maximize student success and enjoyment. ●

START EARLY

Another cardinal feature of good planning is beginning well ahead of deadlines. As mentioned earlier, Ms. Givens made the mistake of waiting until just before materials were needed before heading for the duplicating equipment. One of three "catastrophes" frequently occurred: 1) the duplicating equipment was broken down; 2) someone else was using the equipment; or 3) someone (such as the principal or supervisor) absolutely had to talk with her within that time frame. A better policy would have been to remain after school for a few minutes the previous afternoon and have all materials duplicated for the following day. Because many schools have parent volunteers, student aides, and secretaries available to help with typing and duplicating, you can maximize their assistance by beginning early. They can work your requests into their schedule so that neither you nor they are burdened with last-minute rush jobs.

Perhaps the best time to begin your long-term planning is long before school bells and little voices overwhelm you. If planning is done a little at a time, you can tolerate a certain amount of it even during the summer. In fact, periodic planning will help to dissipate the anxiety you might otherwise experience regarding the upcoming year. If you are like most teachers, summers and vacation periods are often filled with family activities, graduate courses, and supplemental jobs. (*Some* individuals may manage to engage in sunbathing, TV watching, or other frivolous activities during vacation.) Our suggestion is that you set aside at least a week for concentrated preplanning for the next school year; mark it on your calendar in advance. Your "planning week" needs to be scheduled several weeks before school begins, so that you will not feel pressured by time constraints. This planning period should be a time to brainstorm, to let your creative imagination flow, to consider and reflect on new goals and innovative ways to implement them. The end results of this planning effort will be a sense of accomplishment, a clearer formulation of the next year's projects, and a heightened enthusiasm for that September morning when the first bell rings.

DEVELOP A LONG-RANGE CALENDAR

A month-by-month calendar with large boxes can be used in developing an overall picture of your school year. Perhaps the first information to include would be the standard activities that will be occurring at essentially the same time each day and/or week. Lunch, recess, library sessions, and planning periods would fall into this category. The most important information to include will be your class schedule. Also, list before- and after-school duties you will have on a regular basis—bus duty, club sponsorship, and faculty meetings. Because your commitments will vary somewhat from day to day, you may want to map out your schedule in detail for the first couple of weeks. From that point on, you may be able to operate from memory until you encounter a major scheduling change. As you survey the overall school year, mark the times you will not have classes—vacations, holidays, and teacher workshops. As time passes, these entries may become red-letter days on your calendar! Also, identify any atypical events that are definitely scheduled for the school year—senior-class trips, assembly programs, school-wide tests.

You will need to develop a scheme for incorporating special events into your schedule. First, what are the special activities you would like your students to experience—programs offered in your locale, provocative places and exhibits to see, programs that your students could present to parents? It is unlikely that you can do everything that you might desire, so establish some priorities. For example, if you could take only two or three trips a year, what would they be? What would be the optimal points in the year for these trips to occur? Because field trips are often major undertakings, identify the assistance that you will need from other teachers and parents to make those trips a pleasant reality. While you are planning for special events, identify the films you want to use, specify the approximate presentation dates, and order them prior to the school year.

DEVELOP A FILING SYSTEM

A filing system should accomplish at least three things: 1) prevent cluttering of your work environment; 2) protect materials for reuse; and 3) permit quick retrieval of desired materials. The time you devote to setting up and maintaining a comprehensive filing system will later save enormous amounts of time. Something that is worth using one time is likely to have repeated utility. However, you cannot afford to leave those "good" materials lying around until they are to be used again because they will get in the way of other things on which you are currently working and will be lost by the time you really need them.

A fundamental question in establishing a filing system is whether to have one comprehensive system or several smaller files, each devoted to a major conceptual category. We have typically found the latter more functional. When we need to find an item, we can readily identify the file in which it will be found. Having a smaller file to go through greatly reduces the retrieval time. However, if you are unsure of which file to use in storing an item, you should make duplicates to place in all the germane files.

Instructional Objectives. What are some major conceptual categories for which you might develop files? Instructional objectives should be included because hardly any category of materials is more fundamental to your planning. They define what you want to accomplish with students and are thus an absolutely indispensable aspect of your planning. We would advise you to collect sets of objectives from district curriculum guides and from more experienced teachers. Particularly useful would be sets of objectives that build directly on one another. If some lists of instructional objectives are too bulky to place in your file, include brief descriptions that identify the locations of those objectives. Objectives can be filed by subject area and/or skill level.

Instructional Activities. Another major category for which a file may be developed is instructional activities. This may be your largest file of all. You will have some instructional strategies that can be used with the whole class, some particularly adapted to small groups, and others to be used on an individualized basis. Many instructional activities will involve student handouts, so master copies and duplicates should be carefully filed with the original materials.

A clever teacher can develop an extensive repertoire of instructional activities over a period of several years. Many teachers begin by filing away instructional activities developed during their teaching-training program; in later university courses requiring alternative projects, they pursue alternatives that add to their repertoire.

Professional journals are replete with ideas for instructional activities. When you go to workshops or interact with colleagues at school, collect lists of instructional activities as one would collect food recipes. Give special emphasis to instructional activities involving audiovisual presentations and active student involvement. Identify the location of media materials, resource books, and resource people that contribute to an instructional activity so that you will not have to spend time later restructuring the specifics of the activity.

Evaluation Tools. Also included in your filing system should be evaluation tools. If you build your instructional system around objectives, you will need many short criterion-referenced tests to evaluate student progress. Ordinarily, for each objective or each cluster of objectives you will need at least a pre- and a post-test. Ideally, students should write their responses on their own paper so that copies of the assessment instruments can remain relatively intact.

Depending on how you view the role of testing in your classroom, you may wish to develop testing files with different levels of confidentiality. For example, your criterion-referenced test file should be relatively open because it will primarily serve an instructional purpose. It is very possible that students can self-administer and refile these tests. On the other hand, you may develop some comprehensive tests that will be used primarily as evaluation tools. These tests should be housed in a file accessible only to you.

DISCARD UNUSED MATERIALS

Now that we have convinced you to save materials in a comprehensive filing system, we will modify our position somewhat and recommend that you periodically throw away materials also. Trying to keep all the instructional materials you have used can quickly become counterproductive. Eventually, you will be so inundated with materials that you are practically immobilized. We recommend that you go through your files and classroom materials at least once a semester to discard those materials for which you have found little or no utility. There will probably be many materials that seem promising at the time you collect or develop them but seem less relevant as your ideas grow. Do not allow those materials to continue taking up space and obscuring the location of more functional materials. If you are not sure about the future utility of an item, save one copy as opposed to the 500 copies you may have accumulated.

A secondary benefit of thinning your materials is that you will come across germane items that you had largely forgotten. These can be put back in circulation instead of being allowed to remain dormant. Also, materials that have been misclassified can be put in more appropriate categories as you work through your files. The time you take in going through your materials each semester will give your room that clean appearance and will save significant time when you and your students are ready to use the materials the following semester.

ENLIST OTHERS' AID

You need not work in isolation from others. Attempting to do so will diminish the quality of your work. Can you identify another teacher whose teaching responsibilities are similar to yours? This person need not be in your school or even in your school system. However, he or she should be someone you know reasonably well and whose commitment to teaching is similar to yours. Open up your files to each other. Each of you will wind up with at least twice as many resource materials. The interaction between the two of you is likely to stimulate more productivity from each of you.

All of your materials need not be housed in your office. You simply need to know what materials are available elsewhere and how you can get access to those materials efficiently. Librarians, media specialists, and instructional supervisors can be very helpful in preparing lists of instructional materials they have available on a specific topic. Their lists may greatly expand the alternatives you have immediately available in your classroom.

Many essential tasks in the classroom need not be done by you personally. For example, a lot of student work can be evaluated by the students themselves. This is particularly the case when the teacher can objectively specify the criteria the student's work should meet. Spelling tests and math problems that are worked in a step-by-step fashion would be excellent examples. Because most student assignments (including tests) should be used more for instructional than evaluational purposes, students will probably experience greater benefits evaluating their own work than having someone else assume that responsibility. Students allowed to take trial spelling tests and check their own work do better on the subsequent tests than students not accorded the self-checking opportunities (Fitzsimmons and Loomer, 1977). The items that students miss on practice assignments will help you identify what you need to emphasize in your follow-up explanations to those students. However, when student work is primarily used for evaluation purposes, other adults, such as teacher aides, can evaluate work using objective grading criteria.

• Feeling Guilty

Teachers frequently feel guilty when they decide not to do something that they have always done. For example, one teacher recently confided to us that she resented having so many papers to grade. We suggested that she occasionally avoid assignments that generated paperwork and that she consider letting students assist her. Initially, the teacher argued that good teaching required that she personally discover the type of errors students were making. Finally, she noted that her guilt feelings were more difficult to live with than her resentment toward the task. Many teachers feel guilty about saying no and thus end up doing things they could have avoided. Obviously, teachers should not take on more than they are required to do simply to avoid guilt. The bottom line, of course, is how to say no and not feel guilty. The answer may lie in knowing one's strengths. One of our main purposes in having teachers examine their strengths as part of their self-improvement endeavors is to free them from unnecessary guilt. Teachers who know they have strengths can feel good about themselves and what they *choose* to do. They do not have to undertake every task presented to them in order to feel adequate. Uncertainty about one's worth and feelings of guilt go hand in hand. Knowing that one has positive qualities can prevent one from constantly having to do unwanted chores just to "prove" oneself worthwhile. •

MINIMIZE LOGISTICAL DISRUPTIONS

You will periodically need to send information home to parents, collect money for various materials and school functions, make announcements in your room, and make time for intercom announcements. In addition, students will need to sharpen pencils, collect appropriate learning materials, and go to the restroom. All of these activities are legitimate in their own right. However, if these activities continually occur during the day, they can be quite disruptive of your teaching activities and the students' on-task behaviors.

Your major objective should be to group many of these activities into the same time frame or to program their occurrence when they will be least disruptive of the learning process. Except for those routines which may be essential for instruction (e.g., pencil sharpening, getting the learning materials together), most routines should be reserved for the last few minutes of the day. Learning is *least* efficient then, and you are about ready for artificial resuscitation! If all these activities occur at the beginning of the day, they cut into the time of optimal student learning. Of course, you can only control intercom announcements to the extent that the principal respects your suggestions, but most other routines can be directly controlled by you. One possible exception is bathroom privileges. These unscheduled sojourns can be greatly minimized if students are encouraged to take advantage of programmed times for restroom activity. If a student frequently requests restroom privileges, check with the student's parents to determine if the child has a medical or psychological problem.

• Matching Tasks with Energy Levels

If you are wondering what might be the most efficient way for you to use your energies, you should be interested in a strategy developed by Tennov (1977). Tennov believes that each individual has rather consistent daily cycles. For example, you may find that you have an extremely high energy level early in the morning, less energy before lunch, a moderate amount of energy after lunch, and so on. Tennov has classified capability levels into five categories, with level one being the highest and level five the lowest. She contends that to maximize your potential you should match activities with energy levels. You might, for instance, undertake tasks that require greatest expenditures of mental energy when you are mentally sharpest. Less taxing, mundane endeavors could be saved for times when you are not at peak capability.

We recognize that you cannot always dictate when you teach a given subject, but you can schedule many events within your teaching day. You can control when you plan for class, when you grade papers, when you have class discussion, when you show films, and so on. Each of these tasks will require different expenditures of energy and should be scheduled with energy levels in mind. For example, the two of us frequently teach three-hour evening classes at the uni-

versity. Each class typically consists of an array of activities—
for example, teacher lecturing, class discussion, small-
group activity, audiovisual presentations, and short quizzes.
We generally schedule the lecturing and class discussion for
the first part of the period, when we are freshest, and delay
audiovisuals and quizzes, which make less demands on our
energy, until later in the period. Thus, you should consider
your energy levels both across periods of the day and within
periods as you schedule your professional activities. Avoid
lecturing or any other high-energy activity on that portion of
the day or class period when your energy level is lowest. •

LONG-TERM PLANNING

We believe that the bulk of your planning should occur on a
long-term basis. If you try to do your planning largely on a
daily basis, you will find yourself working under constant
pressure. However, if you develop comprehensive long-
term plans, your daily plans will readily flow from that
larger context. By "long-term" we basically mean yearly
planning. If "yearly" sounds too intimidating, then think in
terms of a semester or at least a unit of study. Although your
major long-term planning will have instructional considerations, you can also plan some logistical arrangements
that can be supportive of your instructional pursuits.

LOGISTICAL CONCERNS

Organizing Classroom Space. The physical arrangement of
your classroom can be a source of satisfaction or a constant
provocation to frustration. Among the general outcomes
you want to promote through physical planning are an
aesthetically attractive environment, uncrowded physical
space, and an arrangement that minimizes traffic congestion. Although such planning is definitely evolutionary,
several questions can be addressed early to provide a framework for later planning. For example, what is it about a
classroom that will make it attractive and comfortable for
you and your students? You may think in terms of pictures,
certain colors of paint, curtains for the windows, rugs for

various sections of the room, plants, informal furniture, aquariums, pet cages, and so on. Once you have decided on the amenities you and your students are likely to enjoy, the next step is developing a plan for acquiring them. Whereas you probably have a few things at home that can be used to embellish the classroom environment, most of these items will have to be made by you and your students or acquired from other sources.

A number of practical questions must also be answered about the physical format of your classroom ("The grand plan," 1978). What kind of seating pattern would best promote the kinds of behaviors you want from students? Where will students put belongings, such as lunches, coats, and boots, during the school day? If you plan to use learning centers, how will they be identified and demarcated from the remainder of the classroom? Where will custodial supplies, such as brooms, dustpans, and flyswatters, be stored so that they can readily be found when you need them? Where will audiovisual equipment be placed to capitalize both on available outlets and on students' audibility and visibility? Where will handicapped students be seated to maximize their performance? We are sure that you can add numerous questions to our list. Answering these questions early can prevent lots of confusion and frustration when the events of the classroom start occurring in staccato fashion.

Acquiring and Storing Supplies. First, identify supplies that you will personally need, then supplies that you will need for the classroom as a whole, and, finally, supplies that individual students will need to acquire. The latter list should be duplicated and sent home to parents. Included might be paper, notebooks, pencils, rulers, and so on. The most important supplies will be textbooks and resource materials. Building and organizing a class library will be a high priority. You can check out books from the school or community library, bring some books from home, acquire inexpensive books at garage sales, and solicit unused books from parents. You might also locate a cart to take through your school building so that you can collect instructional kits, materials, and equipment not presently in use elsewhere. These books and materials will need to be arranged so that students can readily locate what they want. A sign-out system also needs to be developed so that you can always determine who has what.

One of the most important areas in your classroom to keep well organized and uncluttered is your desk. Keep only the most essential items there: sufficient writing material, daily plans, major textbooks, and the student gradebook. You might also keep a file of important names and addresses on your desk. "In" and "out" trays for student papers could be appropriately located on your desk as well. Make sure that the two trays are clearly distinguished (by different colors and labels) in order to minimize confusion.

• Finding a Hideaway

Although having a well-organized room and desk can ease the performance of your responsibilities, having a more private space outside the class can also be useful. The two of us have found the planning and preparation of textbooks to be the most demanding and time-consuming facet of our professional activity. A textbook, such as the one you are reading, requires at least a year of sustained activity— anywhere from two to four hours a day. Although our daily schedules may be a bit more open than yours, our regular academic activities must continue while we work on a textbook.

Developing a textbook requires a great deal of special planning, but perhaps the most critical element is finding extended work periods away from interruptions. Whereas you might think that our offices would be the best place to work, we have found the university library far more conducive to sustained concentration. When we are in our offices, we receive many phone calls and visitors that interrupt the development of the manuscript. However, it is possible to find a quiet area of the university library where interruptions will not occur. Most of our textbook writing has taken place there.

Such activities as planning and evaluating student work are best done in sustained time blocks free of interruptions. If too many people know the location of your classroom, is there a hideaway somewhere else in the school building where you could go for sustained work during any free time you may have? •

INSTRUCTIONAL CONSIDERATIONS

The most important long-term plans are those which relate directly to instruction. The long-term planning model that seems most reasonable to us is a linear ends-means model, in which planning progresses logically from one's goals (Tyler, 1950). This model entails: 1) specifying your objectives; 2) selecting learning activities; 3) organizing learning activities; and 4) developing evaluation procedures.

Despite the logical appeal of the linear ends-means model, it does not seem to correspond very closely to actual teacher planning. MacDonald (1965) and Eisner (1967) have proposed an alternative scheme, the "integrated ends-means" model, which they believe more accurately characterizes teacher planning. According to this model, teachers first think in terms of learning activities. Objectives may evolve as students pursue the activities and determine what they can glean from them.

As you might have anticipated, the primary item of planning for most teachers is neither instructional objectives nor learning activities. What would you guess is the first consideration of teachers in the development of long-term plans? If you said content, you are one step ahead of us. A very recent study (Yinger, 1980), which monitored a teacher's planning decisions over a five-month period, confirmed that objectives were not a central part of the teacher's planning.

Peterson, Marx, and Clark (1978) did a fascinating study of teachers' thought processes and behavior in actual planning situations. Teachers were asked to think aloud during these sessions so that their verbal comments could be classified. Teachers devoted the largest portion of their time to discussing what *content* should be taught. Next in terms of time expenditure were instructional strategies and learning activities. Receiving the least amount of attention were instructional objectives. Zahorik (1975) also reported that about 50 percent of teachers initially focus on content and only about 25 percent focus first on behavioral objectives.

The initial dilemma in long-term planning is whether to emphasize what *you* want to cover or the skills and knowledge you want *your students* to acquire. Actually there may be a more judicious beginning point than either of these considerations—what do your students *need?*

Identifying Student Needs. As we consider this issue, a number of questions come into focus. What kinds of cultural and economic backgrounds are represented among your students? What types of skills do these students need in order to cope better with their environmental situations outside the classroom? What types of skills will the students bring with them into your classroom? What types of skills do the students need to develop now to increase their chances of a promising future?

The critical criterion in the determination of student needs is *practicality.* What will really help these students cope better in the world beyond the classroom? Will knowing how to use a calculator be a useful skill? Will being able to express one's views accurately and concisely facilitate social adjustment beyond the classroom? Will knowing the scientific labels for different types of plant life impact greatly on the child's adjustment outside of academia? Will memorizing the counties within one's state promote effective citizenship within that state? Will knowing the practices basic to physical health be likely to improve the quality of the child's physical life? The number of questions one could ask in this vein is practically infinite. Because infinity is rather intimidating, why not begin your planning by formulating ten to twenty questions about the practicality of the skill areas that could be addressed in your classroom? If you do this, you will be a "rare specimen." We fear that too few teachers ever consider the practicality and relevance of what is taught in their classrooms.

Once you have identified some skill areas that would *truly* enhance the quality of your students' lives outside of school, yet would legitimately fall within your teaching domain, you will need to determine the levels on which your students are presently functioning relative to those skills. Anecdotal records, students' cumulative subject-area charts, and prior standardized-test results may give you a general framework within which to work. However, you may need to plan for additional observation and testing at the beginning of the school year to establish more precisely what your students can and cannot do relative to the identified skill areas. As other authors (Shavelson and Borko, 1979; Yinger, 1980) have suggested, most planning decisions should proceed from a base of knowledge about your students—what would be helpful for them to learn, and how much of it they have already learned.

Identifying Instructional Goals. Suppose that you are a language-arts teacher in an inner-city junior high school. Your knowledge of the students' cultural background and their previous academic records all point to gross deficiencies in written communication skills. Nonetheless, you view those skills as critical to the individuals' vocational opportunities and general enjoyment of life. So you determine to focus substantial attention on reading, writing, and spelling skills. Where do you begin? Specifically, what written communication skills will you attempt to develop? If your school system has selected textbooks that are a part of a total curricular system, it is very likely that you will find instructional objectives in the teacher's manuals that accompany those textbooks. Even if you have to refine these objectives, that will be easier than starting from scratch in developing your own objectives.

Your instructional goals should include some statements

of where your students will be going on a long-term basis, as well as the day-to-day skills to be acquired to reach the long-term destination. Your comprehensive listing of goals and objectives should be sufficiently broad to encompass the performance levels of all the students in your classroom at any point in the school year.

• Long-Term Goal and Short-Term Objectives

Long-Term Goal

- Students will increase their reading comprehension scores by at least one grade level during the school year.

Related Short-Term Objectives

- Students will correctly answer questions regarding important details in selected readings.
- Students will correctly sequence four events from selected passages.
- Students will correctly identify the nouns to which pronouns relate in selected passages.
- Students will correctly state the main idea of a paragraph or a group of paragraphs.
- Students will be able to answer questions requiring inferences by providing supportive evidence from selected passages. •

Preparing the Physical Environment. We have already considered general characteristics of the classroom environment. Now we will turn to the specific arrangements you will need to facilitate attainment of the identified goals and objectives. Will your students typically be working in large groups, small groups, pairs, or as individuals? These decisions will be based in part on the similarities in your students' skill levels and their potential for working together in a helpful, nondisruptive fashion.

For the grouping you choose to employ, what physical items and furniture configuration will be needed to work toward the objectives? Will you need desks, tables, bookcases, chalkboards, and capabilities for the use of audiovisual media? If you are going to employ small-group instruction, how will tables, bookcases, and chalkboards be arranged to promote on-task behavior with the group, while minimizing disruptions from other learning activities in the classroom? If you are going to have handicapped students, where will they sit in your classroom to maximize their academic and social growth? What types of special furniture and equipment will be needed for these students?

Mobilizing the Instructional Input. What instructional materials will be needed to teach students how to perform the skills in question? What portions of the standard textbooks address those skills or areas of knowledge? (Never think you have to teach *all* the textbook.) Additionally, can you identify magazines, newspapers, games, maps, charts, graphs, artistic displays, filmstrips, films, audiotapes, and videotapes that focus on the target area? The more resources you have available, the greater the likelihood that each student will find something that teaches the skill or skills in a way he or she can understand.

Once you have assembled your instructional material, how will the content in question be communicated to students? We endorse the "learning center" approach as one dimension of the instructional milieu. Many of the resources identified in the preceding paragraph can be arranged in centers that allow students to have easy access to them and use them in a largely independent fashion. You may also choose to teach many skills through teacher-directed discussion, using some of the questioning techniques described in Chapter 7 on creative instruction. For students with verbal deficiencies, a visual mode of presentation (e.g., films, drawings, or charts) might be preferred. Practical skills can often be learned best through independent or group projects involving activities outside the classroom. Many instructional kits are commercially available for students who like to work independently yet need explicit directions. How will homework assignments be used? We generally oppose the use of homework as an instructional tool unless the child has resources available for learning skills outside the school that are unavailable within the school.

Developing a Contingency Management System. Another important facet of long-term planning is the formulation of a contingency management system that will provide adequate reinforcement for student productivity. Of course, a great deal of reinforcement should come from the students' success as they move through the instructional objectives. However, students with a history of academic failure may not see success often enough to sustain their efforts. For such students teachers may find it useful to develop a token economy system, in which students receive more tangible reinforcement for their academic accomplishments and appropriate conduct. In this system students first earn tokens or points for engaging in appropriate behavior and generating acceptable academic products. The token credit is then exchanged for free-time privileges within the classrooms. This kind of system has proven highly effective with students for whom academic accomplishments are not sufficiently reinforcing. Although you should leave the specifics of such a system for negotiation with your students, it would be helpful to have the overall structure delineated at the beginning of the school year. You can decide ahead of time on the general categories of behavior to be reinforced, the types of consequences to be used as reinforcers, and a method for recording credit and dispensing reinforcers.

• Junior High School Contingency Management System

I. *Being prepared for class*

1. Attending class (checked fifteen minutes after bell)

For attending—earn 1 point

For not attending—earn 0 points

2. Being on time (checked immediately after bell rings)

For being on time—earn 2 points
For not being on time— lose 1 point

3. Bringing paper and pencil

For bringing these items —earn 2 points
Failure to bring either item —lose 1 point

4. Bringing appropriate books

For bringing books—earn 2 points
Failure to bring books— lose 2 points

II. *Working in class*

1. Taking the daily check-up (five-minute check-up at the beginning of class period). The checkup will be based on the previous day's lesson. Homework may be substituted for checkup.

Each checkup is worth up up to 5 points.

2. Finishing the daily learning activity. This may be class discussion, a group activity, seeing a film, reading, or written work.

Each learning activity is worth up to 10 points.

3. Unit exam (given each Friday, made up of material from the daily checkups and learning activities).

The unit exam will be worth up to 30 points.

III. *Negative behaviors*

You will lose 2 points for each behavior that disrupts the learning atmosphere in the classroom. Examples would be hitting other students, throwing objects, and talking while the teacher is giving instructions.

IV. *Grades*

Your grades will be determined by the number of points you achieve. You will be graded each day. On Monday through Thursday, 22 points give you an A+, 17–21 an A, 12–16 a B, and 7–11 a C. Friday will be test day. You will receive a letter grade for the Friday test as follows: 30 points give you an A+, 25–29 an A, 20–24 a B, 15–19 a C, 10–14 a D, and less than 10 an F. You will also be given a grade each week. The weekly grade will be an average of your grades for Monday through Thursday and your grade on the Friday test. The grade you will receive for the nine weeks will be an average of the weekly grades. The semester grade will be an average of the nine weeks' grades.

V. *Privileges*

In addition to grades, certain privileges (honors activities) will be based on the points you earn. If you have earned at least 17 points for the previous class period or at least 25 points on the Friday test, you may have the rest of the period as free time—once you finish each day's learning activity. During this free time you may do any one of the following honors activities:
1. Read comics
2. Read magazines
3. Read books
4. Play games provided
5. Draw

Because some of your classmates will still be working on their learning activity while you are enjoying an honors activity, it is important that you be very quiet while engaging in the honors activity. Talking or any other loud noise during the activity will result in losing the remainder of your free time for that day and having 2 points deducted from your total. If you are not eligible for an honors activity, you may remain in your seat and work quietly with your own materials.

VI. *Daily Procedures*

If you are given written work for the daily learning activity and you feel you have completed it, you may turn in your work to your teacher and engage in an honors activity, provided that you are eligible according to the previous day's total. If you like you may get the teacher's help to see if your work is correct before turning it in.

If you are given group work or other kinds of learning activities, the teacher will let you know when your work is to be completed. Generally, she will make an announcement about ten minutes prior to the end of the class period.

VII. *Ratification*

I,_____, agree to abide by the conditions and consequences specified in this contract and agree to take the grade decided on according to my own behavior and performance on tests.

_____

Student

I, as your teacher, agree to help you with your tasks and award grades and privileges according to the specifications of this contract.

_____

Teacher   •

Evaluating Student Progress. How will you determine if what you have proposed to do thus far is really facilitating student growth? Several types of evidence may be germane: verbal feedback from students and parents, observation data (particularly important for social skills), student diaries, criterion-referenced tests, and standardized tests. Most of these assessment devices can be used to determine whether students are attaining daily objectives, but standardized tests may be more useful in determining if long-term goals are met.

Verbal feedback from students is an excellent beginning point in determining whether progress is occurring. Does the student feel that he or she is making progress in the targeted area? The student's perceptions, accurate or not, are quite important. Students with a history of failure may perceive themselves as making little progress when objective data may suggest otherwise. Therefore, it is important to identify these inaccurate perceptions so that you as the teacher can work toward altering them. On the other hand, the student may have a far more detailed, accurate picture of his or her progress than do you. He or she can point to things happening behind the scene that more conventional modes of evaluation may not detect. If you are truly teaching skills that have application outside the classroom, parents also may be able to document acquisition of new skills by their child.

Observation will be the preferred mode of evaluation anytime a skill has a behavioral dimension. A simple frequency count of the number of times the target behavior occurs is likely to be sufficient. The behavior does not have to be monitored around the clock—only in those situations where its occurrence is most desired. Neither does the behavior have to be monitored by you or another adult. Self-monitoring is often the most effective way for the student to become aware of what he or she is doing and to evaluate his or her progress.

Probably the most systematic way of monitoring students' academic growth is via criterion-referenced tests tied directly to your instructional objectives. "Criterion-referenced" means that the student is attempting to reach a predefined mastery criterion as opposed to competing against other students. Ideally, you would have a pre- and post-test for each cluster of objectives. You may need alternative versions of the post-test for students who have difficulty mastering the target skills; this arrangement will allow the students to recycle through the instructional activities without having to take the same post-test each time. Criterion-referenced tests are likely to be found either in the teacher's manual or in a separate test booklet available from the publishing firm. You may be fortunate enough to be in a school that uses a total management system, allowing a child's progress to be tracked both within and across grade placements by an extended series of criterion-referenced tests. A major side benefit of criterion-referenced tests is that they can usually be graded quickly and by the students themselves, thus saving an enormous amount of time.

The child's progress over the course of the year can also be assessed in terms of performance on standardized achievement tests. Although we do not favor the use of these tests as the primary means of monitoring student progress, others (parents, politicians, or administrators) may view these test data as the critical evidence of student advancement. Consequently, you can hardly ignore the results. However, because the tests may not be tied directly to the skills taught in your class and because some students may experience debilitating test anxiety during such tests, standardized tests often fail to provide a realistic picture of what your students have learned.

To summarize, in order to ensure a successful school year, first identify the major needs of your students, instructional objectives corresponding to those needs, supportive environmental conditions, major instructional activities, a general contingency management system, and procedures for assessing student progress. A great deal of planning will still need to be done on a day-to-day basis, but your long-term plans will provide a context for your daily planning. If you do not plan ahead, your daily planning may be characterized by overwhelming confusion about where to go next.

SHORT-TERM PLANNING

What plans do you need for each day to make the day go smoothly? First, each child should be informed as to what is expected of him or her on that day. Ideally, the child should have a printed indication of the work to be done at any given point in the day. If you are using extensive sets of instruc-

TABLE 3.1

A PLANNING WEB

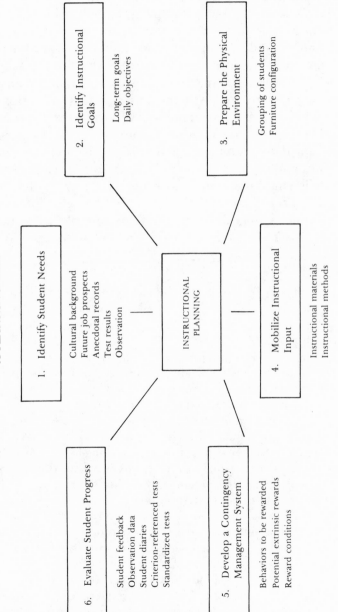

1. Identify Student Needs

Cultural background
Future job prospects
Anecdotal records
Test results
Observation

2. Identify Instructional Goals

Long-term goals
Daily objectives

3. Prepare the Physical Environment

Grouping of students
Furniture configuration

INSTRUCTIONAL PLANNING

4. Mobilize Instructional Input

Instructional materials
Instructional methods

5. Develop a Contingency Management System

Behaviors to be rewarded
Potential extrinsic rewards
Reward conditions

6. Evaluate Student Progress

Student feedback
Observation data
Student diaries
Criterion-referenced tests
Standardized tests

tional objectives (as recommended in the long-term planning section), your daily planning will primarily involve
making the student aware of which objectives to work toward each day. You might operate from a card file so that
the student can simply move through the file as assignments are met. Or you may prepare handouts on which
students can give their responses to assigned tasks.

In your long-term planning you will have identified and
possibly collected most of your instructional resources.
Your daily planning will simply involve making sure that
you know which instructional resources are to be used the
following day and that those resources are ready for use. It is
very likely that you will need to prepare some ditto masters,
duplicate materials, pick up films, and place instructional
resources in the appropriate locales in the classroom.

● Managing Your Daily Activities

One of the most important suggestions of Alan Lakein, a
leading authority on time management, is the development of a to-do list (1973). According to Lakein, the to-do
list is simple to construct. All you do is write down the items
on which you wish to work each day. You can construct your
list before classes begin. As you complete the items, you
mark them off on your list. You add any new items as they
occur to you during the day. Of course, the purpose of the
to-do list is not to give you a false sense of achievement by
having you mark through a lot of trivial items. Lakein sug-
gestes that you concentrate on achieving high-priority tasks
even if only small, beginning steps are taken. Your to-do list
should help you organize your priorities and identify how
you wish to get started on them.

Although the to-do list may sound simple, it is basic to
effective time management. Lakein observes that a major
difference between successful and unsuccessful people in
all fields is that the successful ones use a to-do list. He notes
that unsuccessful individuals often know about the strategy
but either do not use it or use it ineffectively, whereas successful individuals use a to-do list every day to manage their
time more effectively. Do you use a daily to-do list? Other

attempts at remembering what has to be done usually are not effective. Do you set priorities among your activities, write down what you are to do, focus on the most important, and check off each activity when it is accomplished? ●

On certain days you will have atypical activities planned—for instance, films, guest speakers, or field trips. Although we strongly favor the inclusion of unusual activities, we recommend that you have some contingency plans. Films may fail to arrive, projectors may break down, speakers may not show up, and transportation may not materialize. If you are absolutely counting on your atypical plans, you may become very frustrated and waste valuable time. Always have some conventional activities ready in the wings that can be employed if your atypical plans deteriorate.

We suggest that you attempt to do most of your short-term planning during the school day. Most teachers have at least some free time during the day, which they can either devote to socializing in the faculty lounge or to preparing and evaluating student materials. Although socializing sounds more appealing to us, the latter alternative will probably be more beneficial in the long run. It may allow you to get school-related work done at school, thus freeing your evenings for other pursuits. Other ways that you can salvage some planning time during the school day are to arrange for some self-directed learning activities or to provide some personal reading time for students. Even a few minutes of planning and evaluation at school can save a lot of hassle in gathering up and carting papers home.

HOW DO I GET THERE?

Specifying the kind of planning that makes for a productive school year and actually doing that planning are two different considerations. Thus far, we have primarily addressed the first issue. However, knowing what needs to be done is an essential prerequisite to doing it. By virtue of your professional training and your previous teaching experiences, you are likely to have already done many of the things recommended in this chapter. Begin your planning by making a list of those things. Just go through the chapter page by page and mark all the tasks that you have already done. These accomplishments will constitute the foundation on which to build your additional planning.

Now you are ready to identify the remaining tasks that should be done prior to the school year. Next, put these tasks into the most appropriate chronological sequence. We are assuming that task B can best be done after task A is accomplished. For example, instructional activities can be planned more judiciously after instructional objectives have been identified.

Once you have formulated your sequence of planning tasks, think in terms of an overall schedule for completing those tasks. We advised earlier that you formulate a calendar for your school year. It would be equally advisable to prepare a calendar for your summer planning activities. The calendar should indicate *what* needs to occur *when* to have your plans in "apple pie" order by the beginning of the school year.

Once you have prepared your summer calendar, you can focus primarily on one task at a time. Do not be too concerned about task B while you are working on A. Nonetheless, it would be to your advantage to establish a filing system early so that information related to later tasks can be filed for future use. For example, as you go through professional journals looking for information on one theme, you will serendipitously find information related to other planning themes. Obviously, you will not want to retrace your steps through the journal each time you are planning for a new theme. Being aware of your total planning needs, even though you are focusing primarily on one issue at a time, will minimize redundancy in your planning explorations.

We caution you not to linger too long with each task. Once you have developed an approximate scheme for a particular area, move to the next task. After you have completed the initial journey through your schedule, then you can go back and supply the finishing touches. You will also find that you periodically get bogged down with a particular task. Instead of remaining immobilized with that task, skip to something on your calendar that could be done independently of that task. The passage of time plus other accomplishments will often remove the mental blocks relative to earlier tasks.

Environmental support for summer planning is crucial. Because you are not yet faced with the immediate pressure of the school year, many other activities will compete for your attention in the summertime. Establish a reasonable time estimate for each day and/or week. Then identify the work situation that will allow you to be productive. It should be relatively free of distractions and have the resources you will need during your planning sessions. You may be able to develop some space within your home that meets these criteria; however, if you are close to a library containing curriculum materials, that will be a much better place to work. We cannot overemphasize the importance of the work locale. Tasks that you cannot complete in one setting (because of distractions, competing stimuli, or lack of resource materials) will come easily in other settings.

We suggested earlier that you work with another teacher in developing resource materials. If you work with a partner during the summer months, you and your partner can be a tremendous source of encouragement to each other. Exchanging ideas and being aware of what the other person is accomplishing can serve to keep both of you on the task.

Monitoring your progress will be easy if you develop a planning calendar. You can simply check off the tasks as you complete them. This arrangement will allow you to determine at any point whether you are staying on schedule. We are not suggesting that you be enslaved to your schedule. Your initial work schedule may prove quite unrealistic, so allow yourself to revise your schedule as you develop a more accurate perception of what needs to be done and by when.

CONCLUDING THOUGHTS

At this point you may be thinking, "All that you say sounds fine, but where do I get the time to plan plus do everything else that needs to be done at school and at home?" The answer is: "You don't." We are not implying that teachers can perform every possible professional and personal activity. As we suggested earlier, planning is largely a matter of setting priorities and attending to those activities that you deem most critical to your success and happiness. The essence of planning lies in the recognition that: 1) everyone has only a limited, exhaustible amount of time; 2) the value of living (work included) comes from the quality—not quantity—of one's undertakings; and 3) individuals must make choices about how they will spend their time.

One of the major distinctions between successful and not-so-successful teachers is the degree to which they anticipate what they want to happen in the classroom. The latter group often waits until a situation is upon them before attempting to analyze what they would like to have occur in the situation. By that time the demands of the situation are so imminent that little systematic analysis can occur. Thus, these teachers are constantly struggling to keep their heads above water, and they have little sense of overall direction in their work. You can imagine that students in their classroom engage in a good deal of off-task and disruptive behavior as they experience vacuums and misdirections in the academic programming.

Other teachers recognize the importance of defining in advance what they want to have occur during the school year and then planning from day to day in the context of that overall structure. These teachers are likely to spend some time (perhaps only one to two weeks) during the summer months and other vacation periods mapping out their long-term plans. However, the time they invest in advance planning is likely to save significant time during the school year. In fact, failure to do long-term planning can make teaching intolerably time-consuming. Teachers who do not plan ahead put forth a tremendous amount of wasted motion and inefficient activity in the classroom. If these teachers are conscientious about their work, they will attempt to take up the slack by working long hours in the evening. They may personally suffer from exhaustion and anxiety and become disenchanted with their work. Their students will suffer eventually also.

On the other hand, if you formulate the yearly plans identified in this chapter, you can plan for each day with only a modest expenditure of time. A long-term plan is truly "a bird in the hand" in meeting the day-to-day demands of teaching.

REFERENCES

Eisner, E. W. "Educational objectives: Help or hindrance?" *School Review* 75 (1967): 250–266.

Fitzsimmons, R. J. and B. M. Loomer. *Spelling: Learning and instruction—research and practice.* Iowa City, Iowa: University of Iowa, 1977.

"The grand plan." *Instructor* 88 (1978): 10–12.

Lakein, A. *How to get control of your time and your life.* New York: A Signet Book, New American Library, 1973.

MacDonald, J. B. "Myths about instruction." *Educational Leadership* 22 (1965): 571–576, 609–617.

Peterson, P. L., R. W. Marx, and C. M. Clark. "Teacher planning, teacher behavior, and student achievement." *American Educational Research Journal* 15 (1978): 417–432.

Shavelson, R. and H. Borko. "Research on teachers' decisions in planning instruction." *Educational Horizons* 57 (1979): 183–189.

Tennov, D. "How to be more efficient every hour of the day." *Family Circle* 90 (12) (1977): 22.

Tyler, R. W. *Basic principles of curriculum and instruction.* Chicago: University of Chicago Press, 1950.

Yinger, R. "A study of teacher planning." *The Elementary School Journal* 80 (1980): 107–127.

Zahorik, J. A. "Teachers' planning models." *Educational Leadership* 33 (1975): 134–139.

CHAPTER FOUR

THE BOTTOM LINE: IMPROVING CLASSROOM DISCIPLINE

IF YOU COULD do *one* thing to improve discipline in the schools, what would you do? (No, you can't remove the students!) We recently asked this question to more than 100 prospective teachers in our educational psychology classes. The answers were surprising. Over 50 percent of the prospective teachers said that they would do something to improve the home lives of their students. Another 25 percent mentioned the importance of learning techniques to manage specific problems, such as drug abuse and aggression. Other answers included making the schools more academic, returning to the basics, and stricter enforcement of school rules. Possibly the best answer is the one no one gave. Not one of the prospective teachers mentioned having teachers learn better self-control. Just imagine the changes that could flow from teachers' learning to control themselves. Students might begin to imitate the teachers' good behaviors. Parents might even become more effective parents as a result of observing their children's good behavior.

Fortunately, a growing body of research suggests that teachers can markedly influence classroom behaviors despite the background of students—through control of their own behaviors. For example, teachers who have learned to control the amount and type of approval they give have improved the behaviors of elementary students (Madsen, Becker, and Thomas, 1968; Schutte and Hopkins, 1970; Ward and Baker, 1968), secondary students (Hall, Lund, and Jackson, 1968; McAllister, Stachowski, Baer, and Conderman, 1969), and special students (Zimmerman and Zimmerman, 1962). Indeed, teachers who have learned to control their approval responses to students have found far less need for other techniques. This chapter, therefore, will focus on ways in which you can use approval as a principal means of improving classroom discipline. To assist you in learning this important self-improvement strategy, we will take you step by step once again through our self-improvement model. We will begin, though, by examining the close relationship between your responses and the way students behave.

THE RELATIONSHIP BETWEEN TEACHER BEHAVIOR AND STUDENT BEHAVIOR

Why is understanding teacher behavior so important in learning how to control inappropriate student behaviors? First, student misbehavior never occurs in a vacuum: interactions with others always precede and follow any problem behaviors. At some point the teacher is usually involved in the interaction process. For example, whenever a student brings a problem from home to school, the teacher inevitably gets involved. The student may exhibit minimal interest in the day's lesson or act aggressively toward the teacher. How the teacher responds will largely determine whether the student's inappropriate behavior escalates or diminishes. The teacher who criticizes the student for lack of interest or aggressive behavior is simply giving the student more of what he or she is probably already receiving from others. Thus, minimal change is likely in the student's behavior. Conversely, the teacher who is sensitive to the student, gets him or her involved in schoolwork, and recognizes the student's achievements is apt to have a much different impact. Secondly, teacher responses are important. Most students spend a major portion of their lives interacting with teachers. No student can be in school for thirty hours each week for twelve years without being influenced by teacher behavior.

• A Change for the Worse

Have you ever heard anyone comment, "With his home background no wonder he behaves that way"? Such comments tend to depreciate the teacher's important role in shaping student behaviors. A student's home life does not totally account for the way a student acts at school. Others, including the teacher, have a marked effect on students. Don Thomas, Wesley Becker, and Marianne Armstrong (1968), for example, found that a teacher can actually create a "bad" classroom by increasing critical comments to students. These researchers asked a teacher of a class of twenty-eight well-behaved elementary students to withhold approval and increase the amount of disapproval given to students. The results were depressing. Student disruptive behaviors increased from 8.7 to 25.5 percent. When the teacher tripled her disapproval to the students, disruptive acts rose to 31.2 percent. Only when the teacher reduced her disapproval and returned to giving approval for desired behaviors did the students behave more appropriately. Perhaps students are so desirous of teacher attention that they will misbehave in order to receive that attention, even if it has a negative tone. Would you agree that teachers can use the findings of this study to improve the behaviors of students who come from deprived home backgrounds? •

You have probably recognized, however, that the quality of the interaction between a teacher and students need not depend entirely on the teacher. Improvements in interpersonal relationships within a classroom can result from having students alter the way they respond to the teacher. Indeed, changes can be initiated by the students, the teacher, or both. Studies (Graubard, Rosenberg, and Miller, 1971; Sherman and Cormier, 1974) reveal that training students to be more approving of teachers results in teachers' being more responsive to the class, which, in turn, produces overall class improvements. There is considerable merit in students' knowing what they must do to please the teacher. Nonetheless, because teachers are presumably the "experts" in classroom management, it seems as if they should assume the major responsibility for *initiating* class improvements. No one is suggesting that teachers *cause* the problems. What we are saying is that the teacher's training and role places the teacher in the best position to begin the change process—regardless of who is to blame. Students can then learn from teachers what is responsible behavior.

You may be thinking that teachers are not the only persons at school with whom students interact. Nonetheless, teachers have the potential for affecting how others respond to a particular student. For example, if a teacher is friendly or hostile toward a given student, this will indirectly indicate how others should respond to that student. Ultimately, then, it is the teacher who sets the tone for the way students relate to one another.

ASSESSING YOUR INTERPERSONAL STRENGTHS

If you agree that the teacher's behavior is the primary contributor to classroom discipline, you are ready to undertake the modification of your own classroom behavior. We will begin with identification of strengths related to interpersonal relationships because individuals who have talents for getting along with others can use those talents to improve classroom discipline. Strengths identification in this area can also help you feel better about yourself and indirectly about others.

ASKING STUDENTS

The most logical way to start assessing your interpersonal strengths is to have your students identify the positive qualities they see in you. How much assistance you receive will depend partly on how precise you are in giving directions. Asking students "How am I good at getting along with others?" is probably too broad a question to pinpoint your finer qualities. Also, asking *every* student to identify your strengths could prove disastrous. Some students will undoubtedly have negative feelings toward you and would seize the opportunity to "get even" for any perceived past injustices. (The idea of strengths assessment is *not* self-punishment.) Therefore, you might ask only five or six cooperative students who express themselves clearly to answer your strengths identification questions. Your questions could be part of a larger course evaluation. You could inform the class that a few students will be asked to respond to additional items on the course evaluation so that you can improve your behaviors toward the entire class. Appropriate questions for junior and senior high school might include: 1) In what ways has the teacher let you know when you have done a good job on an assignment? 2) How has the teacher been helpful when you have had difficulties? 3) What has the teacher done to make school a more pleasant experience?

With elementary students a class discussion would provide a more appropriate format for identifying your strengths. Of course, whether you are working in a kindergarten or a senior high school, the objective remains the same: you want to ask the type of questions that will lead to a list of your positive attributes. If you feel uncomfortable about conducting a discussion about yourself, ask a colleague to do it. Possible questions for discussion might include: 1) What are some of the things the teacher does to make school more fun for you? 2) How has the teacher shown interest in you? 3) What things has the teacher done to make you feel better about being in school?

NOTING THE "POSITIVES" AROUND YOU

Because you are an important part of your school environment, an indirect means of assessing your strengths lies in identifying what is "right" about your school environment. You can then examine how you have contributed to those positive happenings. For example, if students are seen as being cooperative, perhaps it is because you have modeled cooperative behaviors. Similarly, student interest in a particular discussion may be related to something you have done to facilitate that interest. Even when you cannot pinpoint your own contribution to an environmental event, there are benefits to seeing the good around you. First, recognizing the good around you gives you a more wholesome outlook on life. A positive outlook can inoculate you against overreacting to negative events because negative happenings are no longer your focal point. Secondly, others are more apt to see and communicate positive things about your behaviors when you see and communicate the positive aspects around you.

• Not So Bad After All

A group of North Carolina teachers who were enrolled in a graduate extension course in their county learned through a sharing experience that collectively they were doing a great deal for their students. Each teacher wrote a paper on "What's Right with My School." They later shared the results of their investigations with the class. Because a number of the teachers were from the same schools, the results were especially enlightening. Activities that had become routine for some teachers were recognized as meritorious by others in the school. Collectively, 30 of the teachers from this rural county recognized more than 200 different ongoing positive aspects in their schools. Here are a few of those positive features:

- A math laboratory where students receive individual instruction in basic mathematics.
- A "100 Book Club" to encourage leisure-time reading.
- An extensive community-volunteer program that uses resource persons as support personnel for various classes.
- A continuous-progress reading program for each child.

- Mechanics classes ranging from personal car care to farm-machinery repair.
- Team teaching in math and science at the junior and senior high levels.
- A peer counseling program.
- Regularly scheduled European trips for students.
- Use of "Happy-Grams" to inform parents of student accomplishments.
- A College Partnership Program that enables seniors to receive credit for advanced study in English, math, and science. ●

To get started identifying good things around you, try carrying a note pad and making notes of everything you perceive as good about your classes. You can work outward from your classroom to other aspects of school life. It may be useful for you to categorize positive happenings in terms of people (students, parents, and colleagues), academic and extracurricular activities, and physical surroundings. Anytime you observe something positive, you can list it under one of your categories. Do not hesitate to include the positive comments of others and the role you played in those occurrences. You are not trying to get credit for every positive event; you are simply attempting to recognize your strengths. Furthermore, your records are for your own benefit. Recording positive events within your school should make you more aware of the better side of teaching. We are willing to wager that few days will end with the conclusion that "everything went wrong."

MORE ALTERNATIVES FOR INTERPERSONAL STRENGTHS ASSESSMENT

If the preceding suggestions have not generated an extensive list of strengths, other alternatives are available. You can always seek assistance from colleagues. Asking colleagues for help can be similar to the approach used with students. You indicate to others that you are trying to identify your interpersonal skills that can be cultivated to reach more students. Who can fault that? Or you may want to use the Strengths Bombardment technique, in which you and a colleague share strengths about each other. Another possibility is to use an Adjective Checklist similar to the one presented in Chapter 2. The Minerva Experience, remembered positive experiences from the past, may also be appealing. One option would be to examine notes, cards, and letters you have received. A birthday card, for example, could pinpoint a personal strength. Most persons actually select cards for what they say about the receiver. Irrespective of your method, once you have identified a list of interpersonal strengths, you are in a position to make self-improvements—which leads to the second step in self-change.

RELATING GOALS TO STRENGTHS

Having identified your strengths in interacting with others, you can now establish goals for more fully utilizing one or more of those strengths. Suppose, for example, that you learned from your strength assessments that several of your associates and students believe that you listen well, compliment them on their achievements, frequently ask for their opinions, take time to discuss their interests, have a pleasant tone of voice, and have a nice smile. (We would like to get to know you!) Nonetheless, you sense a general lack of rapport with many of the students in your classes. You may feel negative toward them and find it difficult to be positive in your interaction with them. Thus, your first goal is to become more approving toward students. The strengths listed above clearly involve many behaviors that students would construe as supportive. Your task is primarily to take the strengths you already have and use them in an effective way in reaching your goal. In reaching your goal with others, you will need to consider: 1) the manner in which you approve; 2) the quantity of your approval; and 3) the target of your approval.

MANNER OF APPROVAL

How you show approval will greatly determine the impact of your approval on others. Some teachers, for example, obtain poor results with their approval because they go to extremes. These teachers are usually well intentioned but simply try too hard. They frequently praise too excessively or loudly so as to draw unwarranted attention to students. The trouble with ostentatious approval is that it is usually regarded as insincere. Also, ostentatious approval places students in vulnerable situations. Few junior and senior high school students relish having everyone know they are being praised by the teacher. Such a situation can lead to ridicule and rejection. A student's standing with peers is especially compromised when the teacher says that the student's work is the "best yet" or the "best ever" because others assume that their work is of lesser value. Most students, however, do appreciate discreet comments that recognize their efforts and progress. Part of your goal, then, might be to offer support without being flamboyant.

To assist teachers in improving their approval, Williams and Anandam (1973) have suggested that teachers offer approval that is commensurate with a student's actual performance. That way teachers can be supportive without being overly zealous. For instance, commenting that a student got nine out of ten problems correct is more effective than commenting that the student is a tremendous mathematician. The former statement recognizes student achievement without drawing unnecessary attention to the student. Also, nonverbal cues will help you be supportive without being flamboyant. A study by Kazdin and Klock (1973) revealed that increases in nonverbal approval may be more important in getting students to attend to lessons than increases in verbal approval per se. Making eye contact with students, nodding agreement, standing close to students, changing voice tone, listening to student comments, and smiling are among the important nonverbal signals. The odds are that you will want to capitalize on nonverbal approval because your friends have told you that you are a good listener, have a nice smile, and a pleasant tone of voice. In fact, part of your goal could include making a list of all the verbal and nonverbal ways you can recognize desirable student behaviors. Knowing a variety of appropriate responses reduces the probability that students will tire of your approval. You also will be demonstrating that you care enough about the students to make a comment or gesture that equals their good behavior.

● Let Me Count the Ways

If you are like most persons, you probably have a repertoire of one or two choice comments for showing your acceptance of others. "Good!" and "Great!" usually head the list. Unfortunately, students tire of hearing the same things. They also frequently get the idea that individuals who lack variety in their responses are not really very caring. After all, it takes little effort to say "Great!" To avoid these pitfalls, why not expand your own repertoire of approving comments. You can begin with the following list (we kept it short on purpose) and add or delete as you please:

VERBAL	NONVERBAL
Solicit Opinions	*Gesture*
Tell me what you think.	Smile.
What suggestions do you have?	Laugh.
	Wink.
How do you feel about John's comment?	Nod approval.
	Clap for students.
Let's hear what Sally has to say.	Signal "A-Okay."
How could we improve____?	*Touch/Be Near*
Would anyone like to comment about ____?	Stand beside a student.
What is your reaction to ____?	Sit with a student committee.
	Shake hands with students.
Tell us how you feel.	Touch a student's shoulder.

Offer Praise	*Voice Control*
I'm glad you brought that up.	Change pitch.
Clever thinking.	Inflection on student's name.
Right on.	
I appreciate what you said about ____.	
Good for you	
Hang in there.	
Fine effort.	
Your work shows considerable promise.	●

AMOUNT OF APPROVAL

How much approval should you give? Should you discontinue using disapproval altogether? These are important questions teachers often raise as they attempt to improve their interpersonal interaction in the classroom. The exact amount of approval you should offer a particular student is difficult to calculate. Because of their backgrounds, some students will need considerable positive feedback before they can ever come to feel good about themselves. Other students will get along fine on an occasional positive comment. If a particular student is not responding well, you should probably increase the amount and types of approval you are giving that student. However, in making increases you would be wise to consider a gradual approach. Some students may have become accustomed to receiving very little positive attention. A teacher who responds in a markedly different way from others could be perceived as a "weak" teacher. Students who need the most approval are often the first ones to reject it. Such students may conclude, "We can get away with murder in here." With this kind of possibility, you certainly do not want to change overnight. A gradual approach will permit students to adjust to a new format. Most students will come to realize the difference between a teacher who is being nice because he or she does not know how to manage students and one who is genuinely recognizing others' worth and accomplishments. Also, if you are unaccustomed to expressing a great amount of approval, a drastic change would be awkward for you.

Whether you should attempt completely to stop using disapproval is another difficult question to answer. First of all, even if it were advisable, the chances are that no teacher could ever totally abandon disapproval. Too many student behaviors irritate teachers, and that irritation is occasionally going to surface. Also, no one can unequivocally say that disapproval is always unwarranted. Several studies have indicated that soft reprimands (O'Leary and Becker, 1968) and even an occasional loud one (McAllister et al., 1969), when combined with approval, can be effective in reducing misbehavior. Kindall, Workman, and Williams (1980) found that a praise–soft-reprimand combination more quickly reduced disruptive behavior than a praise-ignore combination.

A major problem in education is that many teachers rely on disapproval. One study (White, 1975), which examined the behavior of 104 teachers in grades one through twelve, revealed that teacher use of disapproval generally exceeded the use of approval. Only in grades one and two did the teachers offer more approval than disapproval. At all grade levels, however, the teachers were reluctant to give approval for managerial behaviors (e.g., being on time, attending to lessons). This condition should definitely be reversed. Disapproval ought to be reserved for extreme behaviors, such as highly disruptive and belligerent activities. Also, the disapproval should be administered so as not to belittle the student. At this point we recommend that you focus your goal on increasing your approval toward students: catch them being "good" rather than "bad." This strategy will probably go a long way in reducing reliance on disapproval.

THE TARGET OF APPROVAL

The difference between success and failure with your self-management project could depend on how you use your approval. Most teachers periodically try to be more positive. Not every teacher succeeds. Some abandon a positive orientation because they are uncertain about how to implement it. Others do not persist long enough to obtain the expected results. To be effective you have to know what you want, and you have to go about your approach systematically. Potentially, there are two targets of your approval: the student and the student's behavior. Positive attention to the person is usually referred to as *noncontingent* or *unconditional* approval. That is, no conditions are attached to your approval. Noncontingent approval is offered because you wish to convey that you care about the individual. To receive noncontingent approval the student does not have to be physically attractive, well dressed, or even a good student. The student is valued for being human—nothing more or less.

The logical time to use noncontingent approval is when the student is engaging in essentially neutral behavior. You should not confuse the students' behaviors with their personal beings. If you always tie your approval to good behavior, students may receive the message, "I am worthy of praise only if I can meet certain standards." Sitting with a student during lunch, talking with students before and after school, and engaging in sports activities with students provide good opportunities to demonstrate noncontingent approval. Such statements as "I enjoy being with you," "You have a nice smile," and "You have a good sense of humor" show you value people. Noncontingent approval is extremely helpful in improving the self-concept of students because they can come to feel good about themselves without the burden of trying to be somebody else. Carl Rogers (1969) and Art Combs (1974) are among the humanistic psychologists who endorse the use of unconditional approval.

The other potential target of your verbal and nonverbal approval is student behavior. Here the intent is clearly to influence the way a student behaves. *Contingent* teacher approval is by far the most widely advocated approach in behavior modification. Like noncontingent approval, contingent approval costs nothing to apply, requires minimal training, and can produce significant results when properly used (Deni, 1979). The two major categories of student behavior toward which you can direct this form of attention are deficit and excessive behaviors. Deficits include such behaviors as tardiness, poor attendance, failure to complete assignments, and lack of class participation. To influence these behaviors via contingent approval, you will probably have to rely heavily on behavior shaping. In other words, you will not be able to wait for the exact behaviors you desire because students may exhibit them infrequently or not at all. Shaping involves approving approximations of desired behaviors, then gradually requiring higher and higher levels of the behavior before offering approval. For example, a student who seldom attends class might initially receive approval for returning to school, then for attending two consecutive days, and then for being in school an entire week.

The second major category of student behavior, excessive acts, includes such behaviors as disruptiveness, defiance, aggressiveness, vandalism, stealing, lying, and cheating. These behaviors are managed somewhat differently than deficits. The key is to look for opposite behaviors that you can legitimately praise. If a student is being impolite, for example, "catch" the student when he or she is being polite. Similarly, be attuned to those small bits of cooperative behavior that even the most defiant student may exhibit. Remember what we said earlier about incompatibility. Opposites cannot occur simultaneously: strengthen one and you will probably reduce its opposite.

Whether you want to increase deficit or decrease excessive behaviors, there are several basic guidelines you should follow in your delivery system. First, you should apply contingent approval on a differential basis. That is, approval should follow desired but not undesired behaviors. The idea is to convey the message that appropriate behaviors pay off, whereas inappropriate ones do not. If you fail to differentiate consistently between what will and will not gain positive attention, students may receive the message, "It doesn't matter how I behave." Of course, to have a maximum impact, approval should be delivered immediately after the desired behavior so that students can see a direct relationship between appropriate behavior and its consequences. Finally, you will want to remember that contingent approval is based on student behavior and not on teacher feelings. If you approve of certain behaviors only when you are in a good mood, the value students attach to that approval will be greatly diminished.

• Clowning Around

Ms. Martin commented that for the life of her she could not understand what made Teddy act the way he does. "He is always clowning around," she said. Several outside observers confirmed that Teddy indeed was the number-one class clown. He practically had the students rolling in the aisles with laughter. Teddy's classmates were not the only ones laughing. Ms. Martin, too, frequently laughed at Teddy's antics. Occasionally, when the lessons were becoming rather "ho-hum," Ms. Martin would ask, "Teddy, don't you have anything to add?" He was usually able to add some humor. The class response to his humor was usually sufficient to precipitate a barrage of humorous comments from Teddy. Seldom was Teddy recognized when he was busy with his classwork. What would you say controlled Teddy's behavior? Are some students simply born to be class clowns? Is there anything Ms. Martin can do? •

MANAGING ENVIRONMENTAL EVENTS

To this point the emphasis has been on identifying your strengths and delineating a goal of using more approval. A fundamental problem still remains, however. How are you actually going to "make" yourself be more approving than you already are? Just telling yourself to be a nicer person probably will not work. If it would we would all have superlative qualities. Much of what individuals do or fail to do is linked to the environment in which they operate. A poorly controlled environment is apt to produce poor responses. Conversely, a properly arranged environment is apt to yield more constructive behavior. This is not to say that one cannot rise above a bad situation. It is much easier, however, to obtain the results you desire when you purposefully structure the environment in which you teach. In Chapter 2 we described strategies for controlling your environment: altering the events that precede your behavior and controlling the events that follow your behavior. Although either strategy alone can prove effective, most teachers employ both to ensure the success of their self-management efforts

ANTECEDENT EVENTS

Any number of antecedent events can be controlled to increase the likelihood of your using more approval with your students. For example, we have known teachers who left notes in conspicuous places to remind themselves to praise certain student performances. (The roll book is a handy place for such reminders.) Other teachers have rearranged the furniture in the classes, placing their own desks in the center of the room, because this arrangement brought them closer to students and made it easier for them to offer praise. Still others have varied their instructional approach as a means of facilitating more interactions with the students. One teacher, for example, found that his standard lecture approach offered little opportunity for student input. By shifting to periodic group discussions, he increased his positive remarks because he generated more student input. Another of our teachers found that thorough preparation for class provided more time to observe and comment positively on student work: she was no longer preoccupied with thinking up something for the students to do. Still others have found that observing positive colleagues and associating with persons who are optimistic predisposed them to be more positive.

If none of the preceding techniques appeals to you, you might consider the merits of having someone (e.g., a student or a colleague) initially provide cues as to when you ought to offer approval. Or you might set aside a specific time in each period to review and comment on student work. Some teachers have found that rehearsing their comments prior to class increased their use of approval in the classroom. A periodic review of the benefits of being more positive toward others could also be useful in triggering approval comments. We know of one teacher who put red, orange, and yellow tags on students' desks to cue her about the need to show approval. The red tags denoted the students whom she felt required the most encouragement. The orange tags were second in priority and the yellow tags third. She shifted the tags as the needs changed. You can probably think of additional events that you could control to help you reach your goal. The objective is to control those antecedent events which will increase the probability of your doing what you already desire to do.

CONSEQUENT EVENTS

To maintain a positive orientation toward others, you must receive some rewarding consequences for your supportive behavior. Unfortunately, positive consequences do not always flow from all your approving behaviors. It is not uncommon for some individuals initially to reject positive overtures. One teacher came to us in tears because she had been "cursed out" by a student whom she had been trying desperately to help. She felt that the student was totally unappreciative of everything positive she had been doing. In disgust she said, "I feel like giving up." Her dilemma arose not from her appropriate behavior but from expecting others to provide reinforcement for her good behavior. Other teachers have had similar experiences. In one study (Long and Mamola, 1978), more than 85 percent of the teachers questioned said that they highly valued positive feedback from students. What they treasured most, however, seemed to be what they could depend on least: the number-one discipline problem listed by these teachers was lack of respect from students. Studies (e.g., Cormier and Wahler, 1973; Cormier, 1970) do reveal, however, that students will eventually give more positive feedback to teachers who employ approval. However, this feedback from students will not necessarily come on a one-for-one basis. Teachers should not rely completely on others to provide the consequences that will sustain appropriate teaching behaviors. To do so is to invite disappointment. Of course, many teachers do get a good feeling out of responding approvingly to others. However, even those feelings can change as a direct result of unfulfilled expectations regarding others' responses.

To combat lack of reinforcement from others, you can arrange for positive consequences to follow your goal-oriented behaviors. This strategy places the responsibility on you, lessening dependence on others. One useful technique is to form a discussion group with one or two colleagues who also are interested in self-improvement. The group can encourage its members' undertakings as well as offer suggestions on strategies that can provide positive payoffs. An entire faculty could become a support group for worthwhile self-improvement projects. Another technique would be to invite colleagues to your class to offer encouragement for the things you are doing correctly. The authors have used this approach from time to time to give each other positive feedback on how each was using approval. Still other techniques involve relaxation and recreation following especially appropriate behavior on your part. A more contrived consequence would be to require yourself to earn a designated number of points before taking a night on the town or making a special purchase. You could earn points for each positive interaction with students. Any payoff you choose, however, should focus primarily on how well you are exhibiting desired behaviors rather than concentrating on the reactions you receive from others. Your hope for changing others has to begin with being able to sustain your own actions. Reciprocity should not dictate what kind of teacher you become.

MEASURING PROGRESS

As individuals interact with each other, atypical encounters tend to make the biggest impressions. For example, after a teacher has lost his or her temper with a student, the teacher is likely to concentrate solely on his or her own emotional reaction or on the behavior of the student and forget everything else that transpired during the day. The teacher may conclude, "I'm making no progress in controlling myself" or "This student will never change." In reality, the teacher and student may have made considerable progress. Individuals simply cannot depend on their memories to put their overall behaviors into proper perspective. Thus, the need to have an objective measure of progress is great in interpersonal interactions.

A number of alternatives exist for measuring your approving behaviors. As with other techniques, you need to select the alternatives that you feel the most comfortable using. Some teachers videotape their classroom interactions before and after implementing self-management strategies. Other teachers have used students and colleagues to provide objective measures of change. In one novel study (Clark and Walberg, 1968), potential school dropouts in an after-school remedial-reading program kept records of the times they received praise from the teacher. The pleasant finding was that students who received increases in teacher praise scored significantly higher on a standardized reading test than did students in a control class where teacher approval remained largely unchanged. If you like this approach, you could tape a record sheet to each student's desk and ask students to record when they perceive that you have offered them approval. A quick perusal of the sheets at the end of each day would provide feedback on how you are progressing and on any need for changes. If you prefer keeping your own records, a record similar to that in Table 4.1 might work for you. You might also wish to measure changes in student academic and social behaviors as a means of judging the effectiveness of your self-management endeavors. Regardless of the techniques you use to measure your progress, keep in mind that changes are usually more gradual than abrupt. So do not be discouraged if your records reveal only gradual change.

TABLE 4.1

TYPE	APPROVAL RECORD FORM DAY				
	1	2	3	4	5
Verbal praise	‖‖ 1	‖‖	1111	‖‖ 11	‖‖ ‖‖
Nonverbal approval	1	11	11	111	‖‖
Display of student work	1	111	11	‖‖	‖‖ 1
Listening to students	1	11	1	‖‖ 1	‖‖
Asking for opinions	‖‖	‖‖ 111	‖‖ 11	‖‖ 111	‖‖ ‖‖
Totals	14	20	16	29	36
	Student or Class_____				

OTHER CONCERNS

Will following the suggestions of this chapter take too much time to be practical? Is it possible for teachers to give too much approval to students? Is the increased use of approval likely to appear artificial? Will the use of approval actually improve student behaviors? These are additional worries that teachers frequently express when considering the increased use of classroom approval. First of all, approval is not likely to be any more time-consuming than anything teachers are already doing. In fact, the use of approval should eventually result in a time savings. Many teachers who are experiencing discipline problems are probably already spending an inordinate amount of time trying to correct misbehaving students. That time could just as easily be spent focusing on what students are doing well. It certainly takes no more time to praise appropriate student behaviors than to correct inappropriate ones. Also, "catching" students being good puts much less emotional strain on the teacher. If approval proves effective, most misbehaving students will improve their academic performances and require less attention from the teacher; students who find that they can be successful in school usually receive considerable satisfaction from schoolwork itself.

When teachers worry about whether students can receive too much approval at school, they are usually most concerned about whether approval actually prepares students for the "real" world. They fear that showing approval will cause students to have unrealistic expectations about the adult world. Students will always be exposed to some non-rewarding individuals. However, this is not sufficient reason for teachers to withhold approval. The odds are that students who come to feel good about themselves and their performances will generate many behaviors that others will approve. Additionally, students who are exposed to a reinforcing school environment might just change the "real" world as they begin responding to others as they have been treated in school. The greatest likelihood of error lies in impeding student growth by withholding genuine approval, not in recognizing the worth of students.

The worry over giving artificial approval is a legitimate concern. The truth is that most teachers who are unaccustomed to offering approval may initially appear awkward in demonstrating concern for others. This is why we have recommended a gradual approach in altering your approval habits. Learning any new skill takes time and practice. However, today's "natural" behaviors are a function of earlier learning. Anyone who has learned to ride a bicycle or ski can attest to the unnaturalness of the first attempts. But with time any skill can become just as natural as riding a bike. Furthermore, any teacher who is going to be successful must be willing to take a chance. You probably will feel uncomfortable at first. Time and effort will make the difference.

The fact that students can improve their behaviors as a direct result of teacher approval is the main reason for focusing on approval as a self-improvement project. Studies over the years have verified the merits of teacher approval. An early fifty-year review (Kennedy and Willcutt, 1964) of the effects of teacher approval and disapproval on student behaviors revealed that praise generally facilitated academic performance whereas disapproval of student behaviors did not. A more recent review by J. R. Deni (1979) also verifies the positive effects of the increased use of teacher approval. We would be interested in hearing from you on the results you obtain from becoming more approving.

SUMMARY

This chapter has emphasized the close relationship between teacher and student behaviors. It has stressed how teachers can improve interactions with students within the framework of a self-improvement model. Specifically, the chapter has described strategies for identifying teachers' interpersonal strengths, for relating goals to strengths, for controlling environmental events to achieve goals, and for measuring progress toward goals. Strategies for assessing teachers' interpersonal strengths included procedures for soliciting input from students and procedures for identifying positive school situations that impacted on teacher behaviors. The manner, amount, and target of approval were discussed as dimensions of approval-related goals. The control of environmental events included a discussion of strategies for cuing and sustaining teacher approval. Videotaping, feedback from students and colleagues, self-recording, and analysis of student work were suggested as means for measuring progress in becoming more positive toward students. The overall theme was that teachers can improve both the academic and social behavior of students by controlling the amount and type of attention shown to their students. Perhaps use of the self-improvement check-list below will aid you in summarizing your efforts as you move toward this important professional goal.

CHECKLIST FOR SELF-IMPROVEMENT OF
TEACHER APPROVAL

Strengths Assessment

What strengths have you identified for working with others?

1. _____   4. _____

2. _____   5. _____

3. _____   6. _____

Relating Goals to Strengths

Do you plan to increase the amount of your

Verbal Approval? (specify form)	Nonverbal Approval? (specify form)	Noncontingent Approval? (when)	Contingent Approval? (directed at)
_____	_____	_____	_____
_____	_____	_____	_____
_____	_____	_____	_____
_____	_____	_____	_____

Managing Environmental Events

Will you control *antecedent events* via
- the physical setting? ——
- the instructional approach? ——
- time for reviewing student work? ——
- signals for offering approval?——

Will you control *consequences* via
- a discussion/support group? ——
- feedback from others?——
- a self-reward system? ——

Measuring Progress

Will you measure your progress via
- student-maintained records? ——
- self-maintained records?——
- video/audio tapes? ——
- student achievements? ——

REFERENCES

Clark, C. A. and H. J. Walberg. "The influence of massive rewards on reading achievement in potential urban school dropouts." *American Education Research Journal 5* (1968): 305–310.

Combs, A. W., et al. *The professional education of teachers,* 2nd ed. Boston: Allyn and Bacon, Inc. 1974.

Cormier, W. H. *Effects of approving teaching behaviors on classroom behaviors of disadvantaged adolescents.* Washington, D.C.: U. S. Department of Health, Education and Welfare, 1970.

—— and R. G. Wahler. "The application of social reinforcement in six junior high school classrooms." *In* J. D. Long and R. L. Williams (eds.), *Classroom management with adolescents.* New York: MSS Press, 1973.

Deni, J. R. "Teacher attention in producing effective behavior change in students." *Education 99* (4) (1979): 406–413.

Graubard, P. S., H. Rosenberg, and M. B. Miller. "Student applications of behavior modifications to teachers and environments or ecological approaches to social deviancy." *In* E. A. Ramp and B. L. Hopkins (eds.), *A new direction for education; behavior analysis 1971.* Lawrence, Kans.: Support and Development Center for Follow Through, 1971.

Hall, R. V., D. Lund, and D. Jackson. "Effects of teacher attention on study behavior." *Journal of Applied Behavior Analysis 1* (1968):1–12.

Kazdin, A. E. and J. Klock. "The effect of nonverbal teacher approval on student attentive behavior." *Journal of Applied Behavior Analysis 6* (1973): 643–654.

Kennedy, W. A. and H. C. Willcutt. "Praise and blame as incentives." *Psychological Bulletin 62* (1964): 323–332.

Kindall, L. M., E. A. Workman, and R. L. Williams. "The consultative merits of praise-ignore versus praise-reprimand instructions." *Journal of School Psychology 18* (4) (1980): 373–380.

Long, J. D. and C. Mamola. "Perceived problems in teaching."

Paper presented at the 2nd Annual Meeting of the Research and Development Association for Education, Alexandria, Va., November 1978.

Madsen, C. H., W. C. Becker, and D. R. Thomas. "Rules, praise, and ignoring: Elements of elementary classroom control." *Journal of Applied Behavior Analysis 2* (1968): 139–150.

McAllister, L. W., J. G. Stachowski, D. M. Baer, and L. Conderman. "The application of operant conditioning techniques in a secondary school classroom." *Journal of Applied Behavior Analysis 2* (1969): 277–285.

O'Leary, K. D. and W. C. Becker. "The effects of the intensity of a teacher's reprimands on children's behavior." *Journal of School Psychology 7* (1968): 8–11.

Rogers, C. R. *Freedom to learn.* Columbus, Ohio: Charles E. Merrill Publishing Company, 1969.

Schutte, R. C. and B. L. Hopkins. "The effects of teacher attention on following instructions in a kindergarten class." *Journal of Applied Behavior Analysis 2* (1970): 117–122.

Sherman, T. M. and W. H. Cormier. "An investigation of the influence of student behavior on teacher behavior." *Journal of Applied Behavior Analysis 7* (1974): 11–21.

Thomas, D. R., W. C. Becker, and M. Armstrong. "Production and elimination of disruptive classroom behavior by systematically varying teachers' behavior." *Journal of Applied Behavior Analysis 1* (1968): 35–45.

Ward, M. H. and B. L. Baker. "Reinforcement therapy in the classroom." *Journal of Applied Behavior Analysis 1* (1968): 323–328.

White, M. A. "Natural rates of teacher approval and disapproval in the classroom." *Journal of Applied Behavior Analysis 8* (1975): 367–372.

Williams, R. L. and K. Anandam. *Cooperative classroom management.* Columbus, Ohio: Charles E. Merrill Publishing Company, 1973.

Zimmerman, E. H. and J. Zimmerman. "The alteration of behavior in a special classroom situation." *Journal of Experimental Analysis of Behavior 5* (1962): 59–60.

CHAPTER FIVE

FOR THE SAKE OF SAFETY: COPING WITH IN-SCHOOL CRIME

THE PRECEDING chapter emphasized how teachers can alter their verbal and nonverbal behaviors to control discipline problems and improve classroom management. The present chapter focuses on strategies for preventing and reducing the probability of becoming a victim of in-school crime. In a general sense a discipline problem can be defined as an event that interferes with the learning process. Thus, school crimes (e.g., thefts, assaults, and vandalism) can be considered as part of the overall problem of discipline in the schools. However, in-school crime differs in a number of respects from "ordinary" interruptions in the learning process.

First, no matter how trivial, crime cannot be overlooked. Most teachers can occasionally ignore being "talked back to" and can appreciate why students may sometimes vent their frustrations in this manner. Teachers, however, should not turn their backs on extortion or threats of physical harm. The latter behaviors not only interfere with learning but can make learning an impossibility. Furthermore, they are crimes. Schools must advocate social order and respect for the rights of others, including the right of teachers and students to have a safe place to teach and learn.

Second, the intensity of violent acts and other breaches of

the law have a more profound impact on teachers than do ordinary disciplinary problems. Teachers can burn out gradually from confronting disrespectful students over a period of several years. Burnout is apt to be swifter and more irreversible, however, when a teacher is the victim of a physical attack or robbery. One traumatic criminal act can scar more deeply than a lifetime of sarcastic remarks and paper airplanes. Teachers who experience or witness criminal acts have told us they are sometimes afraid to go to work. Several have indicated profound doubt regarding their ability to handle criminal activity in school. Admittedly, the strategies that work in managing most classroom disruptions are inadequate for coping with crime in the schools. Certainly, the strategies mentioned in the previous chapter, such as becoming more reinforcing and receptive of student ideas, are necessary components for coping with crime, but alone they are insufficient to ensure the physical safety of teachers and students. It is important, therefore, for teachers to learn additional means of confronting the schools' newest dilemma—crime and violence.

CAUSE FOR ALARM?

When his subcommittee was studying juvenile delinquency, U.S. Senator Birch Bayh commented that a survey of public elementary and secondary schools produced a "ledger of violence confronting our schools that reads like a casualty list from a war zone or a vice-squad annual report" (*School crime and disruption...*, 1978). A recent National Education Association Poll (O'Toole, 1980) indicates that assaults on teachers have dramatically increased in the last five years and that more and more assaults are being committed with weapons. In some inner-city schools the number of annual assaults exceeds the number of staff members. Many persons, however, are uncertain as to whether such reports are exaggerations or understatements. Prospective teachers and others who have never been victimized are particularly interested in determining the true extent of the problem and whether it may be spreading to previously unaffected schools.

• How Good Were the Good Old Days?

When we ask experienced teachers, "Is teaching today more difficult than in previous years?", "Yes" is invariably the answer. Many veteran teachers contend that students are less respectful than in past years. Some say that things happening today were unheard of just a few years ago. For sure, a few disruptive and criminal acts (e.g., bomb threats) are recent innovations. The schools, however, have never been completely free of crime. Many older teachers have probably forgotten some of their earlier students' misdeeds. After all, current dilemmas now dominate their time and thoughts. Nonetheless, Walter Doyle (1978), in comparing American schooling in the nineteenth and twentieth centuries, denotes important differences between the present and the past. Doyle notes that during the nineteenth century less than 50 percent of the school-age youths attended school. Only 50 percent of those finishing the eighth grade entered high school, and of those only 10 percent graduated. He writes that in the nineteenth century crime existed primarily in the streets and was not a problem *within* the schools. Today, because of compulsory attendance policies, more students are enrolled in school. What once happened outside of class is now a reality *in* class. Doyle says that youngsters are not any worse than in previous years, but the schools are now trying to educate those who were not enrolled in school in earlier times. •

Exactly how serious the problem of in-school crime is cannot be precisely determined. The difficulty is that numerous persons do not report the fact that they have been the victim of a crime. For example, the Law Enforcement Assistance Administration (*Criminal victimization. . . ,* 1979), determined from interviews with approximately 22,000 individuals in twenty-six major cities that only one out of ten students and one out of four teachers who were victimized in the schools filed a report with the police.

Why are many individuals reluctant to report an incident when they have been victimized? Sometimes the victim may feel that the incident is too minor to report. In other instances, past experiences may have made the victim cynical: he or she may think that nothing can or will be done. Students have frequently learned through peer intimidation not to "fink" on a fellow student. Teachers also fear reprisals from students. Willard McGuire, a former teacher and officer of the National Education Association (1975), believes that teachers often say that they did not hear or see anything because they "don't want a smashed desk or car or head."

A somewhat different deterrent to accurate self-reporting is the educator's fear of other educators. For example, teachers may fear criticism from the principal if they report violent classroom behavior. In this vein a California teacher was criticized for leaving her classroom to solicit help following an episode in which her hair had been set on fire by students angry over their low grades (McGuire, 1980). Principals may also selectively overlook what is going on in their schools because they do not want the superintendent to think that they are not in control (McGuire, 1975). Superintendents and school board members, in turn, may cover up because they do not want the incident to reflect unfavorably on them.

Although individuals can usually find some "justification" for not reporting criminal acts at school, their failure to report them means that suitable remedies for school crimes are less likely to be found. Too many teachers and students will be left wondering, "Why does this happen *only* to me?"

Although underreporting of criminal activities creates a problem in estimating precisely how widespread various acts of violence and other in-school crimes are, few doubt that a serious crisis exists in many schools. Nonetheless, sensational stories, primarily about rape and aggravated assault, give a nonrepresentative view of what schools are really like. The previously cited study for the Law Enforcement Assistance Administration, for example, estimated that only about one percent of the aggravated assaults (e.g., assault with a weapon) in the twenty-six cities under study occurred at school. Although in-school rapes do occur, they are rare. By far the most frequent in-school crimes are petty theft and assault that results in minor injury.

Do not misunderstand us. We are not trying to de-emphasize the damage to human lives and property that results from in-school crimes. To us *any* level of violence against teachers, students, or the schools is too high. However, we do not want to give the impression that every teacher risks becoming a statistic in a police victimization report. Such is not the case. Statistically, the probability of being seriously harmed while teaching is less than that of being hurt by an intruder in your home. The following findings from a National Institute of Education study (*School crime and disruption . . .* , 1978) should give you a more realistic perspective:

> About 8 percent (or 6,700) of the nation's elementary and secondary schools report having a serious problem with school crime.
>
> Secondary schools are more likely than elementary schools to have problems with crime.
>
> The risk of anti-school crime (e.g., vandalism) is greater in the Northeast and West than in the North Central and Southern regions of the country.
>
> The risk of personal injury is greatest in junior highs and in large communities.
>
> Proportionally, city schools are most seriously affected by in-school crime.
>
> The more students teachers have in class, the higher the teachers' risks of being attacked and robbed.
>
> The risk of being victimized is greater for teachers with high proportions of low-ability, underachieving, behavior-problem, and minority students than for other teachers.
>
> During a given month, 11 percent (2.4 million) of the nation's secondary school students have something worth more than

$1 stolen from them. Only about a fifth of the thefts involve $10 or more.

In a typical month, 12 percent (130,000) of the nation's 1.1 million secondary teachers have something worth more than $1 stolen from them.

About 1.3 percent (282,000) of the secondary students report being attacked in a typical month. Only 4 percent of the attack victims require medical attention.

About one-half of 1 percent (5,200) of the teachers are attacked in a given month. Most attacks result in only minor injury, but more of the teachers attacked (19 percent) require medical attention than do the students attacked (4 percent).

In a typical month, about one-half of 1 percent (112,000) of secondary students have something taken from them by force or threat.

In a typical month, slightly more than one-half of 1 percent (6,000) of all the secondary teachers have something taken from them by force or threat.

During a given month, about 24,000 of the nation's 84,000 public elementary and secondary schools report some vandalism. The average cost for each act of vandalism is $81. Estimates of the annual cost of school crimes run as high as $100 million.[1]

Fear is also quite prominent. Twelve percent (120,000) of teachers report that they hesitate to confront misbehaving students because of fear. Twenty percent of the secondary students say that they are sometimes afraid of being hurt or bothered at school, and about 4 percent (800,000) of the students stayed home from school at some time in the previous month because of fear.

CAUSES OF IN-SCHOOL CRIME

Before attempting any personal solutions to the problem of school crime, you might first explore what others perceive

1. A more recent estimate of expenditures resulting from school vandalism puts the figure at $600 million. That would be enough to buy a year's worth of textbooks or fund 50,000 additional first-year teachers (McGuire, 1980).

as causes of the problem. Perhaps then you will be in a better position to link your own self-management strategies to some of the reasons for the malaise in the schools. McPartland and McDill (1977) discuss five themes in theories of juvenile delinquency and youth crimes. These include the views that juvenile delinquency and youth crimes result from 1) restricted opportunities, 2) subcultural differences in values and attitude, 3) prolonged adolescent dependence, 4) damaged personalities, and 5) labeling and stereotyping.

Proponents of theme one contend that children from disadvantaged backgrounds have fewer opportunities to obtain desired possessions than those in the mainstream of American life. Thus, many of these youngsters become frustrated when they observe the gap between their own standard of living and that of others. Some, then, strike out at the schools and school personnel because the school symbolizes the middle-class goals these youths desire yet feel blocked from attaining.

Supporters of theme two take a quite different position. They argue that some groups do not aspire to the middle-class way of life. One popular variation of this theme is that children from certain neighborhoods have been exposed to so much crime and violence that they have become desensitized to criminal behavior. In brief, they regard criminal acts as acceptable. Acquiring payoffs via aggressive acts and seizure of others' property is not only considered all right but more realistic than expecting rewards from hard work at school.

The third theme of juvenile delinquency and youth crime holds that much in-school crime results from a failure to give youths the opportunity to develop responsible, independent behaviors. According to this theme, many adolescents try to gain some degree of independence by defying adults or by stealing to obtain some freedom from dependence on adults.

The fourth theme interprets school crime as evidence of serious psychological maladjustment. For example, the pleasure that certain youths seem to derive from destruction of property and other criminal acts may reflect deep-seated sadistic tendencies.

The fifth theme emphasizes that certain youths come to see themselves as "bad" because others respond to them as if they are bad. A lowered self-concept, then, leads to a form of self-fulfilling prophecy. Perceiving oneself as "bad" often results in "bad" behavior, which, of course, elicits bad responses from others. Thus, the cycle is perpetuated.

A radically different theme, not described by McPartland and McDill but well known to teachers, is that the victim "caused" the crime. The argument in the victim-as-culprit theme is that the victim "asked for it" through his or her own behavior. While no one can logically contend that criminal behavior is justifiable, many persons do believe that poor teacher attitudes and irrelevant curricula account for *some* in-school crime.

● Who Becomes a Victim?

Do teachers who have been victims of in-school crime view themselves, their schools, and students differently than do nonvictimized teachers? Yes, according to a National Institute of Education School Safety Study in 1978. For example, teachers who have been robbed or attacked are much more likely than other teachers to hold negative attitudes toward students. Generally, the self-reports of victimized teachers show them to be more authoritarian and demeaning. Indeed, one might argue that such teachers occasionally provoke attack. About 90 percent of the teachers who have been attacked report being sworn at in the previous month, whereas only 48 percent of the other teachers report this. Similarly, about 60 percent of the teachers who have been attacked report being threatened at least once in the previous month. Only 11 percent of the other teachers report being threatened. Victimized teachers also are more likely than nonvictimized teachers to dislike the school they are in, to report conflict in their school, and to see the principal as not being fair and friendly.

In all fairness, victimized teachers may only be reflecting the negative behaviors and attitudes around them. Victimized teachers may be more sensitized to recognize and report problems. As noted elsewhere, teachers in grades 7, 8, and 9 (junior high), with large classes (more than thirty students), in urban areas, and with a high proportion of behavior problems in class are more apt to be victimized. Thus, the negative attitudes could be more the result than the cause of school crime. We think that it would be erroneous to indict all teachers simply because a relationship exists between negative attitudes and victimization. This would be similar to placing blame on a rape victim because she was at the scene of the crime. One, however, should never discount the possibility that one's behavior might in some way be contributing to the likelihood of becoming a victim. •

RESPONDING TO IN-SCHOOL CRIME

Is in-school crime simply a reflection of community crime rates? Are the schools, teachers, and students predestined to experience crime and violence because of their surroundings and occupational choices? We do not think so. Much of the school unrest due to integration and busing is past. Government reports (e.g., *School crime and disruption* . . . , 1978) indicate that other types of disruptions are leveling off and may be on the decline. Researchers (Ianni and Reuss-Ianni, 1980) point out that many schools have been able to reduce school violence and vandalism even when the schools were located in communities with soaring crime rates. Ianni and Reuss-Ianni emphasize that school governance is among the most important variables leading to a reduction in school violence. They indicate, for example, that school disruptions and crime have been lowered where students feel that they can identify with teachers and have free access to talk with them, believe the school officials and teachers have ability and self-confidence to maintain order, are aware of the consequences of misbehavior, believe rewards as well as punishments are fairly administered, and have an input into decision making.

Teacher education associations ("How education. . .," 1980) have also become active in introducing and supporting teachers' ideas for resolving in-school crime. The New Jersey Education Association, for instance, has developed a checklist for reporting violence and vandalism. The checklist is intended to help reduce local cover-ups and thus create greater public awareness of incidents in the schools. The New Jersey Education Association has also backed legislation to protect teachers from attack. State law in New Jersey now requires the suspension of students who assault a school employee. Hearings for suspended students are held within four days. Second offenders are suspended until all criminal charges are settled. A number of New Jersey schools have introduced teacher workshops on preventing crime. Teachers at Hoover School in Bergenfield have implemented a program to enhance the self-respect of pupils. They see student self-respect as a key to helping pupils avoid delinquency. Part of the self-respect program includes a contract system for school work and behavior.

The Portland (Oregon) Association of Teachers has instituted an awards system for projects aimed at combating school violence. By offering four $125 awards for the best building-level projects and $25 awards to all entries, the Portland association reduced vandalism costs in some schools by 30 percent in a two-year period. Students and teachers have worked together in conducting surveys and developing student-awareness programs, such as photographic displays, assembly presentations, and in-class discussions.

The Hawaii State Teachers Association has also launched programs to combat violence. A teacher-student version of the big brother/big sister program was instituted in one troubled school. The school staff started holding picnics, organized a volleyball team, and got students involved in painting and sprucing up the school. Reports are that disruptions have decreased at the same time that school spirit and positive student and teacher involvement have increased. Teachers in numerous other associations have learned that through sharing their experiences and combining their expertise they *can* do something about specific problems in their *own* schools.

Other researchers and groups have also suggested additional steps educators can take in addressing violence. Michael Marvin and his colleagues (1977), for instance, have found that most programs to combat violence fall into four categories. These are as follows: security systems, counseling services, curricular/instructional programs, and organizational modification. Examples of security systems designed to reduce violence have included teams of students assisting with hall patrol and the use of intrusion alarm systems after school hours. Changes in counseling services have involved the use of peer counseling and "street" workers to reach troubled youths. Curricular and instructional changes have included the addition of criminal law as an elective course in high school and intern programs at universities to train teachers in crisis-intervention techniques. Examples of organizational modification are the use of career-education programs, parental involvement in school activities, and student-discipline review boards.

In reality, there is no limit to the specific strategies that teachers could initiate. For anyone who is having difficulty identifying strategies that might work in one's school, one could reexamine the causes of delinquency discussed earlier and try to identify techniques that would relate to those causes. If you believe, for instance, that limited opportunity for independence during adolescence contributes to school crime, you could look for alternative ways of involving youth in your class or school. Jack Hruska (1978) cites twelve examples of strategies for involving adolescents in meaningful projects. Among these are ecological projects, aesthetic projects, cultural events, news reporting, inventing projects, human services, arts and crafts, construction, travel, and involvement in business. Do you have any additional ideas for reaching young people and giving them greater independence?

• Wreckreation

Vernon Allen and David Greenberger (1978) have suggested that one important variable in some acts of vandalism is the sheer enjoyment individuals derive from the destruction of an object. Indeed, many persons (including teachers) may not realize just how much fun "wreckreation" can be. One survey ("How education . . .," 1980) of middle school students in Portland, Oregon, revealed that the number-one reason students listed for vandalism was "just for kicks." Apparently, vandalism often occurs without a revenge motive. Unfortunately, vandalism still costs—even though it may be done for its "aesthetic" value.

Drawing from aesthetic theory, Allen and Greenberger offer a number of suggestions for reducing vandalism. Among their suggestions are: 1) immediate repair of damage to deprive individuals of the opportunity to admire their handiwork; 2) lighting directed away from buildings so that potential vandals cannot see the process of their destructive acts; 3) "scribbling walls" or other acceptable outlets for students for altering the school environment; and 4) courses to enlighten students on the psychological processes involved in vandalism. •

Although any of the strategies described above might be used independently of other approaches, we believe that any idea to reduce in-school crime (e.g., vandalism, violence, or theft) will work more effectively when it is fitted into a personal framework for self-improvement. Of course, you may be thinking that one person cannot do much about such a problem as in-school crime. We disagree. Ultimately, most changes begin with one person. Whether you attempt to obtain the involvement of a professional association or try to give more self-responsibility to students, you have to begin with what *you* will do.

ASSESSING YOUR STRENGTHS

As with other matters, the place to begin in coping with such problems as thefts, vandalism, and classroom fights is to examine your own skills, abilities, talents, and interests. In other words, you must assess the personal strengths you can bring to bear on the problem. Maybe you excel in a sport. If so, that skill might be used in organizing after-school activities for students, teachers, or both. Mutual recreational activities could help teachers and students identify other common interests. Or possibly you have good relationships with the principal, certain parents, or community leaders. Such positive relationships might be used to bring parties together to discuss important school problems—such as school violence or the fears of teachers and students. Maybe you hold a position in a professional organization, have a hobby, or have an interest in community affairs that could be useful in addressing the problem of school crime. The point is that, regardless of how insurmountable a problem may seem, you have to begin with some "given." In our approach the beginning is with personal strengths.

Think about it. What assets can you use to confront school crime? Do not be concerned with the global perspective of crime. No one can take on all of society's problems. Focus on your immediate situation. Could you achieve some change in school crime by a change in how you feel or act toward others? Your action might be to influence the teacher next door. Your positive self-assessment might be contagious. Just think of what could happen if thirty teachers in your school really applied their strengths to a single school problem. Constructive changes come about primarily through the positive acts of persons who recognize and use their strengths. We are not suggesting a disappointment-free process. All we are saying is that your actions (beginning with a strengths assessment) *might* make things better than they are now.

RELATING STRENGTHS TO GOALS

Once you have identified your strengths, you are in a position to relate those strengths to personal or school goals for controlling vandalism, violence, aggression, and so on. The goals you develop, of course, will depend on your own experiences, the students with whom you work, the school setting, and any other factors unique to your situation. Two suggestions are applicable regardless of your situation. First, rather than attempting to terminate criminal activity, we suggest that you concentrate on instilling desired behaviors that can compete with criminal responses. As you will recall from earlier chapters, this technique is known as reinforcement of incompatible behaviors. If, for example, certain students intimidate others, your goal could be to strengthen cooperative behaviors that are incompatible with intimidation. Any signs of friendly interaction or helpful activity among students should be reinforced. Similarly, teaching respect for others' property rights would be incompatible with theft.

Second, we suggest that you work primarily on helping others who are victimized by in-school crime rather than working directly on your own problems. This may sound contrary to what has been emphasized so far in the text, but it really is not. We believe that if teachers are to reduce threats to themselves, attacks on themselves, loss of their own personal property, and so forth, they must first show consideration for others—namely, the students. It is the students, not the teachers, who are most likely to be attacked, robbed, raped, or intimidated at school.

Victimized students and their parents will probably view school crime as a problem primarily affecting students. Most parents can identify immediately with their children's needs for a safe learning environment. The students themselves can immediately relate to any teacher who wants to make school a more comfortable place for the students. On the other hand, it is much harder for parents, students, and others to relate to a teacher's problem. They may see a teacher's problem as something less directly affecting them or, at best, as something a teacher should know how to handle. After all, a teacher is an adult and has been educated to manage classroom problems. Also, few parents and students are interested in hearing a teacher always tell about his or her concerns. What others want are solutions to *their* problems. What we are saying is this: the best way for teachers to manage their own difficulties is to focus on resolving the in-school crime problems confronting students. Less in-school crime for students will indirectly mean less in-school crime for teachers. This is a dramatic example of self-interest being best served by recognition of another person's dilemma.

• The Irony of It

Does self-interest dictate the kind of problems that concern various groups? Possibly. At least, Daniel L. Duke (1978) learned from principals, teachers, and students that these three groups were interested primarily in a different set of disciplinary problems. Duke found, for example, that a sample of high school administrators in New York and California ranked skipping class and truancy as their most pressing disciplinary concerns. On the other hand, teachers ranked fighting and disrespect for teacher authority as the most pressing. Interestingly enough, the teachers' major concerns were ranked among the least pressing by the administrators. Students told Duke in informal discussions that theft and fighting (situations where *they* were victimized) were among their chief problems. These findings suggest that too much interest in one's own problems inhibits productive changes that could benefit all. So long as administrators consider teachers' worries not to be pressing issues, little administrative effort will be made to assist teachers. Likewise, when teachers are most interested in protecting themselves, they will receive little sympathy from students. The way out of the dilemma might be for one group to take the initiative to work on the other groups' problems. It is possible that the other parties would then reciprocate. •

MANAGING ENVIRONMENTAL EVENTS

As you will recall from Chapter 2, both desired and undesired behaviors can be controlled by managing conditions that precede (antecedent events) and conditions that follow (consequent events) given behaviors. In trying to determine what *you* can do to address the problem of school crime, there are any number of antecedent and consequent events that can be controlled. For instance, one antecedent event you have much control over is how you view the problems in your school. Some teachers see every act of vandalism in their classroom, every disrespectful statement, and every theft as a personal affront. Such teachers feel that the offending student holds a personal grudge against them. Generally, this is not the case. A delinquent student may simply be striking out against authority or looking for "wreckreation." By taking all inappropriate behaviors personally, the teacher loses objectivity. We are not asking you to view delinquent behaviors as acceptable; we are asking only that you keep crime and misbehavior in proper perspective so that you respond to the problem with less emotionality.

A second means of controlling antecedent events is to arrange circumstances so that undesirable behavior is less likely to occur. Teachers who leave classrooms unlocked while they are at lunch (we have done this ourselves) increase the probability of having unwanted visitors in the rooms. Similarly, leaving pocketbooks and valuables unattended makes thefts more likely to occur. Much in-school crime is a matter of convenience. An appropriate guideline to follow is this: make it inconvenient for someone to commit undesirable behaviors and such behaviors will be less apt to occur.

While you are thinking about ways of reducing the probability of unwanted acts, you should also consider how the environment can be arranged to promote desired acts. Sometimes educators become so preoccupied with trying to stop bad behavior that they fail to get students involved in constructive activities. A few teachers never permit students to get "close to them." Others simply do not give students an opportunity to do good deeds. Similarly, in some schools only the janitor is allowed to maintain the grounds or beautify the setting. Students must sometimes wonder to whom the schools actually belong.

The management of consequences is similar to the control of antecedent events. You might be interested, for example, in increasing the number of times you "catch" students engaged in nondelinquent acts, such as sprucing up the room, showing respect for others' property (e.g., returning a lost item), and cooperating with one another.

Attention and approval directed toward such behaviors could significantly reduce in-school crime. Likewise, demonstrating impartiality in the administration of negative consequences could also be the objective in a self-improvement project. Just remember, whether the objective is to be more positive toward desired performances or fairer in administering punishment, that you can influence student behaviors through your own acts.

MEASURING PROGRESS

Your progress in preventing and coping with juvenile delinquency and youth crimes can be measured in several ways. One logical approach is to compare student behavior before and after you implement a self-improvement plan. You could measure the number of thefts, the incidences of damage to property within your class, the number of fights, or whatever behaviors pose the greatest problem for you. You might also make an assessment of the appearance of your class or school. B. F. Skinner (1968) has suggested that one way to judge how teachers are responding to students is by counting the number of broken windows in the school. He argues that students are more apt to be destructive of school property when the school is governed by threat and punishment. Conversely, he believes that when positive reinforcement is judiciously applied and students are involved in classroom management, the result will be less vandalism.

Your own progress will also be reflected in your physical and mental health. If you have been under considerable tension as a function of turbulence in your school, you may wish to monitor your feelings of well-being. You can log the number of days missed or even the number of days you dread going to work but report anyway. Frequently, looking forward to going to work could be directly related to your initiation of positive interactions with students. One principle you should keep in mind, however, is that behaviors (your own as well as students') typically will not change overnight. Do not allow occasional setbacks to obscure the overall progress you are making toward promoting constructive behavior in your school.

CONCLUDING COMMENTS

If you can survive a verbal or physical attack from a student and still enjoy going to work, you probably do not have to worry about teacher burnout. Unfortunately, confrontations with students and violent acts within the schools have created considerable dissatisfaction for many teachers. As serious as such incidents appear, however, they need not be catastrophic. A serious confrontation with a student could be the basis for assessing one's approach, becoming more determined to succeed, or implementing a plan that has impact beyond mere self-interests. Indeed, the theme of this chapter has been that individual teachers can take constructive actions to counter the problem of in-school crime. The first step is to recognize that you are not alone. Thousands of teachers are experiencing problems at all grade levels. By getting the problems of in-school crime out of the closet, by working with local education associations, by identifying and applying what has been learned from the research of others, and by implementing individual plans, teachers can make things better. No one would suggest that teachers can resolve all their problems. Yet, no one should give up or be forced out of teaching simply because problems exist. The school can be improved, and most improvement starts with one person's taking a step toward that improvement.

REFERENCES

Allen, V. L. and D. B. Greenberger. "Aesthetic factors in school vandalism." In *School crime and disruption: Preventive models.* Washington, D.C.: U.S. Government Printing Office, 1978.

Criminal victimization in urban schools. Washington, D.C.: United States Department of Justice, 1979.

Doyle, W. "Are students behaving worse than they used to behave?"*Journal of Research and Development in Education 11* (1978): 3–16.

Duke, D. L. "How administrators view the crisis in school disciplines." *Phi Delta Kappan* (January 1978): 325–330.

"How education associations fight violence." *Today's Education 69* (2) (1980): 24–31.

Hruska, J. *"The obsolescence of adolescence."* In *School crime and disruption: Preventive models.* Washington, D.C.: U.S. Government Printing Office, 1978.

Ianni, F. A. J. and E. Reuss-Ianni. "What can schools do about violence?" *Today's Education 69* (2) (1980): 20–23.

Marvin, M., R. McCann, J. Connolly, S. Temkin, and P. Henning. "Current activities in schools." *In* J.M. McPartland and E.L. McDill (eds.), *Violence in schools.* Lexington, Mass.: Lexington Books, 1977.

McGuire, W. "Violence in the schools." *Today's Education 69* (2) (1980): 189–199.

———."What can we do about violence?" *Today's Education 64* (1975): 22–23.

McPartland, J. M. and E. L. McDill. *Violence in schools.* Lexington, Mass.: Lexington Books, 1977.

O'Toole, P. "Teachers must face terror in classroom." *The Knoxville Journal,* December 26, 1980.

School crime and disruption: Preventive models. Washington, D.C.: National Institute of Education, 1978.

Skinner, B. F. *The technology of teaching.* New York: Appleton-Century-Crofts, 1968.

Violent schools—safe schools: The safe school study report to Congress. Vol. 1. Washington, D. C.: National Institute of Education, 1978.

CHAPTER SIX

GETTING HOLD OF YOURSELF: COPING WITH STRESS

STRESS is the most critical issue in teaching. When stress is properly managed, teaching can be a joy; when improperly managed, stress can be fatal. Unfortunately, stress is one of the least-understood problems in teaching. Teacher-preparation programs have devoted so much attention to helping prospective teachers learn academic skills and effective teaching methods that little time has been left for addressing the personal development of teachers. Teachers, in turn, have been reluctant to seek information about their own adjustment for fear of inviting criticism about being maladjusted or unfit for teaching.

Stress management, of course, should be central to discussions on teaching and learning. This chapter emphasizes the importance of having teachers learn more about stress management in order that teaching can be a challenge rather than a threat. Specifically, the chapter will examine the meaning of stress, the early signs of stress, the incidence of stress among teachers, potentially stressful situations in teaching, and the effective management of stress.

THE MEANING OF STRESS

Have you ever had a conversation with an individual about some issue and gotten the idea that neither of you were talking about the same thing? Such a situation often prevails when individuals discuss stress. They emphasize their own interpretation of stress, assuming that what they mean by stress is generally accepted by others. In reality, each may have an entirely different conception of what constitutes stress. Stress, as you would suspect, has been defined in a variety of ways. The most common meanings center on 1) demanding environmental events, 2) physiological responses to environmental demands, and 3) psychological responses to environmental demands.

DEMANDS FROM THE ENVIRONMENT

One of the most common interpretations of stress centers on events outside the person that create extraordinary burdens or pressures. The events themselves are considered to be the stress that effects strain on the person. This meaning of stress has its roots in the field of engineering, where stress is defined as a load or force directing pressure or strain on another body. Lay persons find this definition particularly attractive because there probably is no one who has not at some time concluded that certain situations (e.g., the loss of a loved one) are "just too much to bear." Also, there probably is no one who has not also looked outside himself or herself to explain his or her actions. For the scientist this definition offers an objective way of explaining the link between stressful life experiences and the onset of certain diseases. The premise is that stressful situations can lower bodily resistances and thereby increase the likelihood of illness. A growing body of evidence (e.g., Holmes and Holmes, 1970; Rahe, 1968; Wolf, 1965; and Wolff, Wolf, and Hare, 1950) supports the view that stressful life events contribute to a variety of physical ailments.

Several problems arise from equating external events with stress. Foremost, not everyone responds the same way to the same environmental stimulus. What is seen as stressful by one person may be perceived as a challenge by another. Also, what is new and threatening for a person today may be considered less bothersome tomorrow. A related problem with the environmental perspective is a tendency by some individuals to blame their problems on the environment rather than trying to respond more appropriately to the demands of life. Benefits, however, can result from persons' identifying those events which might pose health hazards. Plans can then be developed for avoiding or coping with potentially harmful stimuli.

PHYSIOLOGICAL RESPONSES

Some authorities define stress in terms of bodily reactions to environmental demands. For example, Hans Selye, the most eminent authority on stress, defines stress as the nonspecific response of the body to any demand made on it (Selye, 1956).[1] For Selye the response is the stress, and the environmental demand is the stressor. Selye explains that the body strives at all times to maintain a state of equilibrium. When demands are placed on it, the body attempts to reestablish a balance among its various systems. Selye says that stress does not necessarily mean that a demand is unpleasant, but only that the demand is intense enough to activate adaptive processes. Selye regards stress as being most harmful when an individual is exposed to prolonged or severe stressors. In such instances the body works overtime to cope with the demands placed on it. Changes in heart rate, blood pressure, and the hormonal system can create tissue damage and eventually lead to a stress-related disease. Of course, Selye does not contend that all stress is bad. In fact, he argues that stress can have an energizing impact on the individual. Selye has pointed out that there are

1. "Nonspecific response" refers to body changes that are not an exclusive function of a given stressor. According to Selye, each stressor produces its specific effects, such as exposure to heat-producing perspiration. However, each stressor produces nonspecific effects (e.g., activation of hormonal processes) that also occur as a response to any other stressor. The cumulative wear and tear on the body of these nonspecific responses combine to constitute stress.

actually people who suffer from too little stress (hypostress) and need more activity in their lives. It is important to decide if you are a "racehorse" (thriving on stress and a fast-paced life-style) or a "turtle" (requiring a quiet, tranquil environment).

Stress should be viewed as a signal to initiate effective coping responses, thus preventing a constant physiological fight for survival. Whether stress ends in disease or with successful adaptation depends on the tolerance of the person, on how quickly the person can adjust to different demands, and on the intensity and duration of the stressor. Selye has emphasized that taking a different attitude toward the various events in our lives can convert negative stress into positive stress ("eustress"), which places less demand on the body.

Selye is probably responsible for generating more interest and research in all areas of stress than any other single individual. His interest in the physical aspects of stress has had a profound impact on the treatment of such stress-related illnesses as heart disease, diabetes, and ulcers. His years of research and popular writings have created a greater awareness of the physiological consequences of living in conflict with others. However, Selye's work is not a complete picture of stress. Other components, such as how individuals perceive their environments and how they mentally organize themselves to cope with stress, are also a part of this dynamic topic.

PSYCHOLOGICAL RESPONSES

For many individuals the meaning of stress is drawn from one or more psychological processes. Stress, for example, is often used as a synonym for such terms as anxiety, fear, worry, and frustration. Each of these terms tells something about how individuals feel in relationship to the world around them. Anxiety, for example, indicates that an individual feels apprehensive or uneasy about some impending danger. Frequently, the term is used to indicate that the uneasiness is "free floating" and cannot be traced to any objective, identifiable source. Fear, on the other hand, usually refers to feelings of apprehension associated with real, imminent danger. Both conditions are usually associated with tenseness of certain muscles, queasiness of the stomach, and a sense of panic. Worry suggests that a person feels helpless about a situation and is expending considerable time and energy simply rehashing or dwelling on a problem. Frustration suggests that a goal has been thwarted, at least temporarily, and that there is some feeling of despair, hopelessness, or inadequacy, due to inability to reach the goal.

Any one of the psychological responses described above could occur separately or in combination with a variety of physical responses. They might even precipitate physiological responses. Although our definitions of these psychological responses may be different from yours, you would probably agree that these conditions signal a need for changes either in environmental events or ways of responding to those events. Probably most individuals have come to use such terms as stress and anxiety interchangeably because each suggests an unpleasant psychological state.

MAKING SENSE OF IT ALL

All the different meanings attached to stress create confusion about who is right, about what stress really involves, and about what one can do to manage it. In reality, no one person has been able to provide all the answers to this complex topic. One way to deal with this complexity has been suggested by Lazarus (1966), who contends that stress comes in multiple forms. He says, for example, that the impact of natural disasters on society might be termed sociological stress. Similarly, the effects of environmental demands on bodily tissue would be labeled physiological stress. His major point is that one needs to be very specific in identifying the focus of stress.

In summary, a sensible approach recognizes several different perspectives of stress. Stress can include stressful environmental stimuli (we will refer to these as stressors), physical stress responses, and psychological stress responses (e.g., anxiety). To manage your life effectively, you will need to be aware of all these dimensions of stress. Our subsequent discussion is based on the premise that stress can be any physical, behavioral, or psychological response to real or perceived demands (stressors) placed on an individual.

SIGNS OF STRESS

The long-term effects of stress are easily recognizable. Almost everyone, for example, realizes that peptic ulcers are symptomatic of stress. Similarly, most persons know that coronary heart disease, the onset of diabetes in adulthood, colitis, migraine headaches, skin disorders, asthma, and many psychiatric disorders are often related to stress. Because stress disorders are seldom the result of one incident, one must learn to recognize the early signs in order to prevent serious problems. The signs of stress may be physical, behavioral, or psychological. They may be conspicuous or subtle.

PHYSICAL SIGNALS

The physical signs may include one or more of the following: sweating palms, a flushed face, a lump in the throat, trembling hands, dryness of the mouth, a pounding heart, an increased pulse rate, difficulty in breathing, frequent urination, tension headaches, muscle tension, a queasy stomach, diarrhea, insomnia, backaches, skin rashes, and faintness. Individuals, however, are not always sensitive to what is happening inside and outside their bodies when demands are placed on them. A teacher, for example, may experience a sudden surge of adrenaline (the sensation that occurs when one narrowly escapes an auto collision), a tenseness of certain muscles, and hot flashes on the face when a student "talks back," but may overlook these signs as he or she seeks to quiet the student's behavior.

Lack of Awareness. Lack of awareness does not exempt the teacher from the effects of stress. Greater awareness can be attained by developing the habit of reflection after upsetting incidents. Ask yourself "What happened to me in that situation?" or "How did my body respond?" rather than focusing entirely on "What can I do for (or about) that student?" Also, adjustment is facilitated by learning to take situations "in stride" rather than viewing them as threatening, life-and-death matters. We will have more to say later in the chapter about managing stress. Our main point here is that teachers must be aware of what is happening to them before they can properly manage stress.

• Is Teaching Hazardous to Your Health?

Evidence suggests that most teachers believe that teaching does pose definite health hazards. For example, 84 percent of the 9,000 teachers responding to a poll conducted by the *Instructor* magazine in cooperation with the American School Health Association (Landsmann, 1978) said "yes" when asked "Do you believe there are health hazards in teaching?" Although the majority of the teachers felt that they were in good or excellent health, 27 percent said that they had chronic health problems. Forty percent indicated that they were taking prescription drugs. Seven percent had sought psychiatric help. How many cases of headaches, ulcers, nervous stomachs, and colitis failed to be reported is not known. One can guess from the data, however, that teachers had their share of those problems. On the average they missed four-and-a-half days of school during the year because of illness. Eighty-one percent reported having a cold and 36 percent having the flu during the year. (Individuals are supposedly more susceptible to colds and flu during periods of stress.) Of those responding, the majority named stress as the major factor affecting their health.

The teachers believed that large classes, increases in discipline problems, few or no breaks during the day, and public pressures to manage all the ills of society were major causes of stress. Nonsupportive principals were also seen as contributing to poor teacher health. Interestingly, the majority of teachers (80 percent) said that they had changed their views about teaching since they began in the profession. What is your opinion? Is teaching hazardous? Can future teachers avoid the problems experienced by their predecessors? •

BEHAVIORAL SIGNALS

The behavioral indicators of stress often reveal themselves in interpersonal relationships. A person "under stress" may be unusually irritable, disagreeable, critical, hypersensitive to criticism, withdrawn, prone to outbursts of temper, overly competitive, quick to act, easily distracted, excessively apologetic, or overly eager to please. The behavioral signs of stress can be exactly opposite in different individuals or on different occasions for the same individual. For example, one person may show signs of stress through a hostile verbal attack, whereas another person may become a doormat to avoid an argument. All behavioral signs of stress involve an action that is inappropriate for the situation at hand. People tend to respond inappropriately for two reasons. One, they perceive the situation as more than they can immediately manage, precipitating such inappropriate behaviors as withdrawal, quick acquiescence, and/or using alcohol or other drugs. Second, individuals respond inappropriately because they have never learned more appropriate behaviors. One's initial inappropriate actions may be overlooked by others, but a continuation of these inappropriate behaviors is likely to result in very negative reactions. These negative reactions should signal a need for you to develop alternative ways of dealing with environmental stressors.

PSYCHOLOGICAL SIGNALS

The psychological indices of stress may include depression, excessive fantasy, low self-esteem (a sense of worthlessness), worry, and a feeling of exhaustion in the absence of physical activity. Even certain positive sensations, such as "floating on cloud nine," can have their roots in physical stress. Selye (1956) suggests that being keyed up can be just as indicative of stress as being depressed. In most instances a "low" will follow an extreme "high." We are not suggesting that teachers avoid all exhilarating experiences. However, adjustment to one's personal and professional life comes from establishing a balance. Frequent "highs" and "lows" can lead to more serious problems. Manic-depressives, for instance, are stressed people riding a perpetual high-low roller coaster. Daydreaming, another positive-sounding activity, may also be a stress reaction—indicating a desire to escape the realities of the classroom. Likewise, recurrent negative thoughts about oneself and others may be a response to environmental stressors. Effectively dealing with these psychological indices of stress must be preceded by a recognition of their existence.

IN SUMMATION

We are not saying that teachers should *never* feel elated, be worried, or have an emotional outburst. Everyone occasionally has off days. Everyone has good reason for periodically feeling excited or sad. Our admonition is to avoid frequent extremes. Too many bad experiences can lead to distress (the totally unpleasant side of stress). Distress can lead to a shortened career or a shortened life. Knowing the early signs of stress—physical, behavioral, and psychological—can help you live effectively with stress and give you the balance to enjoy teaching and living.

THE INCIDENCE OF STRESS AMONG TEACHERS

Accurate assessments of the incidence of stress (or distress, if you prefer, because we are talking about unpleasant aspects of stress) among teachers are difficult to obtain. Studies that have addressed this issue have relied on reports from a limited number of teachers rather than on comprehensive surveys or on first-hand observations of teacher behaviors. A problem with these self-reports is that many teachers are unaware of the ways stress can manifest itself. Others are probably reluctant to identify themselves as under stress for fear of reprisals by administrators. When we have asked "To what extent are *you* experiencing stress?" most respondents have indicated that stress is not a major problem for them. When we have asked "To what extent are your colleagues experiencing stress?" the responses have been noticeably different. Most teachers can name any number of associates who are working under considerable tension.

Surveys that have allowed teachers to remain totally anonymous have revealed a strikingly high incidence of self-reported stress. One review of studies dealing with teacher anxiety (Coates and Thoresen, 1976) revealed that as many as 78 percent of the teachers in one survey reported working under moderate to considerable stress (National Education Association, 1967). Only 17 percent of the teachers in a much earlier investigation (Hicks, 1933) reported being "unusually nervous." A more recent survey among 257 British teachers (Kyriacou and Sutcliffe, 1978) showed that 20 percent of the teachers found teaching to be highly stressful. Pratt (1978) administered a Teacher-Event Stress Inventory to 124 primary school teachers and found a positive association between the amount of stress recorded and illness; 20 percent of the sample displayed symptoms of illness. Dunham (1977), who conducts stress groups for teachers, lists anger, self-doubt, lack of confidence in handling difficult situations, exhaustion, depression, hypertension, neurodermatitis, ulcers, migraines, colitis, absenteeism, and early retirement as manifestations of job-related stress in teachers. Of course, the findings in any specific poll depend largely on where and how the poll was taken. Also, the good and bad experiences of a teacher on a given day, rather than long-standing feelings, can affect reported results. We suspect, however, that the figures for self-reported psychological stress among teachers would be

even higher if teachers could anticipate receiving administrative support with stress-related problems.

POTENTIAL STRESSORS IN TEACHING

The potential stressors for teachers can be broadly categorized under two headings: externally imposed and self-imposed. Externally imposed demands include the responsibilities that are a part of one's *professional life* as a teacher and
personal life as husband or wife, father or mother, or friend.
Many of the external demands that others (e.g., superiors)
impose or wish to impose cannot be entirely avoided. They
"come with the territory." Self-imposed demands, however, include a host of problems that individuals bring on
themselves. We have used the term *potential* stressor because whether an environmental "demand" will be regarded as a threat or challenge depends largely on you and
your approach to life.

External Stressors

Professional Life. Perhaps more than any other profession,
teaching embodies the greatest potential for job-related
stress. For example, no other job requires more interpersonal contacts than teaching. In a single day an elementary teacher may be involved in 1,000 interactions, and as
many as 650 are with individual students (Jackson, 1968).
Many teachers consider the strain of maintaining compo-
sure in so many close encounters to be the most difficult
task in teaching. In fact, discipline problems arising from
interpersonal contacts are the most frequent contributors
to teacher stress. Aside from the daily whirlwind of activity
with students, teachers are confronted with the necessity of
interacting with parents and colleagues, completing lesson
plans, grading papers, submitting attendance reports, and
managing many other class routines.

• May I Have Your Attention, Please?

Linda had not been functioning well lately. Typically, she

was a well-organized teacher who liked to have everything operate on schedule. She spent considerable time preparing lessons and arranging activities for her class. Linda was generally sensitive to students and offered them opportunities to contribute to the management of the class. The students seemed to like her because they knew what to expect in her classes. Recently, however, Linda had become ill-tempered with students and critical of the school administration. Linda was not sure of the source of her irritability. She realized, though, that there were few things that she could not do when she "set her mind to it."

The cause of her problem finally became apparent one day following a series of classroom interruptions. At the beginning of the first period, four of her students were invited to the office to serve as guides for unexpected visitors. A few minutes later, the class was interrupted by students who had announcements to make regarding a pep rally for the school football team. During second period six students who had been absent on "picture day" had to leave because the photographer was to take their pictures that day. The principal broke in on the intercom once during the period with messages about a testing schedule and again to inform the janitor to report to the office. Third period included interruptions from band members who were trying to sell candy to finance new uniforms. A fire drill occurred during fourth period, and fifth period included the comings and goings of students to an unscheduled student-government meeting for the preparation for an assembly program.

Linda exclaimed, "I'll just scream if we have one more interruption." About that time she heard a knock on the door. •

What job function is your major source of stress? Is it the work schedule, the pace of the job, interruptions in the routine, too little variety, too many students assigned to your class, uncertainty about assignments, committee work, extracurricular assignments, disruptive behavior by students, administrative or disciplinary policies, or something else? If you have not already done so, why not list those job-related events which tend to precipitate physical, behavioral, or psychological stress for you?

Personal Life. Determining where one's professional life ends and one's personal life begins is difficult because teachers are frequently expected to exhibit high community standards at all times. They also have so many after-hour duties that it is hard to say what time belongs to them. Contrary to what others might think, however, teachers have as many family obligations as any other professional group. They have to perform household chores, meet financial obligations, and provide time and attention to their family and friends. These personal responsibilities in combination with professional duties can put a substantial strain on teachers. Problems carry over from home to work and vice versa. Kyriacou and Sutcliffe (1977) found that one of the most important factors involved in teacher stress is the degree to which the teacher is already experiencing stress resulting from sources *outside* his or her role as a teacher. What personal situations create the greatest demands for you? Are they related to financial problems, marital problems, health of family members, household duties, civic responsibilities, or social norms?

• What Have You Been Doing Lately?

"Well, for starters, I just got married, bought a new house, took a different job, and enrolled in night school. What's new with you?" Are all these changes good? Thomas H. Holmes and Richard H. Rahe are two researchers who believe that the onset of illness is associated with the number and kind of life changes that people experience. They contend that the changes themselves need not be inherently aversive or noxious. The changes need only disrupt an individual's habitual pattern of behavior and thus necessitate some coping or adjustment. The belief is that trying to make adjustments to numerous changes in a relatively short period (perhaps two years) requires many psychological and physical responses that can evoke illness.

As a result of their views, Holmes and Rahe developed an instrument to measure life changes that has been used in a wide range of studies (see Holmes and Masuda, 1974) to measure the probability of the onset of illness. Essentially, the initial instrument developed by Holmes and Rahe assigned life-change units (points) to various life changes. Those changes requiring the greatest readjustment were assigned the highest values. For example, the death of a spouse, divorce, and marriage were assigned units of 100, 73, and 50, respectively. Change in residence and change in working hours, for example, were each assigned 20 life-change units. The more points that an individual accumulates in a short time (either from serious changes, numerous minor changes, or a combination), the greater the likelihood of illness. Because the evidence suggests that persons "may" develop illness from an accumulation of life changes, you may want to avoid too many changes in a relatively short period. •

SELF-IMPOSED STRESSORS

Much of what individuals perceive as imposed on them by others may actually be self-imposed. For example, when a principal asks a teacher to serve on a school committee, the principal undoubtedly has certain expectations in mind. The principal may want the committee members to study an issue, make written recommendations, and submit a report on a certain date. The principal probably expects only that the teachers do a "good" job, but a given teacher might set a goal of submitting a "perfect" report. Similarly, teachers may expect each student to master all the skills at their grade level. Or they may strive to eliminate *all* discipline problems in their classroom; to resolve all difficulties with parents; to be regarded positively by everyone in the school. They worry themselves sick in trying to attain the impossible. Although there is nothing inherently wrong in striving for high ideals, teachers must recognize that problems and imperfection will frequently obstruct their professional paths. Striving for perfection, in our opinion, is a principal source of stress among teachers. No one really expects the teacher to be a replica of Superwoman or Superman. Therefore, a great deal of teacher stress may result from self-imposed ideals of perfection.

The findings of Friedman and Rosenman (1974, 1977)

are closely related to our statements about self-imposed stress. From observing the behavior patterns of thousands of patients, they developed a twofold typology: Type A and Type B persons. Type A persons are characterized by a habitual sense of urgency in whatever they undertake. Such persons incessantly struggle to achieve more and more in less and less time. They constantly compete with time and with others. They assume more responsibilities than anyone else really expects them to. Even when Type A persons are given less to do, they pressure themselves by shortening the length of time in which to accomplish their work. Type A persons cannot stand waiting in line, detest losing in sports, eat too fast, and speak rapidly. They have no time for diversions. In brief, they are swept up in a form of "hurry" sickness. As a result, they are much more prone than others to experience stress-related diseases, such as heart attack. Unfortunately, Type A people are not always the most productive. They tend to be rigid in their approach to problem solving, trying to save time by solving all problems in the same way. Also, Type A individuals deny their own competitiveness and thereby deny themselves any cure to their self-imposed problems.

Type B persons are just the opposite of Type A. They take time to reflect. They can often overcome problems too difficult for Type A persons because they are willing to consider many alternatives and be more creative. Also, Type B persons are less concerned about their status with others. Thus, they do not have to strive constantly for the elusive goal of achieving more and more simply to please superiors. Do you fit into the Type A or Type B categories? If you are a Type A, perhaps you would like to make some changes. Some of the suggestions that follow may help.

THE MANAGEMENT OF STRESS

Personal strategies for managing stress are as numerous as the ways in which stress affects different persons. Strategies may range from taking a short vacation to finding a new job.

Not all the strategies that others advocate, however, may be practical or beneficial for you. What you have to do is determine what best fits your needs in coping with (or managing) stress. By coping and managing, we mean any response that in some way helps you better adapt to your environment.

Perhaps one of the most pleasant ways of identifying coping strategies is to attend a workshop on stress management. Because stress management has recently emerged as a major concern of teachers, these workshops are being offered at almost every college. Many school districts are also hiring consultants to conduct on-site seminars for teachers. Typically, these workshops concentrate on identifying the main sources of stress and on various strategies for handling it. Although many of the workshops do not provide follow-up assistance for the participants, they can serve as a starting point for a self-management project. At the very least, workshops provide opportunities to interact with others and recognize the common challenges that confront teachers.

Another means of identifying coping strategies is to examine educational and psychological journals for current articles on stress management. Teacher-education journals such as *Today's Education, The Instructor,* and *Learning* frequently carry articles written by teachers who have discovered useful ways of managing teacher-related stress. Many good psychological journals also devote considerable attention to the management of stress. A recent comprehensive review of studies dealing with personal and organizational strategies for handling stress appeared in *Personnel Psychology* (Newman and Beehr, 1979). In their review Newman and Beehr divided the personal strategies for managing stress into four categories: 1) strategies aimed at changing one's psychological characteristics or conditions; 2) strategies aimed at changing one's physical/physiological characteristics or conditions; 3) strategies aimed at changing one's behavior; and 4) strategies aimed at changing one's work environment. The first category includes the use of meditation to produce a calming of the mind and body, planning ahead so that one does not rush blindly from one life event to another, and developing a philosophy of life and self and life reassessment as a means of handling stress. Category two, strategies for changing one's physical/physiological characteristics or conditions, emphasizes proper diet and exercise as the principal means of handling stress. Category three, strategies aimed at changing one's behavior, includes behavior-modification techniques (e.g., desensitization) and the social support of colleagues, friends, and family. The final category focuses on actions that would change the nature of one's working conditions.

We will later explore in detail how one technique—relaxation—can help you in changing a wide variety of responses. A detailed examination of this technique should also reveal how a given technique (whatever it may be) can fit within the framework of self-management. We turn again to our self-management model to examine how relaxation can be used to cope with the stressors.

ASSESSING YOUR STRENGTHS

By now you undoubtedly recognize that an important component of self-improvement involves an assessment of your strengths. This is true whether your aim is to be a better disciplinarian, to avert violence, or to remain calm in the face of danger. In fact, identifying strengths that contribute to calmness can have a pervasive impact on other self-improvement goals. Getting excited can complicate a multiplicity of problem situations. What strengths, then, do you bring to bear on being more relaxed?

Suppose, in selecting descriptive terms from the Adjective Checklist in Chapter 2, you described yourself as being calm, confident, cooperative, determined, musical, open, positive, poised, and stable. When you selected those terms, you were thinking of how they applied to one or two situations. Such traits usually have broad implications, however. Certainly, any of the traits just mentioned can be applied to a general goal of being more relaxed. You could use an interest in music (or being musical), for example, to calm yourself after a stressful experience or to become more relaxed prior to a challenging situation. Similarly, being open to others' views has a pervasive utility in a variety of stress-producing situations, particularly those involving interpersonal conflict.

In the event that use of the Adjective Checklist did not yield sufficient strengths for approaching stressors in a relaxed manner, why not consider how your friends view you? Perhaps the strengths bombardment test would be helpful. You might have a close associate, friend, or family member describe a few difficult situations that you have handled particularly well. Let that person tell you what it was that made you seem so effective. Have the associate speculate as to why those situations did not provoke any observable stress responses. Additionally, you might personally review several positive encounters you have had with students or parents. Something in those experiences might be useful in approaching other stressful encounters.

RELATING GOALS TO STRENGTHS

Obviously, no one perceives all of life's demands as stressful. Performing certain job responsibilities may be quite natural for you. Your strengths analysis probably revealed many activities you can perform with ease and comfort. Perhaps some of these activities once produced stress, but you learned to adjust to them. Other job demands, however, may still be quite stress provoking. By following the suggestions given earlier in the chapter, you probably identified the current stressors in your professional and personal life. It is these stressors that should be the focus of your relaxation efforts. If you have a number of demands that are taxing, you will want to deal with each separately. You can start with the least stressful and learn to relax in the presence of that stressor before moving on to the more stressful.

Individuals may manifest stress in the form of shortness of breath, perspiration, headaches, anger, or any number of other signs described earlier in the chapter. These reactions are generally preceded by or accompanied by muscular tension (often people talk about stress by saying that they are getting too "uptight"). The muscular tension may involve a tightening of facial muscles (e.g., brow or lips), stomach muscles, or other body parts. The objective of relaxation exercises is to loosen the various muscle groups that are involved in stress responses. Because relaxation and stress reactions are physiologically incompatible, relaxation can have a profound impact on your total well-being. Relaxation has been shown to be effective in relieving headaches (Haynes et al., 1975), reducing test anxiety (Freeling and Shember, 1970), reducing social-contact anxiety (Dawling, Guidry, and Curtis, 1973), and reducing public-speaking anxiety (Migler and Wolpe, 1967). It has the potential for decreasing both blood pressure and heart rate (Chinnian, Nammalver, and Rao, 1975). Also, individuals who are relaxed in potentially stressful situations have a much greater chance of exhibiting behaviors that will be acceptable both to themselves and others. How, then, can you go about achieving greater muscular relaxation?

Achieving Muscular Relaxation. The technique used in achieving muscular relaxation involves repeated tensing and relaxing of various muscles. The traditional approach consists of tensing a specific set of muscles for a few seconds (5–10) and then relaxing those muscles for a few seconds (10–20) and focusing on the pleasant feeling associated with the relaxed state. Where you begin the process is relatively unimportant, but you should attempt to relax muscle groups throughout the body. You might find it easiest to start with the forehead and move down. Before we help you get started, find yourself an easy chair and get comfortable. Now draw your brow as tight as you can. Hold it for about ten seconds. Then relax. Feel how comfortable your forehead now seems. Next, close your eyes tightly. Hold it for ten seconds. Relax. Doesn't that feel better? Next, try clenching your teeth and tightening your jaw muscles. Hold it. Relax. Now you can move on to your shoulders, then drawing your arms up and tightening your biceps and right on down to your toes. The entire process should not take more than twenty to thirty minutes.

Perhaps you are wondering where you can find twenty minutes during your busy day. Options are available for reducing the time required for achieving relaxation. One suggestion offered by Russell and Sipich (1973) is to pair relaxation with self-produced cue words (e.g., "calm" or "control"). When you have gone through the muscle groups to achieve deep muscle relaxation and are finally totally relaxed, you should concentrate your attention on breathing and silently repeating the cue word as you exhale.

Subsequently, when you become tense (e.g., in the middle of a confrontation at school), you can breathe deeply and silently repeat the cue word (it is better than what you might otherwise say). You must first associate the cue word with a relaxed state if that word is to become effective in inducing relaxation. Another time-saving option for inducing relaxation has been proposed by Bugg (1972). His proposal involves three steps. First, when confronted by a stressor, take a deep breath and exhale suddenly. Bugg contends that this procedure at least produces temporary relaxation. Second, tell yourself "relax." Finally, focus for a few seconds on something pleasant. After completing these steps you can redirect your attention to the stressor. If you still feel anxious, repeat all three steps. What could be less time-consuming? You can probably think of many situations where Bugg's strategies can be applied to help you achieve your goal of being more relaxed.

If you feel that you need more information about relaxation procedures, you could read Goldfried and Davidson (1976, pp. 85–93). They provide a number of relaxation exercises. Also, you could read a detailed account of controlling anxiety in Williams and Long (1979). Or you might prefer listening to a relaxation tape. You can order one from Instructional Dynamics, Inc., 116 East Superior Street, Chicago, Illinois 60611.

MANAGING ENVIRONMENTAL EVENTS

As you recall from Chapter 2, the two major procedures for managing environmental events are control of antecedent events and of consequent events. Both procedures have application for relaxing while confronting any stressor. One specific means of controlling antecedent events is to redirect your thought processes. Prior to experiencing muscular tension, anxiety, or other manifestations of stress, people sometimes say things to themselves. Unfortunately, the self-statements of people confronting stressors are often negative in tone. When confronted with a problem, for example, many teachers say, "I don't see how I will be able to handle this," "I know this is going to get me excited," or "I just can't face this." Such negative self-statements are self-fulfilling. That is, teachers who tell their minds and bodies that they are going to fail are indeed going to fail. They are going to "tighten up." David Meichenbaum (1978) suggests that individuals can avoid this dilemma. Among other strategies, he advocates that individuals prepare themselves for stressors by telling themselves what they *can* do, by thinking rationally, and by abstaining from negative self-statements. Additionally, Meichenbaum recommends that individuals reward themselves for coping with stressors by making approval statements to themselves, such as, "You did it; you can be pleased with the progress you are making."

Personally, we like the idea of controlling your thoughts as a means of reducing stress. Often, a person's negative perception of himself or herself creates the greatest roadblocks to coping with life's demands. However, you may prefer other alternatives. For example, you might want to minimize association with persons who "tense you up," while increasing association with persons who reinforce and uplift you; rearrange your schedule so that the most difficult and tension-producing activities are completed when your energy level is high; undertake a physical-fitness program to increase your overall energy level; or reward yourself with a night out when you successfully cope with a heavy demand. Whatever course you choose, the objective of environmental manipulation is arranging circumstances so that you are more relaxed in the things you undertake.

● Earn Thy Neighbor's Love and Other Sound Advice

One of the major prescriptions that Hans Selye gives for avoiding the stress of conflict, frustration, and hate is to "earn thy neighbor's love." According to Selye, earning thy neighbor's love is neither entirely altruistic nor selfish. It is mutually beneficial. This orientation contributes to your well-being because your behavior promotes a desire from others that *you* should prosper. This is achieved when others can benefit in some way from your prospering. This approach contributes to meaning in your life and minimizes the likelihood that others will seek revenge for perceived harm you have caused them.

In his book, *Stress without distress,* Selye has other equally insightful suggestions for avoiding psychic insults. These include not wasting your time trying to befriend a mad dog; not striving for the impossible goal of perfection; not expending energy arguing over trivial issues; focusing on the pleasant aspects of life and putting aside the ugly and painful; reviewing your achievements, especially after frustrations; taking immediate actions at the heart of an issue rather than procrastinating and rubbing on the surface; remembering your individuality and that what works for others may not be best for you. ●

MEASURING PROGRESS

How often can a teacher experience stress, adapt to the situation, and remain physically and psychologically healthy? Hans Selye concluded from his experiments with animals that the capacity for adaptation is finite. He compares our adaptation capacity to an inherited fortune from which withdrawals can be made but to which deposits cannot be added. If Selye is correct, a great need exists for keeping "books" so that you know how wisely you are using your limited resources.

What kinds of records, then, will you maintain? Because your goal is to reduce expenditures of adaptation energy, you will surely want to log the times you experience muscular tension. A paper-and-pencil technique will probably suffice. You can simply record the situations provoking tension and the intensity of tension in those situations. A gradual reduction in tension would be a good sign that your fortune is not being recklessly squandered by getting uptight over insignificant incidents that come your way. If you prefer an overall measure of your psychological state, you might wish to devise a "Pleasantness Rating Scale" so that you can rate each day (perhaps on a five-point scale ranging from very pleasant to very unpleasant) as to how pleasant you felt. Or you might ask friends to give you feedback about your behavior. A gradual reduction in the number of conflicts with others could be a reliable indication of how well you are coping. Regardless of how you measure your behavioral, physiological, or physical response to stress, the objective of record keeping is to indicate how well your plans are working and what revisions should be made.

SUMMARY AND CONCLUSION

When teachers talk about burnout, they are very likely to mention stress. In fact, avoiding stress is thought of by most teachers as the primary means of preventing burnout. Certainly, no problem is more relevant to burnout than stress. If one experienced excessive stress over a prolonged period, burnout would surely result. An individual might become immobilized to the point of no longer functioning effectively. Yet, stress does not have to end in burnout.

This chapter has emphasized how stress can be managed

effectively. The management of stress begins with an understanding of what stress is. We have described stress as involving physiological, behavioral, and psychological responses, any of which could be warning signals to the teacher. The management of stress begins with recognizing these signals and the concomitant environmental events involved in stress. We have said that teaching, perhaps more than any other profession, has the greatest potential for producing stress. We have also pointed out, however, that an individual teacher's own perception and self-imposed style of approaching life is as much a "cause" of stress as any external demand.

Although many suggestions were made for coping with stress, muscular relaxation was advocated as the major technique for stress management. Learning to approach the demands of teaching in a relaxed fashion will make teachers less vulnerable to the hazards of their jobs as well as more capable of behaving in ways that are acceptable to themselves and others. Whereas relaxation was advocated as a means of defusing one's own tenseness, the approach was not intended as a cure-all for intolerable teaching situations. No teacher should try to render himself or herself immune to truly unhealthy situations. Where changes are needed in the system, teachers should work to change the system.

REFERENCES

Bugg, C. A. "Systematic desensitization: A technique worth trying." *Personnel and Guidance Journal 50* (1972): 823–828.

Chinnian, R., N. Nammalver, and A. Rao. "Physiological changes during progressive relaxation." *Indiana Journal of Clinical Psychology 2* (1975): 188–190.

Coates, T. J. and C. E. Thoresen. "Teacher anxiety: A review with recommendations." *Review of Educational Research 46* (1976): 159–184.

Dawley, H., L. Guidry, and E. Curtis. "Self-administered desensitization on a psychiatric ward: A case report." *Journal of Behavior Therapy and Experimental Psychiatry 4* (1973): 301–303.

Dunham, J. "The effects of disruptive behavior on teachers." *Educational Review 29* (1977): 181–187.

Freeling, N. and K. Shember. "The alleviation of test anxiety by systematic desensitization." *Behavior Research and Therapy 8* (1970): 293–299.

Friedman, M. and R. Rosenman. "The key cause—Type A behavior pattern." *In* A. Monat and R. S. Lazarus (eds.), *Stress and coping.* New York: Columbia University Press, 1977.

————. *Type A behavior and your heart.* New York: Fawcett Books, 1974.

Goldfried, M. R. and G. C. Davidson. *Clinical behavior therapy.* New York: Holt, Rinehart and Winston, 1976.

Haynes, S., P. Griffin, D. Mooney, and M. Parise. "Electromyographic biofeedback and relaxation instructions in the treatment of muscle contraction headaches." *Behavior Therapy 6* (1975): 672–678.

Hicks, F. P. *The mental health of teachers.* New York: Cullman and Ghertner, 1933.

Holmes, T. H. and T. S. "Short-term intrusions into the life style routine." *Journal of Psychosomatic Research 14* (1970): 121–132.

———— and M. Masuda. "Life change and illness susceptibility." *In* B. S. and B. P. Dohrenwend (eds.), *Stressful life events: Their nature and effects.* New York: John Wiley and Sons, 1974.

Jackson, P. *Life in classrooms.* New York: Holt, Rinehart and Winston, 1968.

Knapp, T., D. Dorons, and J. Alperson. "Behavior therapy for insomnia: A review." *Behavior Therapy 1* (1976): 614–625.

Kyriacou, C. and J. Sutcliffe. "Teacher stress: Prevalence, sources, and symptoms." *British Journal of Educational Psychology 48* (1978): 159–167.

————. "Teacher stress: A review." *Educational Review 29* (1977): 299–306.

Landsmann, L. "Is teaching hazardous to your health?" *Today's Education 67* (1978): 48–50.

Lazarus, R. *Psychological stress and the coping process.* New York: McGraw-Hill Book Company, 1966.

Meichenbaum, D. *Cognitive behavior modification.* Morristown, N. J.: General Learning Press, 1978.

Migler, B. and J. Wolpe. "Automated self-desensitization: A case report." *Behavior Research and Therapy 5* (1967): 133–135.

National Education Association. "The American public school teacher, 1965-66." *Research Reports 4* (1967): 3–57.

Newman, J. E. and T. A. Beehr. "Personal and organizational strategies for handling job stress: A review of research and opinion." *Personnel Psychology 42* (1979): 1–43.

Pratt, J. "Perceived stress among teachers." *Educational Review 30* (1978): 13–14.

Rahe, R. H. "Life-change measurements as a predictor of illnesses." *Proceedings of the Royal Society of Medicine 61* (1968): 1124–1126.

Russell, R., and J. Sipich. "Cue-controlled relaxation in the treatment of test anxiety." *Journal of Behavior Therapy and Experimental Psychiatry 4* (1973): 47–49.

Selye, H. "On the real benefits of eustress." *Psychology Today 11* (10) (March 1978): 60–70.

―――. *The stress of life*. New York: McGraw-Hill Book Company, 1956.

―――. *Stress without distress*. Philadelphia: J. B. Lippincott and Company, 1974.

Williams, R. L. and J. D. Long. *Toward a self-managed life style,* 2nd ed. Boston: Houghton-Mifflin, 1979.

Wolf, S. *The stomach*. New York: Oxford University Press, 1965.

Wolff, H. G., S. Wolf, and C. C. Hare. *Life stress and bodily diseases*. Baltimore, Md.: The Williams and Wilkins Company, 1950.

CHAPTER SEVEN

THE ALPHA FILE: RUDIMENTS OF CREATIVE INSTRUCTION[1]

TEACHERS are in a position to facilitate almost anything. Unusual student responses can be achieved with regularity. Miracles usually take a little longer and may happen at unpredictable points, but they can be expected, nonetheless. Truly astounding accomplishments can occur when the classroom teacher perceives teaching as an enjoyable, creative profession. This interpretation of teaching is often affirmed by professional peers and university professors who have a very straight face and sincere voice, and with the "hint of church bells" ringing some distance away.

If a teacher intends to be creative, one of the first things to be removed is this very straight face, and probably the "hint of church bells" as well. Humor and fun are the order of the day, rather than gloom and intimidation. Confronted with the possibility of influencing thousands of students in a teaching career, prospective teachers may focus on the infinite number of errors they might make and therefore may retreat in terror from the profession, or they may choose in-

1. The authors gratefully acknowledge the contributions of Ms. Phyllis O'Donnell to the ideas of this chapter. She has either personally applied or observed the application of many strategies described in the chapter. She is presently studying toward her doctorate in educational psychology at the University of Tennessee.

stead to go forth with gusto at the thought of the things to be learned, the joy to be shared, and the exhilaration of the creative educational experience.

THE CREATIVE ATMOSPHERE

THE CONCEPT OF CREATIVITY

Definition. "Creativity" is a highly regarded concept among contemporary educators. However, its allure may be partially related to its ambiguity. Although most teachers want to foster creativity, they sometimes have an amorphous perception of what creativeness entails. Thus, the elusiveness of the term adds to its mystique. Although we would not dare to detract from the appeal of creativity, we would like to contribute to the clarity of the concept. If teachers are to facilitate student creativity by the deployment of creative teaching strategies, they must have some understanding of what behaviors to include under the "creativity" banner.

The two criteria most often employed in discussions of creativity are uniqueness and relevance. However, even these criteria are not without some ambiguity. Although a unique response is obviously something different from the norm, the question remains as to what constitutes the norm. Is the "unique" behavior different from what that person ordinarily exhibits, different from what ordinarily occurs in that classroom, or different from anything produced by any other member of the human race? Obviously, the third criterion is very stringent (one that few individuals would ever meet in the course of a lifetime), whereas the first criterion makes unique behavior possible for anyone.

The dimension of "relevancy" is even more elusive than "uniqueness." Most teachers would not judge a bizarre response that has no relevancy to problem resolution and no aesthetic appeal as a creative act. If one takes the view that any unusual response is creative, then our mental hospitals would be excellent places to find highly creative people. The teacher need not assume that all student responses defying logical explanation are creative productions. "Off-the-wall" responses are not necessarily counter to a productive classroom atmosphere, but on the other hand they may not represent a corollary to $E = mc^2$.

A basic task in dealing with the issue of relevancy is determining who will judge when an unusual response is relevant. Should an individual make that judgment for himself or herself? Should authority figures, such as teachers or professional experts, make that judgment? Or should society as a whole make the determination? Again, the last criterion restricts creative accomplishments to a very few individuals and to a very few periods in their lives. Unfortunately, the relevancy of one's unusual accomplishments often goes unrecognized by one's contemporaries. Only decades or centuries later does humankind see the relevancy of some great human inventions. On-the-spot judgments of relevancy are also difficult to make in the classroom. Ideas that seem strange and inappropriate when first proposed may eventually evolve into rare insights.

Essence. What is the essence of a truly creative response? Creativeness basically involves the combining of elements in our physical, social, and conceptual worlds—with the resultant combinations being more than the sum of their parts. This particular facet of creativity, referred to as synergy (Parnes, 1971), is illustrated by the use now being made of *garbage* (a term that you dare not apply to our current discussion). Once thought to be totally useless, garbage can become a tremendous source of energy when combined in appropriate ways. Thus, the creative quest is to combine A and B in such a way as to produce something quite different from A and B taken separately. A simple illustration of this procedure at work would be to address two major problems in this society—for example, lack of physical fitness and excessive use of energy—by a common modality—bicycle transportation. We could easily add recreational, social, and aesthetic elements to this one mode of transportation. It is through synergy that those elements are brought together, that one person's junk becomes another person's masterpiece, and that metal hitting metal becomes melodious music.

Operations. The process of generating unique and relevant combinations consists of at least two major operations: divergent and convergent thinking. Divergent thinking refers to the generation of alternatives for dealing with a situation, whereas convergent thinking refers to the formulation of the best alternative. Our later discussion of these operations will relate both to problem identification and problem resolution. A teacher can use these strategies to identify germane problems and then to promote constructive resolutions of those problems.

Both divergent and convergent activities are designed to facilitate certain processes. For example, the first item of business in divergent thinking is fluency, referring to the *plurality* of ideas without regard to quality or type. A slightly higher level of divergent thinking is flexibility, meaning the production of *different* ways of looking at an issue or problem. The most cherished dimension of divergent thinking is originality. Here the focus is on ideas that represent a *new* way of examining the issue. The remaining dimension of creativity, elaboration, is more likely to come to the forefront during the convergent phase when an individual or group is examining the workability of an idea. In the elaboration phase you attempt to develop the specifics of an idea and weigh those specifics as to their practical or aesthetic appeal. Keep these concepts in mind because we will refer to them periodically when we later discuss specific teaching strategies emphasizing divergency and convergency.

● Fluency vs. Flexibility

Our friend John Glover (1980) has provided an illuminating contrast between fluency and flexibility. Persons A and B both generated six unusual uses of an ashtray. However, one received a flexibility score of 2 and the other of 6. Can you determine which received the higher flexibility score?

	Person A		*Person B*
1.	Paperweight	1.	Melt it and make a glass
2.	Bookmark	2.	Melt it for sculpture
3.	Electrical insulator	3.	Hold ice cubes
4.	Melt it for sculpture	4.	Hold marbles
5.	Frisbee	5.	Hold sand
6.	Fill your wallet	6.	Hold gravel

Although fluency of ideas definitely increases the likelihood of original responses, flexibility is considered even more fundamental to genuine creativity. Flexibility requires that we change perceptual sets, an adaptability that is crucial to creative productions. As long as we continue to see things *one way*, it is unlikely that we will generate the next Rembrandt. ●

CREATIVE INSTRUCTION

Suppose, as curriculum supervisor in a large school system, you have been given several thousand dollars to reward creative teaching in that system. Your first task is to identify those teachers whose classrooms are characterized by creative instruction. What would be the atmosphere of such classrooms? What features would distinguish them from more typical classrooms? Do you need some help? Perhaps our comments will get you started, but the final resolution is yours to make. Would a creative endeavor be otherwise?

Problem Orientation. First of all, instructional activity in the creative classroom is oriented toward problems rather than facts. According to Olmo (1977), creativity is basically a problem-solving process in which the creator becomes aware of a problem, generates alternative hypotheses as to how to deal with the problem, tests these various hypotheses, formulates conclusions as to the optimal way of dealing with the problem, and then communicates the results to others in an understandable, usable form. The pursuit of factual knowledge has a place in the creative classroom, but as a tool for problem solving rather than an end in itself.

Facts are primarily to be learned in the context of solving problems. The creative classroom involves little emphasis on memorizing facts unless the immediate recall of those facts is considered vital to the problem solver. The skills that most students need are how to identify sources of factual information that relate to a problem area and then how to extract germane information from those sources.

To contend that creative instruction is problem oriented still leaves considerable room for ambiguity about the nature of instruction. For example, how do you identify pertinent problems? Actually, creativity relates as much to the finding of problems as it does to the solving of problems. A general guideline is that problems should come more from the children's own experiences and current social conditions than from textbooks. However, if the teacher feels compelled to cover material from the textbook, he or she and the students should first identify contemporary problems to which that material might relate.

• Classroom Problems

One of the best places to begin in selecting and solving problems is the classroom itself. Both you and your students could initially make a list of everything you dislike about the class—everything! For example, you dislike the students' failure to turn in homework, the way they get out of their seats, and the fact that they talk so much instead of doing their schoolwork. They dislike having to do homework and being cooped up several hours a day without freedom of movement and expression. The teacher and students need not look far to find some problems begging for solutions.

Focus for a moment on the problems of students talking and getting out of their seats instead of doing their work. They make excuses about sharpening their pencils, going to the bathroom, picking up books off the floor (after first dropping them), and a hundred other things to undermine what you feel is the quiet attentiveness needed for learning. You may initially think that what you need is superglue, both for their seats and their vocal chords. Even if you had a ton of superglue, it would not ensure the students' attention. You want some learning to occur. You cannot get it beyond the biological limitations of the students themselves. So look at it another way. Physical movement and social inter-action are both biological necessities. Some people cannot sit for a long time, get frustrated when they are around their peers all day without being allowed to talk to them, and resent having to do things they did not choose to do, espe-cially when there are so many things in this world they really do want to explore. The challenge of creative instruction is to work in concert with these biological characteristics rather than constantly trying to subdue them. ●

Serendipity. Creative classrooms are also characterized by unprogrammed learning opportunities. We are not recom-mending that teachers operate without specific goals and instructional activities, but opportunities for learning may occur that transcend your planned goals and activities. These learning opportunities often relate to aspects of stu-dents' lives that are far more important than any informa-tion contained in textbooks. The discovery of something really important while looking for something else is referred to as serendipity. The word *serendipity* comes from Horace Walpole's story of the princess of Serendip, who frequently made unexpected discoveries while looking for something else.

If you pay close attention to your students, they will often lead the way to serendipitous discoveries. No matter what your assumed intellectual level, thirty students' heads often make a greater totality of "smarts" than you alone. Some-times the most intelligent thing to do is simply to go with the student flow. For instance, if many people make less than competency level on a particular class test, the test may be woefully deficient. Do not insist on using it except in com-mittee work to identify better ways of asking the questions. If several students emerge with excuses for not having done their homework, look carefully at the nature of the homework assignment. Was it too much? Too hard? Too dull? In the meantime use the students' excuses educationally for you and the students. For instance, you could turn the excuses into an essay on "The Wildest Excuses I Have Ever Heard," which might be followed by a study of myths and American folktales.

If you respond to such situations as those described above by insisting that students do things your way, you have already wasted some of your time and the students' time as well. Bucking the tide by getting angry will only waste more time and psychic energy. View every classroom happening as an opportunity for both you and your students to learn something. Above all, enjoy classroom happenings whenever you can. Your enjoyment will be contagious, leading to a possible epidemic of enjoyment. Remember that creative classroom teaching is a win-win situation. When the students win, you do. When you do, they do.

• "Oh, Those Wiggly Kids"

Do you ever have days when your students cannot stay still and their constant motion "drives you up the wall"? On confronting this sea of movement, one teacher (Chenfield, 1976) challenged her class to wiggle continuously for one minute. Any sign of slowing down was first met with teacher prodding to continue wiggling. After the challenge to wiggle was adequately met, the students were then confronted with the proposition of not moving at all for a minute. When complete immobility had been achieved for an acceptable time, they were instructed to move just one part of the body, then to add a part, and so on until they got everything moving that could move. Can you imagine the scene?

Then "Freeze!" said the teacher. Everyone was asked to sit down and report the body parts that moved. The teacher made a listing of those parts on the board and wrote each student's name by a body part. Each student was asked to memorize his or her body part before the board was erased. Then each child took a turn leading an exercise starting with his or her word. The class guessed the word and followed the exercise. This series of activities was followed by the teacher's writing some sentence stems on the board (e.g., "my toes. . . ," "my elbows. . .") from which the students could compose little verses. Later these verses about their body parts were copied neatly, artistically illustrated, and placed on the bulletin board as a collage on movement.

What did the students learn about themselves from this sequence of events? They have some control over body movement, they know how to read the labels for some body parts, they can write sentences about body movements, they can express body movements artistically, and they can combine all this into an appealing whole. What about the teacher? He or she saved a lot of energy that otherwise might have been wasted trying to repress some very natural tendencies. ●

Student-Teacher Interactions. In the creative classroom both teacher and student assume a very active role. One of the prevailing features of the creative classroom is discussion, as opposed to teacher lectures or student desk work. The creative class is characterized by give-and-take between the teacher and students and between students and students. The baseline requirement for such discussion is that everyone be permitted to express personal views. This type of response is quite different from the more common response of reciting factual information from a textbook.

An interactive atmosphere is best achieved when the teacher's responses to students are predominantly pleasant. Hardly any teacher behavior so undermines student creativeness as criticism, threat, and intimidation. Yet, these behaviors are more common in American classrooms than are supportive responses (White, 1975). In our judgment, teachers depend on punitive responses when they are preoccupied with order and are failing to provide adequate academic stimulation for their students. The whole milieu of the punitive classroom is antithetical to student creativeness. Students become afraid to explore, afraid to express their personal views, afraid to ask questions, afraid to express wild ideas, and most of all—afraid of being wrong. In contrast, when students receive a steady stream of supportive cues from the teacher, they get the impression that they are liked—and not just for their good behavior. With this kind of emotional base creative responses are most likely to flourish.

To make sure that the classroom atmosphere is pleasant for each child, keep a checklist of your students close at hand. Check off the ones to whom you have said something pleasant and encouraging each day. Try not to let a day pass without a pleasant word for every single student. If nothing nice has happened for the student, make it happen. Teachers are in a position to make pleasant things happen for individuals and to make the classroom belong to everyone.

Emotional Tone. Many conceptions of the creative classroom include an affective as well as a cognitive dimension. The thesis is that unrecognized and unexpressed feelings can bottle up one's ability to think differentially. Letting go emotionally is seen as important to letting go cognitively. Thus, "I feel. . ." responses are encouraged just as much as "I think. . ." responses. Peters (1975) affirms that creative instruction allows for confluent education, that is, the harmonizing of affective and cognitive dimensions of experiences. Such harmony can be promoted by providing classroom exercises that emphasize affective communication. Because feelings are often communicated far more vividly through nonverbal behaviors than through words, one way to facilitate affective expression is to provide role-play activities in which communication must take place nonverbally. For example, a role-play situation might be structured such that each child begins with a particular emotional state (e.g., depressed, angry, happy, or calm) and attempts to convey that emotion so emphatically that it becomes the dominant emotional theme in the group. Students are permitted to communicate only through facial expression, body posture, and body gestures.

An emotional response that may be quite apparent in the creative classroom is laughter. Because both humor and creativity involve the merging of apparent incongruities, many creative ideas may sound foolish and funny. The creative teacher does not insist on a sober atmosphere or impede the natural flow of laughter. Nonetheless, some prior discussion with students about the role of laughter may prevent bruised feelings. Many students fear being made fun of when they express their ideas in class. An initial explanation by the teacher that unusual ideas often provoke laughter and that laughter is a positive more than a negative response may neutralize some of the sting from others' laughter. The teacher can also promote the psychological safety of laughter by initiating the laughter, preferably when he or she has exhibited some "less than perfect" behavior. This technique conveys to students that making mistakes is not necessarily bad and that laughing at those mistakes is a good way to adjust to them.

Getting in touch with one's feelings and ideas is not always best achieved through direct interaction. A preface to constructive interaction might be a period of individual reflection when students privately address the issue at hand. Your inner resources might even be mobilized through meditation (Gowan, 1978). The creative teacher might choose to have periods during the day when academic instruction ceases and both teacher and students seek to get in touch with themselves via meditation. The goal is to free one's mind from the onslaught of thoughts, many of which may be threatening and immobilizing. Some students may find it helpful to close their eyes and slowly repeat a word or phrase during the meditation period.

Meditation has been successfully employed by a teacher even at the kindergarten level (Murdock, 1979). This teacher began each school day with meditation and "centering" exercises for her children. The most obvious benefit of the meditation exercises was that the children learned to concentrate on one thing for extended time periods. Such sustained concentration is exceedingly important in the elaboration and convergent aspects of creativity. During elaboration a child allows an unusual idea to germinate and blossom. Consequently, in the convergent phase the child can better assess the workability of that idea. Among the conditions that seem to promote the success of this kind of meditation are: 1) a prearranged signal with which to begin (lights out, a chime, or music); 2) consistency (the same time daily); 3) small groups; and 4) sharing of experiences following meditation.

RELATIONSHIP BETWEEN TEACHER CREATIVITY AND STUDENT CREATIVITY

Teacher Modeling. Another major distinction in this chapter is between the student's creativity and the teacher's. Cochrane (1975) cautions readers not to assume that one follows automatically from the other. His contention is that students can behave quite creatively even when taught in a traditional manner and that student outcomes may be quite conforming even when the teacher is behaving creatively. However, in contrast to Cochrane, we are assuming that creative teaching methods are far more likely to promote student creativity than are conventional teaching procedures.

One way teachers promote creative responding is through modeling. However, it is more important for the teacher to model the *process* of creativity than the *products*. A classroom may be inundated with the teacher's creative accomplishments and yet provide little inkling of the strategies used in generating those products. It is also important for the teacher not to model *too well*. Humor and enthusiasm for the process may be more desirable than outstanding skills. A talented vocalist may be an excellent model for singers with exceptional talent, but a teacher with a raspy, cracking voice who laughs and sings anyway is a terrific support to young people who have not found a voice yet (or who are growing a new one) and who are hesitant about sounding silly. An imperfect, risk-taking model promotes risk taking in students—an essential dimension of the creative process.

Egalitarian Status. Another salient feature of the teacher-student relationship is egalitarian status. Perhaps the word *egalitarian* is a bit too strong because we do view the teacher as ultimately responsible for what happens in the classroom. However, the creative classroom is characterized by the teacher's having what Feldhusen and Treffinger (1977) describe as a "low authority profile." Given the fact that there are twenty to thirty persons in most classrooms, it is unnecessary for one person (the teacher) to be in charge of everything. Manage a classroom much like an office by delegating as much responsibility as possible. For example, all "order" mechanics, such as proper usage and storage of paper, books, art supplies, and closet material, might be handled by students. Because students will probably organize supplies in terms of what best suits their own needs (heights, length of arms, etc.), the teacher need only request proper labeling or charting of what is where. This arrangement allows all persons in the room to know where everything is, thus minimizing delays in getting support materials. Students can use materials as needed and, in the case of short supply, can ration materials equally among themselves. The teacher need not be the keeper of the paper. It takes too much time!

Bulletin boards are another aspect of the classroom that can be delegated to students. A student committee that plans and develops a bulletin board, however simplistic, engages in creative problem solving. Students (like most other human beings) improve with practice. By the end of the year, they can "do" a good bulletin board and the classroom teacher no longer has to spend much of his or her time (other than as facilitator) preparing bulletin boards.

The major purpose of delegating responsibilities to students is to help them develop the capacity for self-direction and self-entertainment. As long as students continue to be told what to do and when to do it, you can be sure that they will not perceive their academic and personal development as primarily under their control. If they do poorly in school, they will be inclined to blame the teacher. If they are bored, they will look to others to entertain them. Not so with the creative individual. He or she will act on the external environment to make it more productive and interesting. Even if the individual finds himself or herself in a hopelessly sterile situation, he or she can call on inner resources (e.g., immagination, daydreaming, or reverie) to make good use of time. The student-oriented classroom creates the response set that the student can usually do something to make his or her life more productive and enjoyable.

• A Suggestion Box for Students

Many business establishments seek feedback from their clientele and employees regarding ways for improving their business operations. A suggestion box is often provided so that individuals can offer their input with whatever degree of anonymity they prefer. Business establishments seek this kind of feedback because dissatisfaction among customers and employees translates into lost profits. Feedback is their way of reducing that dissatisfaction.

Suggestion boxes are not often seen in public schools. Is this because we have captive audiences that are not in a position to hurt us financially? However, in a classroom that maximizes student opportunities and responsibilities, a vehicle for achieving regular student input is imperative. An end-of-the-semester evaluation, such as often characterizes college instruction, is insufficient for helping students who were enrolled that semester. An old-fashioned suggestion box would permit students to give input while they could benefit from it. You could invite students to suggest things they would like to do at school, resources they would like to have available to them, support they would like to have from the teacher, and things that are distressing to them about school. To make a suggestion system work you must be willing to protect student anonymity and implement some of the students' suggestions. A failure on either count could quickly erode the credibility of such a system. •

PROMOTING DIVERGENT THINKING
INSTRUCTIONS TO BE DIVERGENT

The beginning point in promoting divergent thinking is to instruct your students to be flexible and original in their responses. Because most students have learned to give the "right" answer, it may be difficult for them to perceive that it is all right to give wild answers. Informing your students that unusual responses are both permissible and desirable should pave the way for increased originality in the classroom. This is one of many cases where being told the reinforcement conditions seems to facilitate the emission of the selected response (Maltzman, Bogartz, and Breger, 1958).

Other researchers (Glover and Gary, 1976) have demonstrated that students are able to exhibit the different facets of creative responding when instructed to do so by the teacher. Teachers systematically promoted the respective dimensions of creativity (fluency, flexibility, elaboration, and originality) by simply writing on the board the dimension for which students would receive tangible reinforcers. Our point is that you should clearly communicate to your students what you want in order to set creative responses into motion.

GENERAL SETTING EVENTS

Brainstorming. What classroom operations seem to promote divergent responding from both teachers and students? Perhaps the most common setting for accomplishing this outcome is brainstorming. Everyone, including the teacher, is encouraged to join in as frequently as he or she wishes. During brainstorming all evaluation regarding the relevancy of ideas is withheld. No matter how far afield an idea might seem, no attempt is made to establish its adequacy in the brainstorming phase. You may wish to terminate the brainstorming period after a predetermined time or when the ideas become predominantly redundant. It is also advisable to have some means of recording the ideas during brainstorming; otherwise many excellent suggestions will be lost. Writing those ideas on the board will allow everyone to see what ideas have been presented. You will probably need more than one recorder because the ideas are likely to come quickly.

Brainstorming activities often promote "hitchhiking," with one child's idea being directly tied to the previous child's. Hitchhiking, often used in the elaboration phase, is such a fertile phenomenon that the stage may be deliberately set to promote its occurrence. In generating a collective story, play, picture, or ceramic object, you can allow each child to take a turn in adding something to the evolving product. You can be sure that the evolution will take many unexpected turns and may go in some rather awkward directions. One person's addition may preempt another's burgeoning idea, but there will always be other directions. We cannot assure you that the final product will wind up as a best-seller or on display in a museum of fine arts, but you will be facilitating a lot of flexibility of thought.

Brainstorming may lead to more creative possibilities if you start from scratch rather than with current thinking about an issue. Once current ideas are clearly delineated, many students and teachers have difficulty thinking beyond those ideas. Current standards may continue to represent realistic impediments to wild ideas. For example, many sociologists believe that the family structure within our society is destined for substantial change. However, if one begins an analysis of potential changes by outlining the historical and religious significance of the current family structure, many participants will feel more inclined to defend that structure than to contemplate how it could be changed. If one could assume that you simply have men, women, and children without any clearly defined social structure, then perhaps participants could better speculate as to what types of social relationships might best serve the needs of men, women, and children. Once social models have been developed from scratch, they can then be compared with existing models. The modifiability of the current models might become far more apparent with this sequence of activities than if you begin with existing models (Kohl, 1975).

Alternative Resource Materials. Another rather obvious setting event in divergent classrooms is the availability of many different resource materials. Instead of using the single textbook approach, the creative teacher should have newspapers, news magazines, current-events publications, instructional kits, charts, maps, posters, and models readily available for use. In the instructional process, the teacher should make use of media that appeal to different sensory modalities. Included would be records, tapes, slides, films, filmstrips, transparencies, games, and material permitting tactile manipulation, such as clay and models. One of the best ways to organize these multiple resources is via activity centers through which children rotate on a predefined schedule. You can eventually manage three to five such centers in your classroom. Each center can address a different theme or serve to reinforce a different aspect of the same theme.

All resource materials need not have an obvious tie to the mainstream activities in a classroom. Kohl (1977) recommends the unobtrusive introduction of unusual stimuli into the classroom environment just to see what will happen. You might display pictures, models, catalogs, objects, and so on that look interesting to you, even if they do not relate directly to something you are presently doing with students or planning to do with them. The appearance of these stimuli will provide further evidence of your sensitivity to the unusual. You can even encourage students to embellish this collection of the unusual.

Alternative Activities. Another way that you can convey your commitment to divergency is by providing an attractive array of activities that allow students to employ different response modalities. Role playing, dramatic productions, games, invited guests, small-group problem solving, class discussions, and excursions outside the classroom would not be uncommon in the creative teacher's classroom. Some educators (e.g., Allen, 1975) have suggested that students participate in social-service activity, such as beautifying parks, baby-sitting for welfare mothers, and visiting the elderly in nursing homes. Allen further suggests that permitting students to pursue community apprenticeships would allow students to see the relationship between what they learn in the more conventional part of the school program and the real world beyond the classroom.

Earlier, we discussed the students' strong proclivity for peer interaction as a potential problem area to be addressed in the classroom. Instead of repressing this tendency, why not develop some activities to capitalize on it? One way to have movement and communication is to allow students to do it *quietly*—that is, by some sort of nonverbal language. Sign language is one possibility. Invite to your class a person who knows how to sign (for the deaf), and let him or her teach a few people. Get a couple of books on signing and other coding methods, and let the developmental process take its course. You need not personally direct this process; students will mostly teach themselves. You might want to learn a little bit just to show interest, but the whole point is to develop a situation that will allow you to step into the background. More importantly, a nonverbal communication system will allow students to learn from one another, to move their bodies in a way that is physiologically appropriate for their age, to see learning processes as fun, and to function more cohesively.

Another way to take advantage of the natural inclination to interact is to *encourage* the passing of notes between students. If a little structure is added to this process (which has been wrongly *repressed* for generations of teachers), you will find that 1) you have a few additional minutes each day to be creative because it takes considerable time to repress something as rewarding as note passing, 2) students can concentrate better on their academic work after satisfying some of their nonacademic curiosity via note passing, and 3) students develop greater fluency and competency in written communication by virtue of all the practice they get in writing notes.

With these advantages in mind, you might simply tell the students that note passing will be permitted as long as it is done outside lecture time, and that you will not violate the confidentiality of their notes as long as they are willing to avoid critical remarks about other students (and you) and obscene language. You might also ask them to keep the notes in some handy notebook to look at near the end of the year. One teacher insisted that everyone write notes to the next class and vice versa, on the basis that incoming and outgoing students could complain to each other about their respective handwriting skills. Thus, the teacher did not have to complain, and she swore that penmanship and spelling improved in all her classes.

Alternative Perceptions. A major purpose of divergent activities is to encourage students to look at problems, even common ones, from many different perspectives. The creative thinker learns to defer quick judgment about the appropriateness of a solution. This is particularly important when you are dealing with social phenomena. An excellent way of expanding one's perceptions of a social problem is by role playing. Because role play approximates a real-world experience, it is more likely to promote diverse ways of looking at a problem than is individual reflection or routine class discussion of the issue. Role play will precipitate feelings and perceptions that otherwise may lie hidden.

A particularly fertile brand of role play for expanding ideas is role reversal. In role reversal, students who would ordinarily assume one role in a problem situation are asked to assume the role of some other party. In a role play of a student-principal conflict, the leading advocate for student rights might be asked to assume the role of the principal. Such role reversal is not necessarily intended to change a student's views of a problem but rather to sensitize the student to the views of other parties. The outcome should be increased appreciation of both the feelings and the rationale of the other party. This appreciation usually allows the student to be a much more constructive participant in group problem solving.

Closely akin to role play as a vehicle for promoting divergent thinking is sociodrama (Torrance, 1975). According to Torrance, two major benefits of this approach are increased awareness of the problem situation and different states of consciousness (e.g., internal scanning, reverie, suggestibility, and rapture). Thus, sociodrama not only sensitizes one to the many facets of a problem but also to the many resources within oneself for dealing with the problem. Although Torrance has described several different versions of sociodrama, certain elements seem common to most varieties. The major focus is for the group to try to find avenues of approaching a problem of common concern. This is done through an unrehearsed skit in which a problem situation (conflict) is identified. Members then choose roles they wish to play (several members may play the same role) and are given a short time to plan the setting and decide on the direction of the scene: a psychologically safe atmosphere conducive to experimenting with new ideas is sustained throughout; the action is stopped when the actors completely get out of their roles or the episode concludes naturally. One of the creative virtues of sociodrama is that it facilitates the expression of emotional, nonrational ideas, which can then be subjected to logical, practical, and aesthetic analysis.

Alternative Assignments. It is probably apparent to you that a creative classroom is not a lockstep affair in which all students are working on the same materials or even the same problems. A dominant characteristic of creative instruction is providing alternative assignments. This arrangement is based on the recognition that students bring various interests, talents, and skill levels to the classroom and should not be fitted into the same mold. Although effective teachers tend to give less homework than ineffective teachers, the homework they do give allows individual students to focus on different themes (Tschudin, 1978). Creative teachers do not require children to work a certain number of problems out of the math textbook or answer so many questions at the end of the social studies chapter at home. They are more likely to give homework assignments that relate to problems in the child's real world outside the classroom and that call on resources more available to the child outside the school than within it.

Alternative Learning Conditions. Just as the creative teacher allows for alternative assignments, he or she also allows for alternative ways of demonstrating competence in an academic area. Students are encouraged to present evidence that they have met academic objectives in nontraditional ways. Students not having particular skills are encouraged to develop plans for acquiring them through nontraditional experiences in and out of the classroom. For example, a child having difficulty with some basic mathematical operations might propose a plan for mastering them by examining the sports section of the newspaper. Batting averages, yards per carry, net yards per game, and offensive efficiency ratings are examples of sports concepts that might be employed in such an endeavor.

Creative teachers are also very adaptable in the ways they teach subject matter in the classroom, rather than teaching a concept in one standard way and expecting the student to master it or else. Creative teachers seldom blame students when they fail to master a concept. Nor do they accept the proposition that some students just are not going to learn the concept. Creative teachers exemplify persistence. If one example does not clarify a concept, the teacher will use a different example. If a student lacks the prerequisite skills to master the concept, the teacher will arrange for the student to be taught those skills. If the student seems intimidated by the teacher's explanation, the teacher will ask a fellow student to explain the concept to the target student privately. Thus, the creative teacher is likely to employ many different approaches in teaching a series of concepts. Even teachers who must spend a major portion of their time teaching basic skills can employ a diversity of strategies in teaching those skills.

• Don't Forget Me

The creative teacher is particularly adaptable in using perceptual strategies to teach educational concepts. Most instructional strategies are dominated by verbal explanations. This latter approach essentially neglects half the human brain. The left hemisphere of the brain is largely devoted to language and analytical skills, whereas the right hemisphere relates more to perceptual skills. The left hemisphere tends to be overworked at school, whereas the right one may be largely dormant.

Creative teachers are likely to employ pictorial explanations in the teaching of concepts. In fact, they often do the artwork first and the memory/verbal explanation later. For example, the concept of shadow might be acquired by the child's drawing a picture of himself, cutting it out, laying it on a green piece of paper (to suggest grass), and then spraying the picture and the grass with yellow tempera paint (suggesting sunshine). Then, as he or she picks up the self-picture, the child can see that the sunshine went everywhere except where the self-picture got in the way. That part is the shadow. One fifteen-minute period of fun can be worth an hour of verbal explanation. ●

CLASSROOM QUESTIONS

Open-ended Inquiries. Questions that allow students to express personal opinions are perhaps the most critical events for promoting divergent thinking. Such questions can build directly on a factual base (e.g., "How could principle X be used in solving problem Y?"). Or they can relate to highly ambiguous situations (e.g., "Imagine that you are a bird soaring over the landscape. How does it feel? What do you see?"). Student responses to these latter questions might be followed with an analysis of a common analogy, "He or she is free as a bird." The creative classroom will be characterized by the raising of questions that call on students to express views about issues for which there is no one right answer.

A nationally recognized expert on creativity emphasizes a number of dimensions in his model that would make fruitful areas for teacher questions (Williams, 1970). Among these are paradoxes, analogies, and gaps in knowledge. Paradoxes refer primarily to self-contradictory statements or conditions. An example of a paradox is that even though technology allows us to use the resources of the world more efficiently, millions of people are in greater need than ever before. Analogies probe for similarities in relationships. To illustrate, the earth is to the universe as an atom is to a molecule. Can you think of other events and processes that would embody the same kind of relationship? Particularly important to creative instruction is the identification of gaps in knowledge. An example provided by Williams is to have students choose a story from the newspaper and list questions the story stimulated in their thinking. Then they would attempt to answer those questions by reading other articles dealing with that topic.

Student Questions. Obviously, the teacher is not the only one asking questions in the creative classroom. A major focus of creative instruction is the stimulation of question asking by students. In fact, learning to *ask* questions about problem situations is more fundamental to creativity than learning to *answer* questions. Theobald (1975) has affirmed that *training* involves learning to answer questions, and *education* involves learning to question answers. If this distinction is valid, then perhaps little that we presently do in school would qualify as education.

A fruitful area for student questions would be current solutions to social and physical problems. For example, you might articulate the federal government's current stance on the production of nuclear energy and see what questions students can formulate regarding that policy. Especially appropriate would be questions of the "what if?" variety. Such student-generated questions may give the class a richer, clearer definition of the issues to be solved regarding the production of nuclear energy than if you the teacher simply asked the students to assume a pro or con position on the current policy. Also, if you always ask the questions, students may be immobilized in dealing with future situations characterized by ambiguity.

TEACHER APPROVAL FOR DIVERGENT RESPONDING

Once divergent responding is set in motion by teacher instructions, general classroom-setting events, and open-ended questions, what consequent events will serve to maintain and increase those divergent tendencies? The teacher's social response is perhaps the most basic consequence. Because a major purpose of the divergent phase is to promote the expression of ideas, the teacher initially reinforces the expression of views without regard to the quality of those views. Such teacher expressions as "I really like the way you're sharing your views," "Your suggestions will help solve this problem," and "The more ideas, the better" are right on target. The initial intent is to reinforce expression of views without providing any hint as to the utility of any particular view.

The teacher may move from simply reinforcing the emission of responses (fluency) to reinforcing responses that are conceptually different from previous responses (flexibility). Goetz and Baer (1971) demonstrated the effectiveness of descriptive approval in promoting design diversity in the block-building behavior of a group of three- and four-year-olds. Such expressions as "How different, that's nice" not only increased form diversity during the treatment period but produced a maintenance of this tendency in a later follow-up. In a similar study Goetz and Salmonson (1972) showed that the number of different forms used in paintings could be altered through teacher approval. Form diversity was greater when children were given descriptive approval (e.g., "That's a new kind of line") than when they were given general approval (e.g., "That's beautiful") or were simply watched.

PROMOTING CONVERGENT THINKING

TRANSITION TO CONVERGENT THINKING

By providing separate sections on divergent and convergent thinking, we are probably giving the impression that these processes occur independently of each other. However, a more accurate interpretation is that divergent thinking predominates in the early phases of creative problem solving and convergent thinking in the later phases. Both probably occur to some degree in all phases of creative thinking. For example, when you and your students are generating different approaches to a problem (divergent thinking), it may become apparent that certain types of ideas are more functional than others (convergent thinking). During the final phases when you are deciding on the best approach to problem solution (convergent thinking), the evaluative process may stimulate additional alternatives (divergent thinking).

After you and your students have generated many ideas about a problem situation, how do you decide on the best approach to that situation? First, let us make clear that the decision about the best approach is always somewhat tentative. The decision is based on the ideas you have available to you at that time. Despite the tentative nature of convergent decisions, such decisions must be made if problem solving is to occur. How such decisions occur is one of the most elusive aspects of the creative process.

Some writers (e.g., Gallagher, 1975) explain the rudiments of convergent thinking in terms of an "Aha Phenomenon." One suddenly sees the idea or approach that best fits. Although we cannot explain what leads up to the "Aha Phenomenon" in a step-by-step fashion, we can identify certain conditions that seem to promote its occurrence. One condition that apparently facilitates insightful solutions is a relaxed mental state. If one's mental processes are racing from one possibility to another or, conversely, are focused tenaciously on one possibility, one may have great difficulty arriving at the best course of action. As you can see, divergent and convergent thinking make somewhat different demands on one's mental capabilities. Divergent thinking requires shifting focus rapidly, but convergent thinking requires relaxed focusing on one possibility at a time.

Two teaching strategies that may be useful in making the transition from divergent to convergent thinking are to provide a period of meditation or quiet reflection between those phases and to identify some ground rules for evaluating the various options. Meditation will tend to free the mind from the whirlwind of ideas stimulated by divergent activity. It will establish the tranquillity necessary for focusing on each idea intensely. The convergent phase might also be prefaced by deciding on the criteria for evaluating the various viewpoints. In other words, determine the effects of problem resolution that matter most, both in positive and negative directions. Then evaluate each idea in terms of its likelihood to produce those effects. The potential effects of an idea can be weighed in terms of past or present applications of similar ideas. This will help students to determine which of their ideas will have a realistic chance for success. If an idea or an approximation of an idea has not previously been applied, you and your students can establish an experimental situation to test the workability of the idea—at least on a limited basis. That would basically involve monitoring the targeted consequences before and after the idea is applied in some situation. Comparing these before-and-after differences with changes in situations where the target idea was not employed would be helpful.

The most elusive maneuver in convergent thinking is to combine ideas so as to promote stronger solutions. It is very unlikely that any one idea in toto will represent the strongest solution. The same criteria employed in evaluating individual ideas can be used in appraising a combination of ideas. Specifically, do you gain benefits and reduce disadvantages by combining those ideas? A major disadvantage of combining many ideas into one problem solution is that you lose the focus of that solution. Our graduate students often attempt to devise doctoral dissertations that will solve most of the world problems. By the time they get through including everything that interests them in the dissertation, its central focus may be lost. Thus, a major consideration is whether combining ideas unifies or fragments a problem solution.

BALANCE BETWEEN DIVERGENCY AND CONVERGENCY

In implementing any good idea one is tempted to go to an extreme. For example, education has traditionally been so straight-laced that creative teachers may react with excessive divergency. They are contesting the practice of identifying one right answer for every question—an orientation that has characterized American education for too long. In extricating themselves from this myopic perspective, however, teachers committed to creativity may have students perpetually going in thirty-five different directions. Numerous problems are explored in their classes, but a definitive solution is seldom reached on any of them. Is this arrangement any better than the old "one right answer" approach? Life requires that people make decisions about problems. Those who insist on continuing to generate different ideas about a particular problem or who jump from one unsolved problem to another often find that the opportune time for solving life's problems passes them by. The creative classroom should have a balance between divergent and convergent activities. Many problems may be explored and diverse ways for dealing with them may be identified, but problems should generally not be left dangling. Decisions about the best approaches to problem resolution should be made—even though they may be tentative.

THE TEACHER'S PERSONAL GROWTH

STRENGTHS IN CREATIVITY

Having identified several features of creative instruction, we still need to answer the question as to how one creates a creative classroom. The teacher's role in fostering divergent and convergent thinking in the classroom begins with modeling. Because the creative spirit is better caught than taught, it is imperative that the teacher manifest the creative responses delineated in this chapter. If the teacher is a living example of creative responding, student creativity will naturally follow. A checklist for creative instruction is provided in Table 7.1. If you have already incorporated several of these features into your teaching, they can be used as strengths on which to build other creative teaching practices.

Your goals in the area of creative instruction can be twofold: You may wish to increase practices presently exhibited

TABLE 7.1

CHECKLIST FOR CREATIVE INSTRUCTION

Characteristic	Frequency		
	Every Day	Period-ically	Never
1. Problem focus for subject-matter presentation			
2. Serendipitous occurrences			
3. Student discussion			
4. Laughter			
5. Individual reflection time			
6. Teacher risk taking			
7. Low-authority profile for teacher			
8. Self-directed student activities			
9. Divergent teacher instructions			
10. Brainstorming activities			
11. Alternative resource materials			
12. Alternative activities			
13. Alternative assignments			
14. Alternative learning conditions			
15. Open-ended teacher questions			
16. Content-related student questions			
17. Teacher approval for creative behaviors			

only to a minimal degree, or you may want to incorporate totally new strategies into your teaching. With respect to the first type of goal, you may occasionally use a movie in your teaching—which is a start toward multimedia presentations. You can build from this modest basis to use tapes, filmstrips, slides, models, and so on. You can simply expand something you are already doing. On the other hand, you may be following the standard teaching practice of giving the same assignments to all members of your class. In this case, your goal can be to introduce a new instructional concept into your teaching—alternative assignments. By providing several alternatives at each stage of instruction, you will greatly increase the probability that each student will find something that will be reinforcing to him or her.

As with other areas of self-improvement, we encourage

you initially to set goals that will flow naturally from the strengths you already have. Any drastic change in directions may make you feel quite awkward and throw the students off balance. Our recommendation is particularly appropriate if you are relatively comfortable with your present mode of operation. You will not want to make changes that will greatly jeopardize that comfort. Eventually, you may become the paragon of creative teaching, but an attempt to accomplish that goal overnight may contribute more to chaos than purposeful learning.

ENVIRONMENTAL SUPPORT

What are the environmental changes that would support your creative teaching practices? Continuing to expose yourself to workshops, conferences, and professional periodicals that emphasize creative teaching will keep that theme foremost in your thinking. You will also find social support from other professionals who are committed to creative teaching as you participate in these activities. These resources should provide many role models of creative teaching. If other teachers are incorporating creative activities into their classroom, there is no reason you cannot do the same. Workshops also provide a convenient vehicle for you to share your ideas and experiences with other professionals. Planning a workshop presentation will help to clarify your ideas about a creative teaching practice. You will probably also be amazed by the support from other professionals you will receive for your efforts.

You may feel that you need support "closer to home" if your teaching is to become more creative. The responses of your own students will eventually provide a great deal of support for your creative strategies. Students will demonstrate genuine excitement about what is taking place in your classroom. Contrary to everyone's expectation, learning will come to be enjoyable and purposeful. However, if you are teaching in the upper grades, do not expect that enjoyment and excitement to be manifested immediately. Your students may have a long history of inane, boring academic activities. It will take some time for them to be convinced that your classroom is going to be any different. In the meantime, seek support from colleagues who are equally committed to introducing creative teaching practices. Reciprocal discussions and observations of what is happening in your classrooms may sustain you until your students' responses become sufficiently reinforcing.

The way you seek long-term support from colleagues can be a delicate operation. Now that you have figured out some ways to begin enjoying the teaching experience, watch out for your professional image. Your peers may very well suspect you of having fun. Because that will be exactly the truth, you may be tempted to admit it. Wait until later, when your process has the security of time behind it. Now you may need to be reminded of the sacrifice long connected with teaching, the "sound of church bells," and the importance of professional peer pressure. In the eyes of many, teaching is supposed to be a service affair, indeed a somewhat punishing profession. When you get these messages, you had best pay attention to the importance of "suffering" as a visible and publicly supported characteristic of the profession.

This does not mean that you actually have to suffer. It does mean that you may be wise to engage in some behaviors that make it seem as if you are suffering a little. Otherwise, you may be seen as off target, frivolous, irresponsible and perhaps even immature. If you do not have tenure, you could lose your job. Hundreds of students coming up through the years could lose some experiences, through you, that may make a difference in their lives. Risk taking is an indispensible part of creative teaching, but be aware of the risks you are taking and build in some behaviors with which to cover yourself. Some of these could be:

1. Writing down and sharing your overall teaching plan with parents, the principal, and the students themselves.
2. Using educationally acceptable goals and the educational

language supportive of those goals (such words as individualization, convergence, divergence, fluency, flexibility).
3. Frequently making use of the curriculum vehicles supported
by the taxpayer (reading, writing, and arithmetic) and
making obvious that most of what you do involves experiences in these areas. For instance, you could portray note
passing as an activity that uses both reading and writing to
build communication skills.

• A Conversation with Mom and Dad

Ongoing information about your class should be reflected
in your lesson plans, in letters to parents from time to time,
in ongoing conversations with professional peers, and in
summaries provided for students at the conclusion of work
units. For instance, in conversations at home, a typical
parent may ask a typical child, "What did you learn in
school today?" The typical answer may be, "Nothing
much." However, if you explain to students in detail what is
taking place and why—for example, summarizing with
them at the end of a class or day what has occurred—the
conversation can be more like this:

Typical parent:	Well, dear, what did you do in school today?
Typical student:	Well, we did science and math. We did a lot of divergent thinking, and then we had to do some exercises in verbal fluency and flexibility.
Typical parent:	What does that all mean? I thought school was supposed to teach reading and writing.
Typical student:	Yeah, that's what we did. We had to write notes, read them, write on them some more, and pass them back.
Typical parent:	But that's note passing. In *my* day, you could go to the principal's office for that.
Typical student:	Boy! You were lucky! No, we *have* to do this. I mean to tell you that

	it's tough. Every day you have to write, *every day*! And you have to figure out what this guy says in this *terrible* handwriting, and sometimes it's even in *code,* and we're getting tested next week on our fluency and flexibility.
Typical parent:	Is that right! Well, I think that's wonderful! Fluency, did you say?
Typical student:	Right, and it's rough. I'd almost rather do all those dittos like we used to in Ms. M's class. This stuff you have to do *yourself,* but it's not so bad sometimes. It does help you write better.

So ends the conversation. The point is that when students are specifically informed as to what is occurring at school, they can report that accurately, and when they like what is happening at school, they will describe it in a fashion that sounds educationally supportable. •

ADDITIONAL RESOURCES

A major theme of your resource-mobilization program should be fluidity. What is appropriate for September may be outmoded by October. One approach to maintaining fluidity is to organize your collection of resources around seasons of the year. For example, the fall season provides a wonderful opportunity for collecting resources related to nature, football, Halloween, Thanksgiving, or whatever traditions might be more important to your students. The approach you take should allow for regular turnover both in the themes and types of resources available to your students. We once used comic books with disadvantaged youngsters as an avenue of promoting reading skills. For about one week they pursued those comic books with insatiable devotion. Thinking that we had found a really good technique, we kept bringing in more comic books. However, after about seven or eight days of almost continuous reading of comics they began turning to other activities.

Within two weeks *no one* was reading comics. In fact, student interest in comics did not return for the remainder of the school year, and perhaps not for the rest of their lifetime! Our mistake was overwhelming students with one type of resource. A modest diet of comics, along with other types of resource materials, would probably have maintained high interest in our esoteric reading system. So our counsel is to change resource materials often and never provide a excessive amount of any one kind of resource.

A major task in attaining the fluidity just described is locating appropriate media and resource materials. If the school system simply provides a set of standard textbooks, that does not go far toward promoting creative teaching and learning. Several alternatives are available for expanding your classroom resources. First, see what is stashed away in your school. You may be surprised to find unused audiovisual equipment and old textbooks, which could be cut up to form a rich diversity of provocative visual illustrations and activity cards. Federal and state grants are often available for purchasing even more enrichment materials. Check with your curriculum supervisor about the possibility for such funding. Additional resources may be found within your own community. Civic clubs may be willing to sponsor projects at your school with clearly defined educational goals. Some industries may adopt entire schools to assist with educational resources. Church groups, parents, and interested citizens may have an abundance of books, magazines, and trinkets, which they would donate to your classroom for instructional purposes. Individuals within the community possess a rich variety of professional and vocational skills. Many would be thrilled to share their skills by visiting your classroom or having your class visit them in their professional or avocational settings. The educational resources within most communities are practically limitless.

• Loudon through the Eyes of a Child

"Loudon through the Eyes of a Child" was a local community career-education module designed for fourteen academically talented fifth grade students by their teacher. Module objectives were for students to identify the major career opportunities in their small town, the training and responsibilities of the people in the various careers, and the interactions between these careers in the local community. Activities in which the students participated included the following: 1) making a survey—each student sent a letter to a local person representing a specific business, industry, or public service asking for a listing of all job opportunities within that place of employment; responses came from all those contacted, and they were personal and encouraging for the young students; 2) participating in an interview—a visit downtown was planned to tape an interview with people on their jobs to obtain answers to specific student questions; 3) viewing an artist draw caricatures of people in local career roles; 4) planning and constructing from cardboard and paint a miniature Loudon where all of these jobs were carried on; and 5) inviting parents and community members for a sharing of their experiences.

One of the major outcomes of the experience was the positive interactions of students with the adult working community and the support provided by that community to make the experience truly one of educational value. What the students learned about the opportunities within their community simply was not available in any publication accessible to them at school. •

Resources for creative instruction are not restricted to materials and people. You should also develop a repertoire of activities that promote the various dimensions of creativity. We would like to suggest the following texts as rich sources of creative instructional activities:

Cobb, Vickie, *Arts and Crafts You Can Eat*. Philadelphia: J. B. Lippincott, 1974.

deMille, R., *Put Your Mother on the Ceiling*. New York: Viking Press, 1973.

Osborn, Alex, *Applied Imagination*. New York: Charles Scribner's Sons, 1963.

Parnes, Sidney, *Creative Behavior Workbook*. New York: Charles Scribner's Sons, 1967.

CONCLUDING OBSERVATIONS

We operate from the premise that most teachers are very sincere about their commitment to teaching. They genuinely want to help students develop skills that will facilitate their academic and personal growth. It is not unusual, however, for those commitments to get lost or misplaced along the way. Individuals leave our teacher-training programs with high ideals about the potentiality of helping students, but within a very few years they may become thoroughly antagonistic toward students. Teachers who aspire to be innovators may wind up mechanically teaching from the textbook.

We must warn you that the innovative instructional climate described in this chapter is not the norm in public education. Furthermore, teachers can present substantial justification for being content with something less than this climate. However, if you truly want to enjoy teaching and want your students to have useful experiences in school, we suggest that you reflect carefully on the material in this chapter. Although we cannot rival the graffiti you might have available to you as you read our text, you should be much more adept in evaluating its creative quality as a result of this text. What you have in this chapter are only the rudiments of creative instruction. We have provided the alpha file. Beta and beyond rest with you.

REFERENCES

Allen, D. "A baker's dozen education alternatives." *Phi Delta Kappan 57* (1975): 261–263.

Chenfield, M. "Moving moments for wiggly kids." *Phi Delta Kappan 58* (1976): 261–263.

Cochrane, D. "Teaching and creativity: A philosophical analysis." *Educational Theory 25* (1975): 65–73.

Feldhusen, J. F. and D. J. Treffinger. *Teaching creative thinking and problem solving*. Dubuque, Iowa: Kendall/Hunt Publishing Co., 1977.

Gallagher, J. *Teaching the gifted child*. Boston: Allyn and Bacon, Inc., 1975.

Glover, J. *Becoming a more creative person.* New York: Prentice-Hall, 1980.

—— and A. Gary. "Procedures to increase some aspects of creativity." *Journal of Applied Behavior Analysis 9* (1976): 79–84.

Goetz, E. M. and D. Baer. "Descriptive social reinforcement of creative block building by young children." *In* E. A. Ramp and B. L. Hopkins (eds.), *A new direction for education: Behavior analysis 1972.* Lawrence, Kans.: University of Kansas, Support and Development Center for Follow Through, 1971.

—— and M. M. Salmonson. "The effect of general and descriptive reinforcement on creativity in easel painting." Paper presented at the 3rd Annual Kansas Conference on Behavior Analysis in Education, Lawrence, Kans., May 1972.

Gowan, J. C. "The facilitation of creativity through meditational procedures." *Journal of Creative Behavior 12* (1978): 156–160.

Kohl, H. "Creativity in the curriculum." *Teacher 92* (1975): 14–24.

——. "Planning the unexpected." *Teacher 94* (1977): 12–15.

Maltzman, I., W. Bogartz, and L. Breger. "A procedure for increasing word association originality and its transfer effects." *Journal of Experimental Psychology 56* (1958): 392–398.

Murdock, J., "Meditation with young children." *Gifted Child Quarterly 33* (1979): 195–206.

Olmo, B. G. "Developing creativity in teaching: Testing hypotheses." *High School Journal 60* (1977): 269–276.

Parnes, S. "Creativity: Developing human potential." *Journal of Creative Behavior 5* (1971): 19–36.

Peters, W. H. "The open classroom and creative teaching." *High School Journal 59* (1975): 112–121.

Theobald, J. "How community colleges can create America's third century." Convention of the American Association of Junior Colleges, Seattle, Wash., April 13, 1975.

Torrance, E. "Sociodrama as a creative problem-solving approach to study the future." *Journal of Creative Behavior 9* (1975): 182–195.

Tschudin, R. "The secrets of A+ teaching." *Instructor 88* (1978): 66–74.

White, M. "Natural rates of teacher approval and disapproval in the classroom." *Journal of Applied Behavior Analysis 8* (1975): 367–372.

Williams, F. E. *Classroom ideas for encouraging thinking and feeling.* Buffalo, N.Y.: D.O.K. Publishers, Inc., 1970.

CHAPTER EIGHT

NO TEACHER IS AN ISLAND: PROFESSIONAL RELATIONS IN TEACHING

YOU MAY think that teaching would be simplified if you did not have to contend with the views and expectations of persons outside the classroom. For example, you might have more movement activities in the classroom were it not for fear of chastisement from the principal or the teacher next door. You might also think that more time could be devoted to teaching were it not for faculty meetings and other committee meetings. You may even feel that you should not have to contend with expectations of parents, many of whom are quite naive regarding progressive educational practices. Perhaps all teachers go through periods when they desire isolation from colleagues, supervisors, and parents.

A great deal would be lost if the occasional desire for isolation should become a permanent reality. Others' input is vital to professional growth. Teachers need to have others question their purposes and procedures. Otherwise, they may continue interminably with teaching techniques that serve no useful purpose. Having principals, colleagues, and parents to whom they are accountable forces them to open the classroom when they might prefer to operate behind closed doors.

Another unfortunate consequence of isolation would be

loss of a potentially powerful support system. Support from supervisors, colleagues, and parents can have a great impact on morale when monetary payoffs and student progress are limited. However, you cannot assume that this support will occur automatically. As a new teacher, you might expect more experienced teachers to inundate you with encouragement. Unfortunately, they may be so overwhelmed with their own teaching that they have little time and energy to devote to you. You might also assume that as you begin to make significant progress with your students, other teachers will take note and give you some well-deserved pats on the back. Distressingly, the more you accomplish, the less inclined your colleagues may be to applaud you. They may interpret your success as a sign of their own inadequacy and, thus, attempt to undermine rather than support your accomplishments.

Every teacher is also affected by policy decisions that originate from colleagues and supervisors. These policies may relate to the daily teaching schedule, the type of curriculum materials available for classroom use, the selection of students for your classes, disciplinary practices to be employed in the classroom, and learning activities considered legitimate in the school. Obviously, such decisions can significantly affect the quality of your teaching experience.

In this chapter we will examine your interaction with supervisors, colleagues, and parents on both an individual and group basis. Generally speaking, skills in one-to-one interaction can be applied with slight modification in group settings. Normally, you can expect to be a part of faculty meetings, committee meetings (e.g., curriculum, disciplinary, and M-team), formal one-on-one interaction (e.g., teacher-parent conferences), and informal conversation (e.g., gatherings in the faculty lounge). Your interaction in these various settings should contribute to three major outcomes: 1) group decisions that are compatible with your views; 2) positive feelings about your personal involvement in these encounters; and 3) adaptation to group decisions that are counter to your personal views.

ASSESSING YOUR STRENGTHS

Before examining the complexities of group decision making, it is important to determine what you have to contribute to that process. If you have been in a teaching situation for a while, you will want to involve others in identifying your potential contributions. Soliciting input from *all* your colleagues, supervisors, and parents is unnecessary. Begin with one or two whom you trust. These would be individuals who do not criticize others, individuals who have generally made constructive comments in group discussion, and individuals who have given you friendly cues in group interaction.

The way you go about soliciting input from your colleagues can be a delicate matter. Asking them to enumerate your outstanding features probably attacks the issue a bit too blatantly. Preface your request for feedback by voicing your desire to be an effective teacher and staff member. Then you can ask for feedback as to any present behaviors that might contribute to that goal. If you are new to the staff, you might initially pose some alternatives to which colleagues could react. Behaviors that you have seen as only marginally important might be viewed as very valuable by colleagues. Some unobtrusive behaviors, such as looking at the speaker and listening intently to others' comments, might be far more significant to others than you had contemplated.

If soliciting feedback fails to uncover significant strengths, another approach is to think in terms of others' behavior that seems effective. Visualize staff and committee meetings for a moment. What types of behavior have helped the group move toward constructive action? Now take stock of yourself. Which of those behaviors do you have in your repertoire? If you exhibit any of those behaviors in other settings, you can learn to apply them in staff sessions.

If you have little basis for judging what interpersonal behavior would enhance your professional relationships, then think of interpersonal skills in a more general sense. Close acquaintances can help you uncover interpersonal strengths

that could be applied quite effectively in professional interactions. To get the most useful feedback, do not ask for a
comprehensive assessment right away. Alert your friends
and family as to the feedback you are seeking, and ask them
to focus on your interpersonal style for a few days. You
could suggest that they jot down the especially helpful
things you do in your interactions with them. From the
composite feedback you receive from significant others,
you may develop a whole new base of optimism about your
life.

INFLUENCING STAFF ACTIONS

IDENTIFYING STAFF OUTCOMES

You may question the propriety of teachers' attempting to
change conditions within their school. Although these conditions can affect the quality of learning experiences within
your classroom, ought not the principal and other supervisors assume the responsibility for changing them? Perhaps
so, but sometimes your vision for the school will greatly
exceed theirs. In reality, some of the most effective change
agents within schools are regular classroom teachers. Teachers
who say nothing in staff sessions but complain later are not
actualizing their potential as change agents.

Influencing group actions begins with knowing what you
want to accomplish—for example, getting policies adopted,
programs initiated, staff duties changed, and people working on a task. Group outcomes are most manageable when
they are defined in focused, behavioral terms. For example,
people often aspire to improve group morale. That is a
worthy consideration, but how will such morale be manifested? What behaviors would be indicative of good morale
on the staff? You might look for positive statements about
the school, time devoted to committee work, constructive
discussion of school-related topics, and participation in
group planning sessions. Obviously, some of these behavioral descriptions would need to be refined before they
could be reliably monitored (e.g., what would constitute

constructive discussion?), but they do represent steps in the right direction.

Another guideline for specifying staff outcomes is to begin with modest expectations. People often think that accomplishing great things involves "shooting for the stars." Although you may ultimately achieve astronomical success, starting with such goals increases the probability of failure. Many worthwhile outcomes are not realistic for a particular group at a particular time (e.g., total individualization of instruction or 100 percent parent attendance at a school program). The euphoria initially generated by proposing lofty outcomes will quickly dissipate into cynicism when it becomes obvious that such outcomes cannot be attained. It is wise to set attainable goals even if you underestimate what the group can do. Achievement beyond the group's fondest expectations is hardly a catastrophe! Besides, you can always upgrade your expectations after initial ones are met.

• Show Time

Recently, an all-campus film committee at a major state university undertook a spring festival to sensitize the campus community to cinematic art. The initial objective was simply to showcase two films per day for three consecutive days. The films were selected from the works directed by a renowned alumnus of the university. However, by eliciting the involvement of various campus organizations, the committee gradually developed more ambitious objectives. The end result was that the director of the films attended the festival, numerous experts in film conducted seminars during the three-day festival, and the university curriculum committee began exploring the possibility of a film curriculum on campus. Thus, the group accomplished far more than it had originally intended, while experiencing the satisfaction of achieving several upgraded goals. •

STRATEGIES FOR ACHIEVING GROUP OUTCOMES

Now that you have some procedures in mind for defining

group outcomes, how do you promote their attainment? A basic question is whether to use positive or negative input in working toward change. Some feel that change can best be achieved by exerting pressure on those who make the decisions. Pressure often is effective in producing change at the institutional and system level. However, we consider the logistics of strikes, demonstrations, and insurrections to be beyond the intended scope of this chapter. We prefer to speak in terms of gradual day-to-day changes, which usually can be achieved best through the deployment of positive strategies. Your interpersonal strengths are at a premium in achieving these gradual changes.

Establishing Your Reinforcement Value. The beginning point in influencing staff actions is to establish yourself as a reinforcing person within the group. People will probably respond to your recommendations as they respond to you personally. Neglecting to establish your reinforcement value in a group may render your recommendations null and void. Informal contacts (e.g., in the lounge, over lunch, or at parties) probably provide the best means of enhancing your reinforcement value because these occasions permit you to discuss aspects of others' lives (such as family, friends, sports, career aspirations) that they find most reinforcing.

Your reinforcement value within the group can also be enhanced by your being present and prompt for staff sessions. These behaviors may sound mundane, but they are one avenue of indicating to staff members that you consider the staff sessions important. Failure to attend certain sessions will reduce the impact of your comments when you are present. In a sense, attendance at planned group sessions earns you the right to express your views not only at those sessions but at future sessions. It is equally important to be in place at the appointed time. Coming in late could make you unpopular with other staff members and increase opposition to your views at staff sessions. Also, arriving late contributes to an image of disorganization, an image not likely to add weight to ideas you express in staff sessions. If you have problems getting to staff meetings on time, you may wish to identify a personal goal in this area as one step toward influencing staff decisions.

Another behavior that affects your reinforcement value is the way you nonverbally respond to others in meetings. These responses will create a receptive climate for the comments you will later make. A beginning point is to make it very obvious that you are listening to others. If you are fumbling through your papers, dozing off, or carrying on a side conversation while someone else is speaking, you can be sure that that person will not give you rapt attention when you have your turn to speak. Looking directly at the person speaking, nodding your head to indicate understanding or agreement with what is being said, and smiling occasionally will convey a spirit of goodwill toward the speaker. Although these behaviors sound like the most rudimentary elements of good conversation, you will be surprised at the extent of their absence in staff sessions. If you exhibit these behaviors, you will find that others will more frequently make eye contact with you and speak directly to you in staff sessions. Thus, your personal goals in this area might focus on nonverbal behaviors, such as visual orientation to the speaker, head nods, and smiles.

How you *verbally* respond to others is another major contributor to your reinforcement value. The basic verbal response you want to make is to reflect what the speaker has just attempted to communicate. Before voicing agreement or disagreement with the speaker, you want to be sure that you understand what has been said and that the speaker knows you understand. An active listening response often begins with "Your point is. . . ," "You're saying that. . . ," "You feel. . . ," "You're concerned about. . . ," or "You're upset that. . . ." Stating the message that you have received from the speaker indicates that you value that message even though you may later say that you disagree with it.

What we are really addressing in this section is the issue of reciprocal reinforcement. The likelihood that others will listen to, consider, and approve of your recommendations is very much related to how you treat their suggestions. Many times we do not attend to others' views because we are so anxious to voice our own recommendations. If the other person perceives that you lack appreciation for his or her recommendations, he or she may well reciprocate in kind. If you have been reading your magazine while the other person has been making a recommendation, do not expect him or her to jump for joy when you offer your suggestion.

Recognizing the value of others' ideas and accomplishments is one of the most efficient ways of reducing feelings of jealousy. If you are exceedingly effective in working with students, your behavior may be threatening to individuals who are less effective. This threat may engender opposition to your recommendations. Jealousy results when people see you receiving, or about to receive, reinforcers they are not receiving. Although you cannot control all group reinforcers, you can control the amount of reinforcement others receive from you. The most potent way to neutralize another's jealousy is to become a source of reinforcement to that person. When you point out the achievements of others, they will feel better about themselves and about you as well. Go easy at first. If you have seldom interacted with that person, excessive approval will surely be looked on with suspicion.

Being an Effective Role Model. A multitude of group behaviors can be changed through modeling. Suppose others are behaving distractingly in committee meetings. You should not only avoid attending to the distracting behavior but also avoid exhibiting the behavior. If it is important for others to express their views concisely in committee meetings, you should be careful to express your views concisely. Modeling of this type occurs even when we do not intend it. We heard recently of a university faculty in which all the male professors started wearing ties. When asked about the new dress code, a member of that faculty had difficulty explaining how the change had evolved. Finally, he recalled that a visiting European professor who had worked there for six months always wore a tie. Since that professor was viewed as a charming and brilliant person, the male faculty members had unwittingly adopted his standards of dress.

Role modeling is perhaps the most effective way to add credibility to your verbal comments. If group members see you behaving consistently with your recommendations, your later recommendations will be treated more seriously. However, if you say one thing and do another, your verbal declarations will eventually be held in contempt. Over an extended time period no strategy can rival role modeling in its potential for changing groups.

• "It's Not What You Say But. . ."

Total consistency between speech and actions is rarely exhibited. For example, some medical personnel who treat cancer and heart patients are perpetual smokers. Some religious leaders who teach charity accumulate great wealth for themselves. Some parents who punish their children for lying or cheating falsify their income-tax returns. Some counselors who stress unconditional positive regard for others cannot get along with their colleagues. You could undoubtedly add many examples of individuals publicly saying one thing and privately doing another. Unfortunately, every inconsistency erodes the credibility of what we say.

Over time the most influential staff persons are not those who talk the longest and loudest in staff meetings. In fact, influential persons are sometimes relatively quiet in staff discussions. People who make the greatest impact over an extended period are those whose private responses to students and colleagues are consistent with their public pronouncements. Before offering a recommendation in staff sessions, it is important to ask oneself, "Is this what I really believe and do?" •

Finding Common Ground. It is important for you to be able to work with anyone on the staff. Although your views and another's may be vastly different, you still share many convictions with the other person. A classic illustration of our point is the dialogue established between construction workers ("hard hats") and college students in the turbulent summer of 1970. You may recall that this was a period of great campus unrest. Whereas construction workers and college students had perceived themselves as at opposite poles, discussion revealed many common concerns—for example, inadequate garbage collection, traffic congestion, inflation, and air pollution (Postman and Weingartner, 1971). To say that you cannot work with a certain human being is unfair. The two of you may never be bosom buddies, but you can work together toward attainment of common goals.

Making Recommendations. Changing existing practices usually brings a certain degree of pain to some members of the group. Normally, individuals have established territorial prerogatives within the existing regulations. Any change in current regulations may be viewed as a threat to those prerogatives. In addition, long-standing policies assume a kind of sacred status within groups. When you question a procedure, you are likely to be told, "That's a policy around here" or "That's the way we've always done it." Few people dare to question long-standing policies. So a major delicacy in achieving group change is questioning existing policies without posing a mortal threat to others. Delaying your recommendations until you have become a reinforcing person within the group would be prudent. Your recommendations will then be considerably less threatening to others.

Perhaps the most appropriate place to begin your questioning of established policy is in a private, informal setting. If you initially broach the subject in a formal group meeting, many individuals will feel reluctant to voice their opposition to established policy. However, if you privately ask close associates how they feel about policy X, you may find that they share many of your sentiments. When you subsequently make your recommendation to the group, they may perceive you as speaking for them rather than in opposition to the group. For example, several students in the junior author's department once proposed a modification of the departmental curriculum. Before formally presenting their recommendation to the department as a whole, they privately spoke with key staff members about the proposed change. In these private conversations it became apparent that faculty members shared many of the students' concerns. Subsequently, when the students made their recommendation in a departmental meeting, they were viewed as helping rather than attacking the department.

How you *word* your recommendation to the group is critically important. Deriding the current policy will not enhance the chances of your recommendation. In fact, pointing out the historical utility of the present policy will make the proposed change more palatable. If you speak disparagingly of the existing policy, you will antagonize the group members who had a part in formulating that policy or who have lived by it. Institutional and societal changes should be presented as the reason for your recommendation. Maybe the present policy was highly appropriate when the school was smaller or when societal demands were different. Indicate that these changes, not the policy per se, are the factors necessitating new action.

Rather than speaking of a "brand new" policy, it would be preferable to speak of modifying the existing policy. The latter has a less drastic ring to it. Viable components of the old policy should be emphasized at the outset of your comments. As you introduce your suggested modifications, describe how these modifications would benefit the group. However, do not go overboard in stating the benefits. Others will want to know what reinforcers they can expect from the recommended changes, but they will surely be suspicious of a hard sell. Probably the best way to elucidate the potential benefits would be through reference to research findings. Professional people are especially amenable to this approach. You could further capitalize on their scientific sensitivity by recommending that your proposal be adopted on an experimental basis. Whatever you do, do not present your proposal as the only truth on an issue. Few persons will be naive enough to buy that appeal.

Whenever possible, shape your recommendations from the comments of others. Perhaps no one will express your idea in toto, but several persons may introduce portions of the idea. At some point in the discussion you can pull those comments together into a unified recommendation. Be sure to give other people credit for their ideas. You might say, "I liked Roger's idea about. . ., and I thought Darlene made a good point relative to. . ., so why don't we. . .?" By formulating your recommendation in this way you are likely to have the support of both Roger and Darlene.

Reacting to Group Objections. Once you have offered your recommendation, be prepared for objections and amendments. These reactions are seldom an attack on your competence or character. So try to find merit in others' suggestions rather than attempting to keep the original recommendation intact. Your basic response to others' objections should be a nondirective one, such as, "You disagree with. . ." or "You object to. . . ." Following this response, you can either provide a fuller explanation of why you have made a particular recommendation, or you can amend the recommendation along the lines of others' objections. What you are looking for is not simply the acceptance of your views but rather a recommendation that can best serve the needs of your department and school. Thus, if someone can improve on your original recommendation or propose a superior one, applaud their contribution rather than resisting it.

Sometimes group members exhibit behaviors that are insulting to you. Although you word a recommendation in a totally diplomatic fashion, two or three group members may laugh outright, others may whisper something to each other, and the group leader may abruptly move on to another issue. In this kind of situation do you ignore the behaviors, confront the offending parties on the spot, or confront the offending persons outside the group situation? If an important recommendation is about to go down the drain, you need to confront the individuals immediately. Your reactions should identify your feelings and the specific changes you desire in others' behavior. For example, you might state, "I'm disturbed that my recommendation isn't being treated very seriously. This recommendation is important to me and I would like to hear your reaction to it." If your recommendation is not critically important to you, we suggest that you handle your confrontation outside the formal group situation. Confronting people in the presence of others may simply make them more defensive about their behavior. In a private moment you might say, "John, I noticed when I made recommendation X in our staff session today that you and Mary laughed. Were you laughing about what I said or something else?. . . I would appreciate your considering my suggestions seriously."

● "They're Not Listening"

It is not unusual for female staff members to find that their suggestions are not taken as seriously as those of male members, especially if the person chairing the meeting is a male and if the group has a substantial male representation. The chairperson may direct most of his comments to males, make eye contact with males more frequently, be more likely to recognize male hands, and give more attention to comments made by males. These tendencies are obviously related to the pervasive sex-role stereotyping in this society. This stereotyping has led to the erroneous belief that the ideas of males are inherently more valuable than those of females.

If a female staff person finds that her ideas in staff sessions are routinely overlooked, what can she do to increase her visibility without alienating the staff? Under such circumstances she may be tempted to respond aggressively toward male staff members because the behaviors in question often do reflect insensitivity and ignorance. However, the attention gained in the short run by aggressiveness may be negated by resentment created over the long run. When staff members are treated in an abrasive, condescending fashion, you can be sure that they will strike back. Unfortunately, many of these staff reactions will occur covertly, making them more difficult to counteract. Thus, a bad situation for a female staff member may degenerate into an untenable situation.

A course of action more likely to produce positive attention to your ideas is to engage in a great deal of active listening, to support constructive ideas expressed by others, and to confront privately those staff members who appear not to be taking your ideas seriously. Those confrontations should occur in a nonjudgmental climate, without impugning the competence or integrity of the other individual. Such pervasive indictments as "You're sexist!" seldom prove constructive in ameliorating bad behaviors. A better tactic is to identify the specific behavior that is offensive to you and describe the way you feel when the other person exhibits that behavior. •

Adjusting to Group Rejections. What if the group rejects your recommendation outright? Do you support the group decision, complain about it, withdraw from the group, or take the next plane out? If the group is vital to your happiness, the latter three options would be ill-advised—though we have seen those responses numerous times. On the other hand, blind allegiance to a group decision is not wise. Your dissatisfaction with a decision should be voiced while the group is still formally convened. If you value the group, you should not couch your dissatisfaction in threatening language, such as "I'll just quit if. . . ." That is infantile behavior which could quickly place one in an untenable position. Simple indicate that you are disappointed with the action and why you are disappointed.

Once you have indicated your dissatisfaction with a group decision, accept the decision in the same good faith as you accept decisions consistent with your views. This does not mean that you pretend that the decision represents your personal view, but rather that you are willing to abide by the decision. You might indicate, "I felt we should have done such and such, but I respect the group's decision." For example, a particularly controversial speaker was being considered for an all-campus symposium at one university. This speaker was considered in poor taste and too costly by one member of the selection committee. After seeing that she was the only person holding this view, she requested that she be placed on record as the minority faction on this issue. Her disagreement with this portion of the total program did not force her from the committee or cause her to resign. Once on record as opposing the selection of that speaker, she proceeded with the tasks delegated to her and worked for the best interests of the selection committee.

Periodically, group decisions may be made that violate your code of ethics. Group judgment does not ensure ethical acceptability. When a group makes a decision that you find unconscionable, you must indicate to the group that you simply cannot abide by that decision. It is not necessary to resign or to threaten resignation. That course of action prevents the group from having to respond. If you are to be purged from the group because of noncompliance, let the group make that judgment. That will be a painful ordeal for the group and may force it to reconsider the decision. If you are excommunicated because of your ethical standards, you have to ask, "Is this the kind of staff with which I want to be affiliated?" Groups can play a significant role in one's life, but when groups demand that one set aside personal ethics, one should question the value of those groups.

We encourage you to take strong stands on very few issues, particularly to the degree implied in the preceding paragraph. In his book *Stress without distress,* Selye (1974) contends that one can live a less stressful life by not fighting over every issue but rather only over those one perceives as highly important. Most things seem to come out about the same regardless of whether one gets excited. So why get emotionally aroused except over a basic principle? "Going to the well" too often seems to undermine one's logic when the big issue does come along. The big issues are those which relate to human rights, especially student rights. When students are being treated in a demeaning or arbitrary fashion, you will have good reason to be upset. The exclusions of married, pregnant, and handicapped students from the educational mainstream are historical examples in this area.

Dealing with Conflict between Others. Most staffs will be characterized by a certain amount of infighting. Crow and Bonney

(1975) have proposed that the "authoritarian personality syndrome" in educators is a root cause of unsatisfactory collegial relationships. Such relationships may cause a teacher greater unhappiness than an unsatisfactory class-room situation. Therefore, it is important to acquire con-flict-management and mediational skills that can be utilized during clashes of personalities and views. Lines of conflict may be sharply drawn and reemerge on issue after issue in staff sessions. You will have to work hard to avoid being identified with one clique or another. You can prevent that from happening if you establish a reputation for listening respectfully to *everyone's* views.

Conflicts may evolve over such issues as extracurricular duties of teachers, funding of different departments within the school, grading practices, curriculum reform, and text-book choices. When these conflicts emerge, you can render an invaluable service to the staff by assuming a mediational role between staff factions. Mediation involves being able to speak rationally and calmly in the midst of heated contro-versy. However, intense conflict often produces tension even among those who are only observing the conflict. Therefore, you may find some of the stress-reduction strat-egies of Chapter 6 quite fundamental to your effectiveness as a mediator.

When people are involved in controversy, they often ex-hibit three types of behavior, which intensify rather than ameliorate the controversy: 1) they do not hear what the other party is saying; 2) they overgeneralize or erroneously generalize from available data; and 3) they make comments that are irrelevant to the current discussion.

You can help with the first behavior by intervening with some active listening responses. This will help clarify for one and all what is really being said in the meeting. An enor-mous amount of staff time can be wasted in responding to misconceptions of others' views. An active listening response not only clarifies but also reaffirms the value of each partici-pant and tends to have a tranquilizing effect on the meeting. Usually, it takes only one calm voice to have a quieting ef-fect on a volatile group situation.

Inappropriate generalizations can best be counteracted by pointing out exceptions and alternative interpretations of the available data. In an M-team meeting someone may affirm that a child appears generally unmotivated to do schoolwork. However, you might identify a number of occasions when the child has willingly participated in school-related activities. Or a staff member may contend that a particular child is intellectually slow because he or she is failing all of his or her courses. Alternative possibilities would be that the child has a motivational problem or a subtle physical handicap.

Comments irrelevant to the current discussion often focus on past transgressions of various group members. Consequently, group members (especially those being attacked) get caught up in answering those charges. Group attention to the pertinent issue is lost. Other irrelevant comments focus on issues already resolved in past meetings, issues that could more appropriately be addressed weeks or months later, or current issues that are too complex for group resolution. Because such comments often sound legitimate, staff members almost always take the bait and pursue discussion of them. Such discussion serves to divert attention from the current issue or clouds the issue so badly that the group is immobilized in dealing with it. If such a diversion is to be thwarted, it is best done early. One approach is to recognize the importance of another's concern but to point out past staff actions dealing with that issue or the appropriateness of dealing with the issue at some future date. Teachers should be spared from too many "reinventions of the wheel" in staff sessions or too much attention to the problems of the year 3001.

● "Where Were You When. . . ?"

One of the authors is associated with an academic department that has a policy of optional attendance at staff meetings. Although that policy is particularly nice on rainy Friday mornings (the scheduled time for staff meetings), it does pose difficulties in reaching decisions on issues. Even though some staff members do not want to attend all staff meetings, they do want to participate in all decision making. Consequently, these staff members will often bring up issues resolved in previous meetings. Because they miss a great deal of information transmitted at staff meetings, they are prone to discuss issues from an uninformed perspective.

The net result of sporadic attendance has been that these staff members become unpopular within the group. Even when they periodically make perfectly germane suggestions, other staff members may fail to appreciate those suggestions. As a third-party mediator, you can be helpful in keeping irregular attenders on track in staff discussions and pointing out their pertinent suggestions to other staff members. •

We should not leave the impression that conflict between staff members is necessarily bad. In fact, some authors (e.g., Swingle, 1976) contend that the absence of conflict is a bad sign, suggesting pervasive lethargy or suppression of open dialogue. Our concern is not staff disagreements but staff conflicts that divert discussion from relevant issues. Your major contribution in conflict situations is to refocus the group's attention on pertinent issues. However, even with continued focus on germane issues, staff members may have such sharply different views that an impasse is reached. In that case your role may be to suggest a compromise. Look for a way that will allow all staff members to have some portion of their needs met. If staff member X insists on a policy of free smoking in the faculty lounge and staff member Y wants a total prohibition of smoking, could some compromise (such as smoking only in a circumscribed area of the room or smoking only when the windows are opened) provide an acceptable resolution?

ACQUIRING ASSERTIVE BEHAVIORS

A popular response in psychological circles these days is assertive behavior. Many behaviors already described in this chapter (e.g., making recommendations to the group, expressing dissatisfaction with a group decision, and mediating interpersonal conflicts) would be labeled assertive. One can safely assume that a nonassertive person will have minimal impact on a group. It takes some "speaking up" to produce even modest changes in group practices and policies. How many times have you seen a discussion proceed in the "wrong" direction because you were reluctant to intervene?

Where does one begin in increasing assertive behavior?[1] As with all behavioral goals, you begin not too far above where you are presently functioning. If you never say a word in group meetings, challenging the principal in a formal staff meeting probably would not be a good first step for you. It is imperative that your initial goal represent a behavior that will produce immediate reinforcement. Selecting an initial goal that is likely to produce punishment is one of the most effective ways to make you forever non-assertive! Before you designate that initial goal, look around and see what kinds of assertive responses are typically reinforced within the group. By all means select one of these as your starting point. You might begin by defining a hierarchy of assertive responses that you want to exhibit in group meetings. That hierarchy would perhaps include the following: 1) volunteering a comment during group discussion; 2) expressing your feelings about an issue; 3) asking another person to explain his or her view more fully; 4) changing the discussion topic; and 5) verbally disagreeing with another viewpoint expressed in the meeting. You may also want to identify a hierarchy of group situations in which you would have difficulty with each behavior.

Having identified behavioral targets, how do you attain those goals? If trying out the behaviors in formal group sessions is initially too difficult, some very productive practice can occur outside the group setting. Role playing is one of the best ways to get ready for the real thing. There is great virtue in getting the feel of a behavior before attempting to exhibit it in the formal group situation. You may have

1. If you want very explicit directions on how to become assertive, you could order A. Lazarus's tape on assertive behavior from Instructional Dynamics, Inc., 166 East Superior St. Chicago, Ill. 60611.

friends who would be willing to role-play some group situations, or you might ask others who are nonassertive to work with you in role play. With the latter arrangement all parties would benefit from the experience. If role play is too advanced, you can covertly work through your entire behavioral hierarchy. In this case you would visualize each situation and the assertive response you wish to make in that situation. Being able to visualize yourself exhibiting a particular behavior is often a prerequisite to emitting that behavior.

A strategy that therapists have frequently used in helping people become more assertive is modeling. Modeling should enhance assertive activity both in and out of formal committee meetings. Usually, you can find appropriate models within your group. Look for people who not only express their views but get positive reactions to those views. What distinguishes these individuals' behavior from that of other individuals who talk just as much but get poor results? The answer may be found in domains previously discussed in this chapter—for example, how the person responds to others' views, or how reinforcing the individual is outside the group setting. If your group lacks appropriate role models, you may want to obtain a commercially available tape or film that portrays assertive behavior.[2]

The likelihood of your responding assertively in staff sessions is very much related to how the stage is set. Perhaps you have had the experience of expecting to talk a lot at a staff session but ending by hardly saying a word. No strategy assures that you will respond as freely as you desire, but several strategies increase that probability: 1) If a staff agenda is provided in advance, study the issues on the agenda and consider what you might say about each. Jot down some salient questions. Just asking some questions about the issues will get you interacting and make it easier for you to express your opinions on the issues later. 2) Arrive at staff sessions a little early and interact informally with other early

2. Audiovisual materials of this nature can be obtained from Instructional Dynamics, Inc. (cf. note 1).

arrivers. This gets you in the interactive mood and makes it easier to respond assertively in the formal staff session. 3) Sit near the person who is chairing the meeting. Because your major interaction will probably be with that person, proximity allows your interaction to flow more easily. 4) Make your initial comments supportive rather than confrontational. A few supportive comments will make the group more receptive to your points of disagreement.

Another major way to shape assertive behavior is through feedback. Video- or audiotapes provide the best means of getting objective feedback. For example, if you have an audiotape cassette recorder, you can listen to an interaction enough times to discern clearly the nature of your behavior. You are likely to uncover discrepancies between what you thought you were saying and what was actually being said. Audiotapes also make it easy to self-record interactive behaviors. However, as you can imagine, it is very difficult to interact and self-record simultaneously. If taping is out of the question, solicit feedback from a trusted member of the group regarding your emission of the target behavior.

GETTING HELP FROM SUPERVISORS

Although you should value your relationship with all staff members, the relationship between you and your supervisors (particularly the principal) is of special significance. These individuals make decisions regarding your salary, tenure, and promotion plus day-to-day conditions within the school. So in some rather fundamental ways they can affect the quality of your professional life. We have found two considerations exceedingly important in relating to administrative superiors. Number one—provide periodic social reinforcement. This does not mean obsequious bootlicking. It does mean taking the time to let administrators know that you appreciate certain of their behaviors. Administrators function almost in the absence of social reinforcement. Teachers expect supervisors to applaud their achievements, but they seldom communicate with their superiors unless they are making a complaint.

A second consideration is forthright expression of your opinions. Because of the power represented by administrative positions, teachers are sometimes intimidated by principals and supervisors. When asked for their opinions on issues, teachers may give answers they think the administrator desires. In the process they lose self-respect and probably a certain measure of the administrator's respect. We have come to the conclusion that if a superior asks for your views, he or she deserves to know no less. Over the long haul, supervisors will appreciate you more for having views of your own than for trying to parrot their viewpoints.

Administrators often become largely inaccessible to feedback from within their organization. Because of the threat of negative input, they isolate themselves from the source of that input. But even the most isolated of administrators will come out of his or her cocoon occasionally. It may be at a luncheon, a reception, or a party, but sometime you will have an opportunity to interact with your administrative supervisor on a personal basis. Whereas flooding the administrator with compliments would be highly inappropriate, airing your grievances would be even more inappropriate. Why not simply interact in a very positive, friendly fashion—possibly passing on one or two compliments that you have heard about the person? If you pursue this course at your initial meeting, you will find it far easier to establish additional contacts with that person.

• The Root of the Matter

What is the root cause of most problems between teachers and administrators? Is it collective bargaining, political confrontations, or something else? Many sociologists and psychologists contend that collective bargaining and political conflicts are merely symptomatic of the more basic problem—lack of communication and trust between teachers and administrators (Hoyle, 1979). Communication is so deficient in some schools that administrators and teachers have little understanding of what the others' jobs involve.

Lack of information and misinformation invariably lead to suspicion and resentment.

Where does the individual teacher begin in transcending the chasm between himself or herself and school administrators? A possible beginning point is indicating one's desire to work cooperatively with that person. This beginning must be followed by a steady stream of supportive input from the teacher. Administrators can easily become isolated from the instructional staff or interact only under problematic circumstances. This kind of role may contribute to abrasive and paranoid personalities.

When you drop by the principal's office during the school day, you need not always discuss professional issues. Questions about his or her family or pets convey a sensitivity to the personal side of the principal's life—something that should not be forgotten in academia. •

Not only is the principal in a position to provide valuable support for you, but he or she can be a tremendous source of reinforcement for your students. One principal spent fifteen minutes a day playing basketball with a third grader as a reward for the reduction in his disruptive behavior (Brown, Copeland, and Hall, 1972). This positive approach proved highly facilitative in improving the child's performance in the classroom. Traditionally, the boy would have been sent to the principal for disciplinary action. In another study (Copeland, Brown, and Hall, 1974), the principal's approval was given for improvement in academic performance. The principal went to the target class twice a week to announce which students had shown improvement in their math assignments the previous day and to approve these students publicly. It took the principal three minutes or less to complete each visit, but the payoff was improvement in math performance for the entire class.

Perhaps you are saying that it would be wonderful to have a principal who would volunteer this kind of support for students. The key word here is "volunteer." Seldom can you count on a principal's taking the initiative in such an endeavor. Most principals probably feel that teachers would be threatened by their presence in the classroom. Could they be correct? If you want the principal in your class for any reason, you will probably need to invite him or her to your class. Principals would probably be delighted to perform many positive functions in the school if asked to do so. Traditionally, principals have been inundated with requests for disciplinary action. If you seek the principal's assistance in issuing reinforcement to students, you will undoubtedly be viewed as a breath of fresh air. Getting the principal to perform the kind of functions described in the article by Copeland and his colleagues may be as simple as asking him or her to do those things and then expressing your appreciation for his or her doing them.

Above all, we would remind you that principals and other supervisors are ordinary human beings who appreciate attention and support from others. Try to spend a little time each day communicating with your supervisors. If you do not have time for a one-on-one conference, they would certainly appreciate a supportive note. Although you will periodically need assistance with classroom problems, your interaction with administrators should mainly involve positive input. If you provide that, they will look forward to seeing you and will be accessible when the hour of travail comes.

MOBILIZING PARENTAL SUPPORT

Parents often constitute a major threat to young teachers. Parent-teacher conferences are approached with expectations of criticism rather than support. This perception of parents is quite unfortunate because no other group is more concerned about students' progress and more willing to assist in their education. Thus, the major objective of this section is to identify ways that you can mobilize parental involvement in the formal education of children.

We often ask our classes in educational psychology to identify the types of support they would like to receive from parents. Frequently mentioned are parental attendance at school functions, parental assistance with homework assignments, parental application of reinforcing activities for academic work, parental support for the teacher, and periodic parental assistance with in-class activities.

Although some schools have already established a tradition of parental involvement, most schools do not even approximate their potential in this area. As an individual teacher, what measures can you take to capitalize on the tremendous resources possessed by parents? The type of input you receive from parents is very much related to the type of input you give them. Parents often avoid contact with the school because school is aversive to them. The parents may have experienced punitive treatment when they were in school and now as adults may receive input from the school primarily when their children are having problems. Thus, contact with the school is something to be feared. Parents often fear teachers in the same way teachers fear parents.

The one strategy that has the best chance of producing desired parental involvement is to increase the frequency of positive input to parents. In establishing a trusting and cooperative relationship with parents, you must somehow convey to them that you genuinely care about their children. A step in this direction is to communicate something positive about those children. We recommend that instead of contacting parents primarily when their children are doing badly, contact them when they are manifesting improvement.

Another way that you can demonstrate genuine concern about children is to give parents more frequent feedback than that traditionally provided in the formal grade report. An outstanding program for providing frequent feedback to parents has been developed by the Anne Arundel Learning Center (AALC) in Maryland (Cohen et al., 1971). Teachers in this center introduced the idea of "Good Friday" and "Excellent Friday" letters to parents, informing them that their child had been doing good or excellent work during the week. To earn a "Good Friday" or "Excellent Friday" letter, the student had to complete a certain number of academic tasks. The reinforcement value of the letters was further enhanced by pairing them with rewarding activities at school.

At some point you may wish to invite parents to the school to see their children's classes in action. This invitation should be preceded by the types of communication mentioned above, or you will probably get little response from the parents. When parents arrive on the scene, make every effort to let them see their children functioning positively. If the parent comes during an evening session, be sure to have some of the child's productive work ready to show.

• When Parents Come Calling

When a parent visits the school, he or she is generally concerned about two issues: 1) How is my child doing in school? and 2) What is the school doing for my child? Whereas the first issue must be dealt with largely on an individual basis, the latter can be handled quite effectively on a group basis. In fact, it would be highly inefficient to explain your school program on an individual basis to parents.

One teacher (Brewer, 1979) posted a list of general objectives for each learning center in her classroom. These were printed on the same color tagboard as the center sign, so as to make them easily identifiable. Thus, parents could readily determine the purposes of the various activities in which their children were engaged. The posted objectives were particularly helpful when parents were allowed to see the learning centers in operation. They could readily evaluate the ongoing activities in the context of the posted objectives for the various centers.

An example of this concept is provided by the following series of objectives for a puppet-stage center in a kindergarten classroom:

The puppet stage encourages the child to
- identify with characters in stories
- overcome excessive shyness
- express ideas with confidence
- discuss stories for enjoyment

- tell original stories
- use new words correctly
- retell favorite stories to peers
- speak the part of more than one character by changing the voice and portraying various feelings and moods.

Brewer's article includes objectives for fifteen areas ranging from dramatic play to music. The major point of her article is that you should maximize the visibility of your instructional objectives and strategies when parents come calling. Additional suggestions for improving parent visits and parent-teacher conferences have been advanced by Long (1976), Cronin (1977), and Rabbitt (1978). ●

It would be nice if all teacher-parent interactions could be serenely reinforcing. Realistically, that will not be the case. Parent-teacher encounters tend to become unpleasant when a parent accuses the teacher of negligence, favoritism, or prejudice. When a parent takes such a stand, it is quite natural for you to feel hostile toward that parent. How can a parent be so insensitive to the incredible effort expended in your teaching? One reason why a parent may accuse you is to direct attention away from his or her own inadequacies. In other words, parents' accusations may be defense mechanisms. By defending yourself you do exactly what the parents expected and probably reinforce their accusing behavior.

When you are confronted with accusations from a parent, we recommend that you acknowledge the parent's feelings by saying something to the effect that "I didn't realize you felt that I've been. . . . Could we talk about why you feel that way?" We recommend that you have some practice sessions in which you visualize these situations and then verbalize the responses you would make to a parent. You might practice in front of the mirror.

Probably the most unpleasant type of encounter with parents is when they issue threats because of something that has happened at school. These threats cause different types of teacher reactions, including fear, hostility, self-pity, or a "to hell with it all" kind of attitude. It is legitimate for you to have these feelings. Before you act, however, we propose that you think about the following: The parents who seek you, whether in a positive or negative way, are probably more concerned about their children than parents who never seek you. Your response to those parents should recognize and reinforce that concern.

What can parents do to enhance their child's success at school? First, they can help to keep the child in school. A school's impact is severely limited by irregular student attendance. The parents may contend that if school were interesting their child would stay in school. No one can refute this contention. Yet, parents can help in identifying activities that would make school stimulating and reinforcing for their children. Some of these activities (e.g., drawing, reading comics, or listening to music) can be incorporated into your regular school program. Unfortunately, many of the privileges that would be the most reinforcing to students are not available for use in the school setting. Some of these privileges—such as watching television, being with peers, attending movies, going to the pool hall, attending an athletics contest, and purchasing new clothing—are at least partially under the control of parents. Your task is to get parents to use these privileges to reinforce the child's attendance at school.

By telephone or home visit you can arrange a "deal" between parent and child. This parent-child deal would bring some of the aforementioned privileges to bear on appropriate behaviors, such as attending school (MacDonald, Gallimore, and MacDonald, 1970) and completing assignments (Cantrell et al., 1969). One of the first tasks in negotiating this agreement is to identify the specific privileges that will serve as reinforcers for the child. One study (Trovato and Bucher, 1980) found that inviting a friend home to play and going with the family to a hamburger restaurant were two of the most popular reinforcers among second to fourth grade students. Reinforcement priorities will undoubtedly differ widely among students. A common-sense way to find out what is reinforcing to a particular child is to ask the parent or child how the child's free time is spent, what the child would like to do if given a chance, and what things the child would work to obtain. Some of these reinforcers may already be freely available to the child. In developing your plan, then, it would be advisable to depend primarily on new privileges. Otherwise, the child may feel that he or she is getting a raw deal—that is, he or she is now having to work for rewards that were formerly freely available.

The kind of plan we have just described includes certain commitments from you, the child, and the parents. We have seen many contracts become ineffective because of teacher failure to follow through on commitments (e.g., not recording behavior accurately, not providing in-class reinforcers on time, or not communicating appropriate information to parents). Keeping your part of the agreement may require a little self-management. A checklist of things to do each day, prominently displayed on your desk, would be a starting point. This list will serve as a definite reminder, and it will give you a sense of satisfaction as you check off completed items.

CONCLUDING THOUGHTS

This chapter has been based on the recognition that individuals outside the classroom can affect what you and your students do inside the classroom. Although your major sense of satisfaction in teaching will probably come from what happens in the classroom, your relationships with your students' parents, with your colleagues, and with your supervisors also have something to contribute to that sense of satisfaction. Good relationships with these respective groups do not happen magically or result from forces beyond your control. We believe that these relationships are very much affected by your behavior.

The recommendations of this chapter were not designed to produce quick and dramatic changes in behavior. The power of these recommendations can best be felt over an extended time period. Pressure strategies may initially produce quicker changes in staff policies and practices; however, that pressure may undermine the trust and comfort necessary for constructive long-term staff development.

REFERENCES

Brewer, J. A. "Keep your parents posted." *Clearing House 9* (5) (1979): 72–74.

Brown, R. E., R. Copeland, and R. V. Hall. "The school principal as a behavior modifier." *Journal of Educational Research 66* (1972): 175–180.

Cantrell, R. P., M. L. Cantrell, C. M. Huddleston, and R. L. Wooldridge. "Contingency contracting with school problems." *Journal of Applied Behavior Analysis 2* (1969): 215–220.

Cohen, S. I., J. M. Keyworth, R. I. Kleiner, and J. M. Libert. "The support of school behaviors by home-based reinforcement via parent-child contingency contracts." *In* E. A. Ramp and B. L. Hopkins (eds.), *A new direction for education: Behavior analysis 1971.* Lawrence, Kans.: University of Kansas, Support and Development Center for Follow Through, 1971.

Copeland, R. E., R. E. Brown, and R. V. Hall. "The effects of principal implemented techniques on the behavior of pupils." *Journal of Applied Behavior Analysis 7* (1974): 77–86.

Cronin, J. "Parents and educators: Natural allies." *Phi Delta Kappan 59* (4) (1977): 242–243.

Crow, M. L. and M. Bonney. "Recognizing the authoritarian personality syndrome in educators." *Phi Delta Kappan 57* (1) (1975): 40–44.

Hoyle, J. R. "Teacher versus administrator." *Education Digest 44* (May 1979): 20–22.

Long, A. "Easing the stress of parent-teacher conferences." *Today's Education 65* (3) (1976): 84–85.

MacDonald, W. S., R. Gallimore, and G. MacDonald. "Contingency counseling by school personnel: An economical model of intervention." *Journal of Applied Behavior Analysis 3* (1970): 175–182.

Postman, N. and C. Weingartner. *The soft revolution.* New York: Dell Publishing Company, Inc., 1971.

Rabbitt, J. "The parent/teacher conference: Trauma or teamwork." *Phi Delta Kappan* 59 (7) (1978): 471–472.

Selye, H. *Stress without distress.* Philadelphia: J. B. Lippincott and Company, 1974.

Swingle, P. *The management of power.* New York: John Wiley, 1976.

Trovato, J. and B. Bucher. "Peer tutoring with or without home-based reinforcement, for reading remediation." *Journal of Applied Behavior Analysis* 13 (1) (1980): 129–141.

CHAPTER NINE

IN THE COOL OF THE EVENING: LIFE OUTSIDE THE CLASSROOM

THE REDDISH hue above the horizon signaled the day's last rays of sunlight. It was the time of day that Sarah appreciated most of all. After spending several hours in a hot classroom, she could fully appreciate the coolness of the evening. Besides, the continuous activity of the school day made her more than ready for the tranquillity of her back patio. The lightning bugs and crickets were as much stimulation as she needed at that moment. Despite the serenity of the occasion, however, Sarah had other things to do, a thousand other things! Dishes and clothes had to be washed, her children had to be helped with their homework, and her own preparation for the next school day had to be done. She dared linger no longer to enjoy the cool of the evening.

Contrary to what your students may think, a teacher's life does extend beyond the school day. It may not be an exaggeration to claim that the most important part of a teacher's life begins with the ending of the school day. During the subsequent fourteen to sixteen hours, one must find the rest and renewal to return for another day. Professional burnout may be intimately related to what is happening (or not happening) in those after-school hours. If one attempts to manage the teaching day effectively but treats the non-teaching day as simply an extension of the school day (e.g., grading papers or preparing lesson plans), vital dimensions of one's personal life will be left unattended. Consequently, one eventually will have less to offer in the classroom because of personal deprivation. Such deprivation can also result from involvement in nonacademic work responsibilities, such as a second job or a plethora of domestic responsibilities at home.

Teaching is a physically, mentally, and emotionally demanding profession. In after-school in-service programs we have seen that washed-out look on teachers' faces too many times! The impression we get is that by the completion of the teaching day many teachers are physically fatigued and emotionally depleted. Some crucial things must happen in the next fourteen to sixteen hours to get those teachers ready to function effectively again the next day. Our suspicion is that those "crucial" things often do not happen and, thus, teachers return the next morning in a semiexhausted, depleted state. That obviously makes the day exceedingly tough for them.

The purpose of this chapter is to raise some possibilities for beginning the school day in a refreshed condition and perhaps even concluding the day in a semirefreshed state. We are going to divide your nonteaching time in the evenings and on weekends into six areas: rest, physical fitness, recreation, social relations, domestic responsibilities, and academic preparation. We will discuss how each area can best be handled in the nonteaching hours to bring you back to school with some sparkle in your eyes.

REST

Rest is one of the most neglected areas in discussions of professional effectiveness. In fact, there is virtually no professional literature on optimal rest patterns for teachers. Despite this neglect, rest is a critical feature of your nonteaching hours. As your teaching and nonteaching responsibilities accumulate, there will be a tremendous tendency for these responsibilities to encroach on your resting time.

After all, "burning the midnight oil" is a revered educational value. Unfortunately, if you burn too much of this oil, both you and your students will be the losers.

The first item in managing the resting portion of your life is to determine your optimal patterns and conditions of rest. Because people differ so widely in their requirements for rest, only you can really specify the amount and type of rest that you need. A beginning point in making that determination is to do some self-monitoring. For several days record all resting activity. We are defining "resting" as time when other activity ceases and resting becomes the central focus. Although sleep often occurs during these periods, simply sitting or lying down for a few minutes could qualify as resting. Thus, you need to record all sleep time (naps and at night) and additional times that you sit or lie down for the purpose of resting. Be sure to record when and for how long these rest periods occur.

Another important aspect of your self-recording is to assess how you feel at various times of the day. We suggest that you rate how rested you feel three or four times a day on a ten-point scale. Let 0 represent a state of fatigue in which you cannot stay awake and 10 a state of boundless energy in which you feel that you could take on the universe. It is critically important that you evaluate these states in the absence of medication. For example, certain antihistamines may make you feel unduly drowsy, whereas many amphetamines can produce temporary alertness. Obviously, these states are artificially induced and severely complicate rational judgments about the natural effects of rest on body states.

Some prime times for rating how rested you feel would be at the beginning of your teaching day, at the end of your teaching day, at the midpoint of your evening hours, and at bedtime. It would not be unusual for a self-management program to affect some of these assessment points much more than others. However, at this stage you are simply interested in determining what pattern of resting gives you the most enduring rest.

If you seldom achieve the desired rest pattern, that pattern may become a self-management goal. For example, you may determine that you function best on seven hours of sleep and a fifteen-minute nap in the late afternoon. The next task is managing your evening hours so that that rest pattern can be sustained. Because rest is so fundamental to effective teaching and living, we will begin with your rest requirements in determining how you will use the fourteen to sixteen hours that separate your teaching days. We will make that a must on your schedule and build other activities around that requirement.

PHYSICAL-FITNESS ACTIVITY

Another potential facet of your "in-between" hours is physical-fitness activity. Perhaps you feel that you are so tired when you finish your teaching day that you cannot even consider the possibility of physical activity. Paradoxically, you may be experiencing extreme tiredness because of too little physical activity. A physical-fitness program can prevent fatigue during the school day and give an immediate energy lift in the morning or evening. Additionally, regular physical exercise is likely to enhance your self-image and sleep, while diminishing anxiety and depression (Pollock, 1979). Rhythmical exercise of moderate intensity has greater potential for reducing the muscular tension often associated with anxiety than meprobamate, one of the most popular tranquilizers (deVries, 1975). It is no wonder that teachers who have recovered from professional burnout often cite physical-fitness activity as part of their prescription for recovery.

• "But Will It Help My Personality?"

The physiological benefits of regular physical exercise for adults are well documented. More recent attention has turned to the effects of exercise on personality characteristics. An investigation (Young and Ismail, 1977) was begun at Purdue University in 1971 to establish the long-range effects of a systematic exercise program on both physiological and personality variables. Included in the study were forty-eight Purdue University staff members and local business people. Three groups were established from this subject pool: (A) those who were physically active on a regular basis before and after 1971, (B) those who were inactive before 1971 but took the Purdue Adult Fitness Program for one semester and continued to exercise regularly during the subsequent four years, and (C) those who were inactive before 1971 and took the fitness program but became inactive again.

Only the two active groups (A and B) significantly improved their physical-fitness status from 1971 to 1975. Perhaps the most revealing personality variable assessed was Factor 0 of Cattell's 16 PF, which, according to Cattell, is a major factor in anxiety. Although none of the groups changed significantly on this factor over the four-year span of the study, the longtime regular exercisers (Group A) scored significantly lower at both test periods. This suggests the long-range effects of regular exercise on self-confidence and emotional stability. The major personality growth of the exercise convert group (B) was in becoming less conservative in temperament from 1971 to 1975. This finding may suggest a willingness to pursue a greater diversity of reinforcement possibilities. •

Time is at a premium in the pursuit of exercise activity. Although you might like to spend two hours each evening playing tennis, going to a dance class, canoeing, or mountain climbing, some of these activities will not be available to you on a daily basis and, even if they were, you would not have the time to pursue them. They might constitute excellent weekend excursions or biweekly outings, but you can hardly invest two hours a day in physical-fitness activity unless you are an experienced teacher and your workday is well organized. What is attainable is a physical-fitness routine that requires no more than thirty minutes a day and that is adaptable to varying weather conditions and locales. Probably the most accessible physical-fitness activity to most teachers is vigorous walking or jogging. Any teacher who devotes thirty minutes a day to such activity will probably be a very fit individual. If you have been a sedentary person for some time, your initial goal should not be thirty minutes a day but something far more modest, such as five minutes. You never need to push yourself or go beyond what is comfortable to you. However, after a few five-minute walks you may discover that you can easily walk a little longer or faster.

You can almost always find a place to walk or jog. Many neighborhoods have running tracks. However, many individuals prefer to do their walking or jogging in more scenic areas, such as side streets or parks. Many cities are developing scenic par courses to enhance the enjoyment of running. The course typically follows a one-mile, winding path covering several landscaped areas. Along the way are exercise devices, such as chin-up bars, balance beams, and push-up bars. Each exercise station posts a recommended par for that station (Paradine, 1974). If worse comes to worst (if the wind chill factor is -40°F or if you stand a good chance of being mugged when you step outside your house), you can always jog in place or jump rope right in your own house as you watch television or listen to music.

A complement to walking or jogging is some stretching exercises done before and after walking or jogging. They will give your body a relaxed feeling as well as minimize the likelihood of muscle strains and pulls from your running. Stretching also makes you more aware of your body and its available energy, thus making vigorous exercise such as jogging more palatable. A particularly good target for stretching exercises is the lower back, which suffers from fatigue and tightness due to the extensive sitting that frequently characterizes teaching activity. The back exercises diagramed in Figure 9.1 should help you become a "looser" person. Do not emphasize how far you can stretch. Pressuring muscles to stretch will cause them to tighten rather than loosen (Anderson, 1979).

FIGURE 9.1

STRETCHING EXERCISES FOR LOWER BACK

Directions: First week–4 of each, twice a day
               Second week–7 of each, twice a day
               Third week–10 of each, twice a day
               After third week–at least 10 of each, twice a day, more if possible

| | Starting
Position | Exercising
Position |

Semi-situp

Lower back arch

Leg pull up

Leg lifts

(one leg at a time)

We are not suggesting that your exercise program consist solely of walking, jogging, and stretching, but that these activities constitute the basic ingredient of your program. Actually, there are approximations of these activities, such as biking or swimming, which may be just as accessible and more enjoyable to you during certain periods of the year. You will certainly want to embellish your basic exercise program with other movement activities that you find enjoyable. Such activities as dancing or backpacking may be employed on at least a periodic basis.

If you really look forward to these activities, they can sometimes sustain your morale throughout your teaching day—or even your teaching week. Another major benefit of these activities is that they may become totally absorbing, causing you to set aside other concerns while engaging in them. The aftermath of such involvement may be that you see your work responsibilities in a much more balanced perspective. The authors have been impressed with the calmness and serenity that joggers seem to bring to their work. Apparently, something happens as a result of jogging that allows them to see their work-related problems in less critical terms.

What are the factors that you need to change in your life to make exercise activity a regular part of those in-between hours? First, view your involvement in exercise as an unconditional part of your schedule, not as something you do if other things get done first. Otherwise, other activities will often crowd out exercise. Secondly, identify the portion of the day that would be most compatible with exercise. Do not try to force exercise into the busiest or most exhaustive part of the day. Also, do not relegate it to the last part of the day. Fatigue may cause you to rationalize omitting your exercise for one day and then two days—until it is completely curtailed. We have found that shortly after the completion of the workday and the midpoint of the evening hours are good times for incorporating exercise into the routine.

Another consideration is whether you exercise alone or with others. For most individuals, exercising with others works better. The activity is usually more enjoyable because of the social stimulation, and the likelihood of participating in the activity is greater because of mutual commitments. One of the biggest hurdles to exercise is getting to the exercise site. Teachers often report that they enjoy sports activity once they get involved in it, but that they have difficulty getting prepared for the activity and getting to the exercise site. If you have made a commitment to a friend to join him or her at a particular time and place, you are far less likely to set aside your exercise plans.

The inclusion of exercise in your daily schedule is one of the most tangible steps you can take to remediate or, even better, to prevent professional burnout. In addition to raising your energy level, exercise will help you keep the events of teaching in a much more positive perspective. It is usually our subjective interpretation of events rather than the objective reality of those events that poses the problem. A person who is physically tired is far more likely to attach ominous overtones to a problematic event than one who is energetic. Likewise, an individual who has few exhilarating involvements outside the classroom is more likely to have a pessimistic perspective on what happens in the classroom than one who has satisfying pursuits beyond the classroom. Regular physical exercise is more likely to raise one's energy level and to give a greater sense of personal enhancement than anything else we could recommend. Besides, presenting a healthy image to one's students is sure to facilitate their acquiring effective life-style practices.

RECREATIONAL PURSUITS

For many individuals, sports involvement and recreational pursuits are practically synonymous. Enjoyment of your exercise activity is one of the surest ways to sustain it. However, there are some very good reasons for having some nonphysical recreational options. Perhaps the most notable reason is that physical illness and injury will occasionally preclude exercise. Another possible deterrent to ongoing exercise is a slump in your exercise activity. You may be continuing the activity but not deriving much satisfaction from it. During such periods, particularly, the availability of other recreational possibilities can buoy one's spirits.

By "recreational options" we are not necessarily referring to weekend trips, nights on the town, or vacation ventures. Those events have a place and provide for much positive anticipation, but they may not be enough to sustain one on those rainy Monday mornings. What one needs then is something to look forward to on Monday afternoon!

What types of recreational activity could be included in one's daily schedule? Reading, playing a musical instrument, listening to music, painting, working with crafts, gardening, collecting various items, and playing games are only a few possibilities. As enjoyable as some of these activities might be, how can one defend including them in a daily schedule already laden with professional and personal responsibilities? Our answer is, in part, related to our perspective on life's basic purposes. We strongly believe that among the fundamental purposes of life is the enjoyment of life. That seems to be the reason many give for working so hard—so they can enjoy life at some "later time." Our conviction is that those "later times" come too late and too infrequently for many people. A better approach is to include enjoyable activity in each day's schedule. That way one partakes of life's fundamental purposes as one proceeds through life.

If you prefer to be less philosophical about the inclusion of leisure-time activities in your busy schedule, we would point to the monetary potential of many avocational pursuits. Becoming a master craftsperson, for example, may require several years of practice and a considerable financial investment, but the skills, once learned, are completely portable. They can become sources of added income during vacation periods at school. Ceramics is perhaps the most popular of the crafts, although many individuals are supplementing their income and having a very good time working with fabrics, leather, wood, metals, and glass (Coyne, 1976).

Perhaps you are concerned about the adverse effect that recreational activity may have on your professional productivity. If the recreational activity indeed does "recreate" and provide for renewal experiences, then you are much better prepared to tackle the next teaching day. Beyond general personal "renewal," recreational activities can provide for specific skills and information that contribute directly to teaching. For example, leisure reading can provide a wealth of examples to use in one's teaching. An awareness of contemporary music can provide a common ground for relating to many of your students. Your artwork can be used to embellish the atmosphere of your classroom. Stamp and coin collections can provide for enrichment of geographic and monetary concepts. Playing a musical instrument can serve as entertainment and stimulation for your students. There is hardly any recreational activity that cannot contribute in direct ways to your teaching effectiveness. As a matter of fact, leisure-time activities often evolve from one's work interests. Blum's concept of fusion between work and leisure should be particularly relevant to teachers (Blum, 1953).

Despite the multiple benefits of recreational activity, you may still have difficulty incorporating it into your schedule. Because such activity is inherently enjoyable, it can be included on your schedule when you might otherwise experience fatigue or boredom. In other words, it need not cut into your most energetic evening hours. Because recreational activity can recharge your spirits, you may wind up accomplishing more in the evening hours than if you had devoted the additional time to work. For example, two periods when individuals often experience a lull are when they return home after their workday and after they have eaten the evening meal. Instead of going through the motions of working during these periods, why not involve yourself in an absorbing recreational activity for a few minutes? Or you may prefer to give yourself a list of work responsibilities leading up to leisure-time involvement. The list should be sufficiently short so as to motivate rather than overpower. If the recreational activity is well within sight you may breeze through your work in record time.

Decisions about the amount of time you invest each day in recreational activity will obviously have to be made in the context of other time commitments. Nonetheless, we would encourage you to keep your recreational time at a modest level on weekdays, saving up for a double or triple dose on weekends. By "modest" we mean something on the order of thirty minutes to an hour a day. Greater time investment runs the risk of undermining other commitments, thus creating guilt feelings about work and interpersonal relationships. What should be a source of motivation and enrichment may become an albatross under those circumstances.

A second danger of excessive involvement in daily recreational activity is that you preempt the reinforcement value of such activity—that is, you get so much of the activity that you tire of it. An axiom often applied to eating, "Leave the table a little hungry," is equally applicable to recreational involvement. To ensure that you are investing enough time in recreation but not an excessive amount, you might record your participation for a period of several days.

• Resting for the Big Weekend

The New Zealanders seem to have cultivated many values about leisure time that would merit consideration in our society (Ramsay, 1976). Actually, they seem to value their leisure-time activity about as much as their jobs. Once a person is employed, a major priority is extending past hobbies or cultivating new ones. Because all parts of the island are relatively close to the sea, many avocational pursuits relate to the sea, such as sailing and boat building. However, sports clubs are also very popular. Because of the emphasis on leisure time, it is not unusual for a person to become better known for his or her avocation than for his or her profession.

Admittedly, many facets of life in New Zealand are especially conducive to the cultivation of recreational activity. Most businesses close at 5:00 P.M. each weekday and are closed all day Sunday. The island is replete with natural beauty—rolling terrain, towering mountains, breathtaking fiords, sandy beaches, and ten national parks. It is no wonder that New Zealanders jokingly say that they rest during their workweek in order to be properly prepared for the weekend. ●

SOCIAL RELATIONS

Another crucial facet of your nonteaching hours is relationships with significant others. Teachers who become deeply immersed in their profession have a tendency to let social relationships slide during heavy work periods. The requirements of teaching periodically become so great that spouse, family, and friends may be neglected.

We are convinced that intimate social relationships contribute more to the quality of life than anything we have discussed thus far. Particularly important to us are long-term intimate relationships. Over time these relationships have contributed immeasurably to our sense of meaning and enjoyment in life. Such relationships have provided indispensable support during "down" periods and exhilaration during periods when "all's right with the world."

Despite our idealized fantasies, significant relationships seldom just happen. One or both parties usually work at initiating and maintaining those relationships. Intimate relationships are unlikely to be sustained unless the needs of both parties are met to a substantial degree. Most relationships are quite reciprocal in nature—that is, you provide affection for the other person and you will probably be the recipient of much affection. However, if you neglect the other person, you can expect to be neglected at some point.

An issue discussed throughout this chapter is equally applicable to maintaining and enhancing social relationships—time allocation. Significant others not only deserve time from us but high-quality time. A good beginning point is to share exercise and recreational time with family and friends. Such sharing should enhance the experience for you, as well as enrich the life of your close affiliate. Consequently, he or she will have more to contribute to the relationship, even beyond the sharing of exercise and recreational time.

Another type of sharing, which might even be incorporated into exercise and recreational activity, is communicating some of the more positive occurrences each day. It is unfortunate that sharing time with significant others is often problem oriented. By the time one finishes "dumping" all of his or her problems on another, sharing may become an oppressive experience. In contrast, one should anticipate spending time with those who focus on positive events in their life. Besides, if one selectively attends to the positive aspects of each day, one is sure to feel better about the quality of one's day.

We feel that there should also be time to share your deepest concerns with intimate others. If your sharing time is consumed in small talk, you may feel even more existentially alone following your conversation. However, if you share some of your deepest aspirations, anxieties, dilemmas, and perceptions of life, that sharing time will be invaluable. Others often long for that kind of communication and could provide vital support and feedback. Research (Kohen, 1975) indicates that self-disclosure is quite reciprocal. You share intimate aspects of your life with another, and he or she is likely to share at an equally intimate level with you. Tragically, many people continue to function in isolation from significant others because they deny others access to the deeper aspects of themselves. Consequently, others are left with only a superficial version of the individuals' lives. How richly stimulating their lives would be if they would share at a deeper level!

We consider quality time with significant others fundamental to the maintenance of the teacher's morale. Note the emphasis on "quality." Simply spending time in one another's presence may not be valuable. As a matter of fact, when individuals are tired and cross, attempting to interact may be counterproductive to the relationship. If one restricts interaction to the sharing of exercise, recreation, mealtime, work responsibilities, and positive and deep conversation, that interaction will surely have a positive valence for both parties. It will serve not only as a source of tremendous enjoyment during productive periods at school, but as a source of vital encouragement when things are not going well at school.

• When Marriage Is Real

The afternoon soap operas on TV seldom portray what it takes to make a marriage, or any intimate relationship, really work. One researcher (Williams, 1979) has investigated *real* marriages in terms of the quality and quantity of communication that characterizes happy and distressed couples. Quality related to such dimensions as pleasantness, reciprocity, and noncontingency (i.e., the recipient not having to do anything in particular to get a positive stroke from the partner). As you would expect, happy and distressed couples differed both in the quantity and quality of communication time. These two dimensions were found to affect each other reciprocally. For example, there was a threshold of time that couples needed to be together before they could communicate intimately and positively.

Williams's findings may be interpreted in the context of Gottman and his colleagues' (1976) "Bank Account" theory of behavior exchange. According to this model, satisfaction in a relationship is largely a function of the positive versus negative and contingent versus noncontingent quality of communication. A contingent comment would be directed toward behavior and a noncontingent comment toward the person. These researchers proposed the following continuum of satisfaction in a relationship:

Happy			*Distressed*
Noncon-tingent	Contingent	Contingent	Noncon-tingent

————————————————————————————➤

| Positive | Positive | Negative | Negative |

The happiest couples are those who exchange a high rate of noncontingent, positive comments. The triggering stimulus for the comments is the partner's presence. Gottman and his co-workers proposed that these positive deposits on the left end of the continuum are more than adequate to cover occasional negative exchanges or withdrawals. ●

DOMESTIC RESPONSIBILITIES

Because few teachers are affluent enough to hire someone to take care of their habitat, some domestic activity is almost inevitable in the evening hours and on weekends. Domestic responsibilities can become extremely aversive and undermine other pursuits in the areas discussed in this chapter. We are convinced that such an eventuality can usually be avoided. Three concepts useful in keeping domestic responsibilities at a manageable level are sharing equitably, balancing daily loads, and sequencing responsibilities.

When a teacher reports that he or she is overwhelmed with domestic responsibilities in the evening hours, we usually find that the teacher has assumed a disproportionate share of the domestic tasks in his or her household. During most of your life you will probably be living with others. It is imperative that any person living in your household assume his or her portion of the domestic responsibilities. A good format for initiating and sustaining equitable sharing is a family contract. You and your domestic partners might begin by listing all the work to be done around the house. Do not forget those less pleasant cleaning tasks (e.g., cleaning the oven, the top of the range, the bathroom fixtures, the plastic shower curtains), to which most members of your household may be largely oblivious. You might attach a time estimate to each task to aid in the distribution of responsibilities. You could then begin choosing the work responsibilities that each person finds most palatable. Continue choosing tasks until the time investment is approximately the same for all adults in the household and until the children have assumed a reasonable portion of the work responsibilities. Obviously, as a child approaches adulthood, he or she should gradually assume an adult level of responsibility.

Two impediments to the distribution of tasks will be the claim by some that they do not enjoy or do not know how to do certain tasks. The cruel reality is that many household chores are not inherently enjoyable. "Enjoyment" will not be a very workable criterion of "who does what" around the house. You may enjoy seeing a clean, attractively arranged house, but it is unlikely that you will ever get much exhilaration from washing dishes or vacuuming the floor. Lack of skill in doing certain tasks is also offered as an excuse for doing little in a given area. Admittedly, certain members of the household, especially males, may have meager knowledge of how to perform many domestic functions.[1] However, if anyone in the household knows how to do a particular task, he or she can teach others in the household to do that task. No aspect of domestic work is too difficult for a person of normal intelligence to master. Achieving an equitable distribution of tasks may require a good deal of in-service training for some members of your household.

A fun way to teach and learn domestic skills has been suggested by Schmelzel (1974). Cleanup tasks and easy cleaning methods for those tasks are typed on separate cards. The tasks include some really tough orders, such as cleaning a rusted steel knife, a scratched ceramic sink, a greasy spatter, a wooden salad bowl, an egg-coated plate, a flour sifter, and a "smelly" refrigerator. Schmelzel has developed a card game for teaching/learning the most efficient way of performing each task. The specific rules of the game plus all tasks and cleaning methods are included in Schmelzel's article. The scoring of the game focuses on achieving matches between tasks and cleaning methods. We would suggest this

---

1. An initial assessment of who knows how to do what might be achieved by administering a cleaning IQ test ("What's your cleaning IQ?", 1976). The normative categories for scores on the test are: washing wiz, washing wipe-out, and all washed up. We won't reveal how we personally scored on the test.

game as a painless, nonthreatening way of teaching all members of the household how to perform a myriad of tasks.

An equitable distribution of domestic tasks should reduce each person's load to a very manageable level. An extension of the distribution concept is the distribution of tasks across days. A few things may need to be done every day (e.g., preparing meals and washing dishes), but many things may be done only once or twice a week (e.g., washing clothes and vacuuming the house). Taking on only one or two major tasks each day should prevent you from feeling overwhelmed by what you have to do. Furthermore, your house will retain a semblance of order and cleanliness, which will make it a far more pleasant place in which to abide. This will prevent domestic disarray from undermining other work and play possibilities. We would estimate that given the sharing format we have proposed, no person would need to do more than an hour of actual housework each day.

Perhaps the most crucial dimension of this daily scheduling is the sequencing of tasks. The optimal time to grocery-shop is before the pantry is totally barren. The optimal time to wash clothes is before every stitch of clothing in your household is filthy. Develop a schedule that anticipates needs and prevents you from getting in desperate domestic straits. Also, think in terms of how one task affects another. Task B may be considerably easier to do after task A has been completed. (Have you tried preparing the evening meal when the pantry is barren? Vacuuming the floor when clothes and papers are scattered hither and yon? Mopping the kitchen floor before it has been swept?) Look at the full gamut of domestic tasks to be done during the week. How can you best sequence those tasks not only to prevent dire circumstances but also to make subsequent tasks flow more easily? Such an approach can save hours of work and much psychological discomfort each week. It can also put you in control of an area of life that has a tendency to get out of control.

ACADEMIC PREPARATION

Academic responsibilities have a way of going beyond the school day and infringing on your personal time. Every effective teacher probably does some school-related work at home. The two major academic activities done at home are planning and evaluating student work. Because you spend most of your school day interacting with students, you may find little time at school for either of these activities. However, teachers are not the only ones bringing work home from school. Students are also having to deal with academic work that infringes on their evening hours and weekends.

It is our conviction that the spillover into the evening hours is caused by teachers' trying to accomplish too much with students or mismanaging professional responsibilities during the school day. We prefer to operate from the premise that a child's formal education should occur within the context of the school day and that 90 percent of what the teacher does professionally should occur within the school day. Actualizing this premise would require two things: 1) keeping student assignments at a modest level; and 2) providing time and support for the completion of those assignments at school.

● Are You Sure about That?

Joan, a dedicated fourth-year teacher in a suburban elementary school, took work home with her every night. Generally, she spent approximately two hours each night grading papers and making preparations for the next day. Joan claimed that she did not mind the extra hours she spent on paperwork. She felt that the amount of time invested after school hours paid off in the classroom. She had good control of her class and was never at a loss as to how to get students involved in their work. She liked her students and they appeared to like her as well. Joan had a problem, though. It "burned her up" to see other teachers leaving school with nothing under their arms. She complained at home that other teachers were uncaring. She felt that most teachers did not really have the interest of the students at heart. "How could they," she asked, "when they never put in an extra minute?" Although our analysis could be wrong, we suspect that Joan has some uncertainties about her professional and personal priorities. Individuals who are sure of what is good for themselves do not have to spend much time worrying about what is good for others. A clue to one's own satisfaction may lie in whether one can let others also "do their own thing." •

Several guidelines would aid in the fulfillment of these requirements. As a teacher, do not make any assignments for which prompt, systematic feedback cannot be provided. Requiring work from students that is never carefully checked is absolutely taboo. If students are required to do the work, then it is your responsibility to see that the work is thoroughly checked. If you keep this guideline in mind, it may serve to temper your judgment about massive assignments.

Another guideline that may reduce everyone's work load at home is to minimize repetition within assignments. Five problems related to a mathematical concept or manipulation may serve as well as twenty problems related to the same concept or manipulation. Repetition across many problems is likely to produce fatigue and boredom, conditions that are counter to the enjoyment of that activity. Make your assignments just long enough for the students to demonstrate comprehension of the concept or procedure under question. Generally, give assignments that illustrate only one or, at most, a few major concepts.

A third guideline for reducing your work load at home is to provide time at school for completing and checking all assignments. Remember, the purpose of assignments is basically instructional. This requires that students be given prompt feedback and corrective instruction in areas of difficulty. To accomplish this requirement, you will need to institute a lot of self-checking procedures and peer tutoring in your class. This arrangement in many instances will permit students to determine their own deficiencies and will allow students who have mastered particular concepts to assist others having difficulty with those concepts.

If students are given time at school to work on and correct assignments, this will provide some planning time for you during the school day. The ideal is for planning, completion of assignments, feedback regarding assignments, and corrective instruction to occur within the time frame for a particular subject area. Consequently, when the reading period is over in the morning, both you and your students should be able to turn to other matters until the reading period the next day.

• Strategies for Juggling Professional and Family Lives

The following strategies for managing one's life outside the classroom were suggested by a graduate student who is also a single parent and a full-time teacher. Her suggestions bring together most facets of one's personal life discussed in this chapter.

1. Each Sunday evening review the week ahead and make your game plan. Jot down all family appointments and obligations, school-related activities and responsibilities, and social events. For the "light days" pencil in laundry, baking, grocery shopping, or miscellaneous household chores. For "heavy days" plan "slow-cooker" or microwave-oven dinners and the bare minimum of household maintenance.

2. Make a daily list of calls to make and things to do; keep it handy all day long and check off items when they are completed.

3. Consolidate errands. By careful planning you will need to go to the supermarket, the library, or the bank only once a week or every two weeks.

4. Assign chores to everyone in the family; you cannot do it all! Children can be given monetary incentives or points to be traded at the end of the week for tickets to a movie or skating, for example.

5. No matter how busy you are, take a few minutes each day to talk to each child about the events of the day and share a laugh, a game, or a snack.

6. Learn to say "No." Because you already have plenty to do, you need to learn the skill of assertive refusal when being pressured to help with the church bake sale, to take on another committee assignment, or the like. (You will be of little assistance to anyone if you spread yourself too thin.)

7. Streamline your daily work as much as possible. Can you give a multiple-choice test rather than an essay test that will be more time-consuming to grade? Can students grade each other's papers instead of your carting them all home? Can you delegate some routine tasks?

8. Stop feeling guilty about your housekeeping; you cannot possibly do as much as your neighbor who does not work. Post this sign conspicuously on your bathroom mirror: "No one will know in 100 years if I dusted the furniture today or not."

9. Do something each day just for *yourself* to relax or "recharge your batteries." Take a walk, listen to music, take a relaxing bath, read a good short story, or visit or phone a friend. You deserve it!

10. Find a place where you can get away from both work and family. It might be a café, a health spa, a public park, or someplace else. This spot will provide you with an opportunity just to be a person—a rare opportunity in our fast-paced, highly organized society.

11. Plan a minivacation once a month—take the family hiking, to the lake, or to an out-of-town ball game, for instance. Just getting away now and then from the usual environs refreshes everyone. ●

CONCLUDING OBSERVATIONS

We readily admit that this chapter has taken a much broader perspective on the teacher's life than that advanced in most educational texts. However, we strongly contend that a teacher's effectiveness in the classroom cannot be divorced from his or her life outside the classroom. Inevitably, a troubled or sterile life outside the classroom will infringe on a teacher's productivity in the classroom.

We also admit that some recommendations run counter to established educational philosophy. Who ever heard of minimizing homework for both students and teachers? We believe that academe's infringement on the evening hours for both teachers and students operates much like a malignancy in the human body. A malignancy feeds on the body until it ultimately kills its own source of life. Extending work responsibilities long into the evening ultimately undermines the enjoyment and energy necessary for teaching and learning to occur most effectively during the school day.

REFERENCES

Anderson, B. "Stretching." *The Journal of Physical Education 76* (6) (1979): 130.

Blum, F. H. *Toward a democratic work process.* New York: Harper, 1953.

Coyne, J. "Handcrafts." *Today's Education 75* (November 1976): 75–76.

deVries, H. A. "Physical education, adult fitness programs: Does physical activity promote relaxation?" *Journal of Physical Education and Recreation 46* (September 1975): 53–54.

Gottman, J., C. Notarius, J. Gonso, and H. Markham. *A couple's guide to communication.* Champaign, Ill.: Research Press, 1976.

Kohen, J. "The development of reciprocal self-disclosure in opposite-sex interaction." *Journal of Counseling Psychology 22* (5) (1975): 404–410.

Paradine, M. "Parcourse—How to enjoy jogging." *Journal of Physical Education 71* (July 1974): 170.

Pollock, M. L. "Exercise—A preventive prescription." *Journal of School Health 49* (1979): 215–219.

Ramsay, R. L. "New Zealand: Leisure as a priority." *Journal of Physical Education and Recreation 47* (October 1976): 11-12.

Schmelzel, C. "The big sweep." *Forecast for Home Economics 20* (December 1974): F32.

"What's your cleaning IQ?" *Forecast for Home Economics 21* (9) (May 1976): F47, F59.

Williams, A. M. "The quantity and quality of marital interaction related to marital satisfaction: A behavioral analysis." *Journal of Applied Behavior Analysis 12* (1979): 665–678.

Young, R. J. and A. H. Ismail. "Comparison of selected physiological and personality variables in regular and nonregular adult male exercisers." *Research Quarterly 48* (1977): 617–622.

CHAPTER TEN

A FINAL LOOK: MAXIMIZING YOUR SUCCESS

ALMOST everyone has something to say about what is needed to produce and to retain good teachers. We obviously have our share of opinions. Ultimately, however, you must decide if aspects of your professional life need to be changed and how you will attempt to accomplish those changes. In large measure, teachers control their own destinies. Of course, some would prefer to transfer that responsibility to others. Most persons, however, want to direct their own lives and to make the most of their chosen profession. Because you have read this far, we assume that you are in the latter group. Unfortunately, not everyone reaches his or her goals. Obstacles always exist along the path toward self-improvement, and many acquiesce to those hardships. Nonetheless, our contention is that those who persevere can increase their professional effectiveness. In this final chapter we want to offer additional encouragement as you undertake your self-improvement projects.

BETWEEN SUCCESS AND FAILURE

In the past several years we have seen a number of prospective and in-service teachers embark on self-improvement projects. Those persons using our model successfully have attributed their successes to a variety of factors. Many teachers, for example, have felt that analyzing their strengths was the key to self-improvement. Others have said that establishing clear goals was the most important factor leading to improvement. No single factor has emerged as the sole reason for success or failure. However, as we have analyzed the self-improvement projects submitted to us, a number of salient differences have emerged between those which have been reported successful and those which have not.

The emergent differences between reported successes and failures can be categorized under each of the four steps in our model. First, persons reporting success have generally been more *direct* in talking about their strengths. For example, those reporting success have made such statements as "I find it easy to diagnose my students' math skills" rather than "I enjoy determining what my students can do." Although these statements may appear quite similar, there is actually a marked difference between them. Saying that one *likes* to perform a task is less direct than saying that one *can do* a task. To enjoy tennis is not the same as being able to play tennis well. Interest, of course, is essential and can serve to build strengths. Reluctance to admit that one can perform a task well is a characteristic of those who report less success in their efforts.

We recognize that individuals do not want to appear as braggarts. Yet, as we have stressed in other chapters, recognizing your strengths is not bragging. Your strengths need not be announced over national television! Individuals who are willing to admit (at least to themselves) that they have strengths can use that knowledge to persevere when the going becomes difficult.

Successful self-managers have also been quite *specific* in identifying their strengths. For example, successful persons have said that they were good at such specific skills as paraphrasing and summarizing the views of others as opposed to saying merely that they were good at working with others. Again, we find that persons who strive for accuracy in identifying their strengths have something specific they can use in confronting problems.

Another major difference observed in the projects submitted to us relates to goal-setting strategies. Successful projects have almost unanimously emphasized positive goals, whereas most of the failures have sought to eliminate bad behaviors. In one in-service class two teachers dealt with the same problem but obtained opposite results. We believe that the critical factor was the way they chose to approach their goal. Both were interested in talking less. The unsuccessful teacher sought only to be less verbose. She did succeed in saying less, but she reported that her relationships with others had suffered. Friends thought that they were being snubbed. The successful teacher also wanted to talk less, but she chose to pose more open-ended questions for others. She reasoned that she could achieve her goal better by focusing on what she should be doing rather than on something she should not be doing. Reportedly, she became more reinforcing to others because they were allowed to speak more in response to her inquiries. She was forced to listen more and to talk less. Finally, she came to appreciate others more as she learned about their lives and what she had in common with them.

In relation to controlling environmental events, we have found that those achieving success invariably mention a functional relationship between how they behave and what happens to them. For instance, successful teachers have repeatedly told us that when they increase such behaviors as active listening and giving of praise, something good usually happens to them. In other words, those teachers note that their situation changes as a function of their own behavior. Conversely, with self-reported failures, there has been a conspicuous absence of suggestions that a relationship exists between behavior and its consequences. We recognize, though, that it is easier to take credit than to accept blame. Nonetheless, successful self-managers tend to be alert to how their own behaviors impact on both positive and negative events in their lives.

Finally, successful reports typically contain a system of record keeping that is self-revealing. By "self-revealing" we mean one that suggests where strengths and weaknesses lie and what actions might be appropriate. A record of non-verbal behaviors that includes such labels as "smiles," "eye contact," "nods," and "special distance" allows individuals readily to assess progress as well as to identify areas needing improvement. On the other hand, we have seldom seen a diary approach work very well. Persons who record everything they do without categorizing their actions cannot seem to make "heads or tails" of what they did rightly or wrongly. In brief, persons who make the effort to develop a written record that is sensible to themselves and to others are prone to be more successful with their overall self-improvement projects.

MAINTAINING ENTHUSIASM

Although people's enthusiasm is often tied to their successes, maintaining enthusiasm when setbacks occur may be more fundamental to long-range self-improvement. Maintenance of enthusiasm in the face of difficulty is largely a function of expectations and rewards. Much loss of enthusiasm in teaching occurs from expecting too much too soon. Students did not get to be the way they are overnight. A teacher, therefore, is not likely to produce radical changes in students in a short time. Likewise, few teachers are apt to transform themselves immediately. A part of the task of maintaining enthusiasm, then, lies in knowing that slight, gradual progress is to be valued. Slight day-to-day changes that you thoroughly understand are far more likely to be maintained than dramatic changes attributed to mystical factors.

The need to reinforce gradual changes is just as important as the need to expect gradual change. Often, efforts alone may need to be reinforced. A teacher, for example, should never conclude that no teaching has occurred simply because there is no immediate, concrete evidence of learning. Occasionally, youngsters will regress slightly before they progress. Also, some may never acquire certain skills. However, such results should not remove the teacher's enthusiasm for trying. In other words, we think that trying per se is worth at least a self-administered pat on the back. To deprive yourself of any joy because everyone else has not changed as a result of your efforts is asking too much. A question of importance is: Have *you* changed for the better? If so, then, a reward is rightfully deserved. The positive impact on others will eventually be evident.

● It's Different from Factory Work

Tom recently told friends that he was disgusted with teaching because he could not see the results of his work. He commented that "it's not like working in a factory where you can see a tangible product at the end of the day." Although we empathized with Tom, we do not agree with him completely. Perhaps Tom cannot *always* see how others are changing, but what about himself? Is Tom the same today as yesterday? Need he be the same tomorrow? What about Tom's students? Are their skill levels this month any different than last month's? Could it be that Tom has become so habituated to slight day-to-day improvements that he is failing to see how they add up to substantial improvement over extended time periods? ●

WHAT LIES AHEAD?

Will your efforts to improve yourself eventually lead to your graduating summa cum laude or being chosen a national teacher of the year? Possibly. No one can predict exactly how much an individual of your talents can achieve! However, our own goals are less oriented toward products (e.g., honors from others) than they are at finding personal satisfaction in what we do. We have seen too many persons become unhappy as a result of trying to obtain tenure, promotions, and esteem from others. Those things do not necessarily bring happiness when they are sought directly. In other words, when people engage in activities that they do not really enjoy just to obtain a prize, they are usually left with a sense of emptiness when the prize is obtained. Immediately, they start seeking other things. We know of one teacher, for instance, who made her life miserable by trying to outdo everyone else with "showy" projects so that she could be considered for an outstanding-teacher award. She would much rather have been doing something else, but her upbringing taught her to seek end products.

We have nothing against awards. They can be highly valued. However, awards and recognition should flow from others as a by-product of doing what is enjoyable. In brief, what lies ahead for you is largely a function of what you work toward. There are a lot of goals to attain, but we hope that you choose those goals which *in and of themselves* can enrich your life and the lives of your students.

• "I Don't Know What to Work On"

Persons are not uncommonly at a loss regarding an initial self-improvement goal. We have offered a number of suggestions for projects throughout the text. The major chapter topics themselves may have caught your interest. If so, you may wish to work on becoming more creative or to manage stress more effectively, for instance. However, in the event that these initial goals are not quite right for you, perhaps one of the following may be applicable:

- Becoming more assertive
- Beautifying work/study space
- Increasing positive self-statements
- Developing a file on positive occurrences at home/work
- Organizing a special-interest group for teachers/students
- Sharing classroom management/domestic responsibilities
- Increasing nonverbal approval of others
- Developing a daily to-do list
- Participating in staff meetings
- Obtaining new ideas from friends •

A FINAL WORD

A major theme of this text has been that you can change your life. Although we have offered a model for your consideration and have applied the model to a number of major problems confronting teachers, the emphasis has remained on what *you* can do. We can only inform; only you can implement. You possess more knowledge about yourself than anyone else could ever possess. You know your likes and dislikes, and you are in the best position to evaluate what works for you. If there were only one piece of advice we could offer you (we realize we have offered a great deal already), it would be that you trust your own judgments. Do not accept our prescriptions or anyone else's unless you can adapt them to your own special talents. In a word, we have faith in you, and we hope that you share that faith.

INDEX